Anna Nowak

Growing Up Laughing

Growing Up Laughing

My Story and the Story of Funny

Marlo Thomas

WITH GUEST APPEARANCES BY

Alan Alda ★ Joy Behar ★ Sid Caesar ★ Stephen Colbert
Billy Crystal ★ Tina Fey ★ Larry Gelbart ★ Whoopi Goldberg
Kathy Griffin ★ Jay Leno ★ George Lopez ★ Elaine May
Conan O'Brien ★ Don Rickles ★ Joan Rivers ★ Chris Rock
Jerry Seinfeld ★ Jon Stewart ★ Ben & Jerry Stiller
Lily Tomlin ★ Robin Williams ★ Steven Wright

HYPERION

NEW YORK

For Terre and Tony,

who lived it all with me

in the house on Elm

Contents

Contents

Acknowledgments

Growing Up Laughing is my first and only memoir, and my most personal project. So I am deeply grateful to those who lent me their wisdom, inspiration and support throughout the eighteen months it took to complete this book.

To my attorney of many years—and throughout six books—Bob Levine, for encouraging me to tell my story, and then finding the perfect publishing house to guide me through the adventure.

To my publisher, Ellen Archer of Hyperion Books, and my editor, Gretchen Young, for their endless enthusiasm and imagination, which gave me the freedom to put my life into words. And thank you, Gretchen, for the perfect subtitle.

To the extraordinary funny men and women—comic icons, all of them—who generously lent their time and boundless gifts to my exploration of the magic of laughter: Alan Alda, Joy Behar, Sid Caesar, Stephen Colbert, Billy Crystal, Tina Fey, Larry Gelbart, Whoopi Goldberg, Kathy Griffin, Jay Leno, George Lopez, Elaine May, Conan O'Brien, Don Rickles, Joan Rivers, Chris Rock, Jerry Seinfeld, Jon Stewart, Ben and Jerry Stiller, Lily Tomlin, Robin Williams and Steven Wright.

To my talented (and tireless) illustration team, whose dead-ringer caricatures exquisitely capture the sparkle of the comic mind: Tim Foley, Chris Galvin, Bob Kurtz, Chris Morris, Gerardo Orlando, Stephen Silver, Brian Smith, Taylor Smith, Zach Trenholm and Greg Williams.

To my colleague Debra Newman and personal assistant Karen Marsh, who kept me booted up, logged on and linked in throughout this extraordinary journey. And to Phyllis Maniero, Ken Haywood and Aliou Kone, who pitched in and filled in whenever, however and wherever it was needed.

To Orlando Munguia, for his lightning-quick transcription of countless hours of comic banter. And to Phyllis Halliday, who helped in the joyous task of searching for just the right kind of jokes we all like to tell (and retell).

To my faithful army of advisors, experts and pals, each of whom in their own way provided sage advice or hands-on help the moment I came calling—notably, Bruce Kluger, who helped me find jokes, artists and anything else I thought of at three in the morning. And for being a shoulder no matter the time of day.

And to Steven Rice, Leslie Lopez and Matthew Rolston (what artists you are!), Walter Anderson, Ken Feisel, Bob Lowry, Stephanie Pesakoff, Dan Potash, Gary Tobey, Jerry Chipman, John Zacher and the gang at St. Jude Children's Research Hospital.

To my dear and cherished close circle of friends, who were often the very source of love and laughter that fill these pages, and who were more than happy to relive those moments all over again with me: Kathie Berlin, Elaine May, Bill Persky and Julian Schlossberg.

And to my husband, Phillip, who I can always count on for his honest critiques and loving support, and who listened with all his heart to every word as soon as I had written it—and cheered me on till it was done.

Growing Up Laughing

The Set-up

A Prologue

Sometimes in the wee hours of the morning I'd hear that funny sound of an audiotape being rewound. Running backwards it sounded like a Swedish movie. I'd get out of bed and go into Dad's study. And there he'd be—listening, taking notes, going over his act from his last engagement and getting it ready for the next.

"You hear that, Mugs?" he'd say. "That's a big laugh, but the one after it is weak. See, they're tired. You have to pace the laughs. I'm gonna put a song in here. Then I'll come back with the *Whoopee* routine."

He had an ear for the rhythm, the music of the comedy.

"You can never lie to the audience," he'd tell me. "They'll follow you down any yellow brick road as long as you don't lie to them. Once you go off that road, you've lost them."

My father's respect for the audience was his compass. When he hunched over the tape recorder like that, he was shaping the act for *them*—not for himself, not for the critics. And when I went to Las Vegas and saw the act working the way I had watched him put it together, it was exciting. I felt like a co-conspirator, a rooting section, a student—not only of his, but of all of the funny guys he hung out with and with whom I grew up.

I was a lucky kid to have a seat at the table (often our dinner table) with those comic warriors who had the audacity to stand up in a room full of strangers with the conviction that they could bring them all together in laughter. The stories of those times have been humming in my head all of my life, and I decided at last to write them down. They also bring back the many wonderful performances I have seen.

Father-daughter evening out. Most dads take their kids to a movie.
We went nightclubbing.

My father, Danny Thomas, was famous for telling *looong* stories. He would take his time setting up the story and the characters in it. There were always big laughs, and along the way some smaller ones that made you chuckle. And even in his shortest jokes, you could see the characters.

As the funeral cortege passed by, an old man approached
a cop on the corner.
Old Man: "Who died?"
Cop: "The gentleman in the first car."

How did he know when to swing for the fences and when to just put the bat on the ball? What inner voice told him the best rhythm, the best sequence? He knew that the big laugh, the killer laugh, would only come if what came before was carefully, artfully built. But how did he know?

On February 8, 1991, my family occupied the front pew of Good Shepherd Church in Beverly Hills, inconsolable and in disbelief, unable to speak through the tears.

Daddy was the gentleman in the first car.

Since then, I've thought about all that I had the chance to witness. The performances, the love of the work, the banter of his friends. Growing up with all this, it's no mystery where my sense of humor and my appreciation of the craft of comedy come from.

And it made me wonder: How did the seeds of humor get planted in the DNA of the comedians who fill our lives with laughter today? How do we explain the need that all comedians have—that childlike "Watch me!"? Why didn't Seinfeld and Tomlin choose law? How come Conan and Whoopi didn't wind up selling ties at Macy's? What made Sid and Milton run?

So in addition to my own stories, I asked some of the men and women who make us laugh to open a window onto the funny in their lives. And they took me down the unpredictable and sometimes desperate road that led to their own unique brand of comedy. They shared some very honest personal thoughts with a little girl who once had a seat at the table with the giants on whose shoulders they stand today.

I asked my father once if he'd been in the army. He said not as a soldier, but he had spent a year behind front lines, entertaining the troops with Marlene Dietrich in North Africa, Europe and the Pacific.

"Oh, so you weren't a *real* soldier," I said.

"No, we didn't carry the guns," he said, "but we helped heal the boys who did. You know, Mugs, right after the Red Cross comes the U.S.O."

—Marlo Thomas
New York City, Summer 2010

CHAPTER I

Celebrations

*D*id you kill 'em, Daddy?"
"*I murdered 'em, honey! I left 'em for dead.*"

Dialogue from *The Sopranos*? No, just a call from my father, the morning after his opening night at the Sands in Las Vegas (or the Chez Paree in Chicago, or the Fontainebleau in Miami, or any number of other nightclubs around the country).

I didn't realize until I was older how violent the language was for a profession that was so filled with laughter. It was life-and-death, all right—to all of them. But what a celebration when Daddy left 'em for dead. We were big celebrators anyway.

We celebrated everything in our family. My grandmother (the Italian one—my mother's mother) never missed a holiday, and sent us elaborately decorated cards on every conceivable occasion, with all the good parts underlined, followed by exclamation points. Tucked inside the card was always a hanky and a dollar (or, as we got older, two dollars). What a character she was. She looked like a dark-haired, dark-eyed Sophie Tucker (her idol, by the way) and sang in that same kind of husky, raucous voice.

But Grandma did Sophie one better—she also played the drums. In her seventies, she was playing drums with her little band called Marie's

5

Merry Music Makers. In a beer garden in Pasadena. During the week she billed herself as "Danny Thomas's Mother-in-Law." On the weekends, to get the younger crowd, she billed herself as "Marlo Thomas's Grandmother." She was some entrepreneur, my grandma.

Grandma and her beer garden band. That's her on the drums—
flowers in her hair and a big smile on her face.

Of course, everyone tried to get her to act her age and give up the drums—or at least the beer gardens. My mother wished she would just retire to babysitting and making pasta. My father wished she was Bob Hope's mother-in-law. I adored her.

In a family of celebrators, there is always work to be done, and the work was divvied up. My sister, Terre, was the cake committee (she still is, to this day). I, being the oldest—and having a bike—was in charge of buying the cards. I'd ride over to Beverly Stationers on Beverly Drive, where Gladys, the ever-present, ever-dependable proprietor, helped us pick out school supplies each fall. She was also the maven of the card section. Sometimes she'd have a few already put aside for me. I'd pick out something clever and funny for my card; something with a sweet princess and a loving message from Terre; and one with a picture of a lion or a puppy from little Tony.

One year on Father's Day, Terre had gotten Bailey's Bakery to create an elaborate cake with pictures in frosting of all the characters on Dad's TV show. I had done my job of choosing a custom card from each of us, and after dinner the ceremonial opening of the gifts began.

My present was first. As was the custom, Daddy would read the card aloud, and since mine was always a funny one, we'd all laugh. If it was really funny, he'd read it aloud again, and the laughter would start all over.

Then came Terre's card. Daddy read it aloud. Inside, the saying was beautiful—Hallmark had outdone themselves. It was about how Dad was "the best father in the world," "caring and loving," a man who would sacrifice anything for her, who guided her and who was always there for her. Quite beautiful. Tears all around. I was very proud. But then Daddy looked up from the card.

"Terre, do you believe all of this?" he asked.

"Yes, Daddy," Terre said.

Daddy paused. "Because if you really believe what's written in this card," he said, "you'd do the things Daddy wants you to do, wouldn't you?"

"Yes, Daddy."

"Like right now. Where is your retainer?"

"It's upstairs, Daddy."

"Upstairs?! I didn't spend my hard-earned money for you to put your retainer in a drawer upstairs. It belongs in your mouth!"

His voice rose. "I bought it for you so you would grow up to have beautiful straight teeth, with a smile to be proud of."

His voice got even louder as his body began slowly rising out of his chair. Suddenly, the festive room had become very quiet.

Terre looked at me accusingly and said, "You couldn't have given me the other card?"

Within seconds, the tense standoff in the room had dissolved into what was more customary under the Thomas roof: laughter.

This still makes me laugh.

And my father? She murdered 'im.

Terre—looking angelic (without her retainer)
on the day of her First Communion.

CHAPTER 2

A Kid at the Studio

I sat on the lap of director Henry Koster for weeks. I was eight years old, and my father was filming a movie at Warner Bros. with child star Margaret O'Brien, who was nine. It was summer and school was out, so I went to the studio with Dad as often as I could. I loved the whole workday, which began with cueing my father on his lines as we drove to the studio. He'd tell me how well I read Margaret's part, and I'd feel so proud and useful.

Then we'd get to the set.

And I remember watching as Dad and Margaret worked on the scene that we had rehearsed in the car.

And I remember wishing she'd fall over in a dead faint. And then somebody would shout, "Is there a little, dark-haired girl here who knows these lines?" And I could rush in and save the day.

It was so much fun for a kid to run free around the studio—wandering through the wardrobe and makeup departments, visiting other sets, going to lunch in the commissary and sitting next to a man dressed like a pirate or a cowboy.

But the best part was watching the filming from Koster's lap. He would wave his arms around me as he directed the action. Then when the take was over, he'd bellow in his thick Hungarian accent, waving his arms,

Dad working with Margaret O'Brien.
Was I jealous? Was I ever.

Margaret and me. I knew all of her lines, just in case . . .

"Cut! Print it! Very good! We try it again." He'd never say that the scene was bad. It was always, "Very good. We try it again."

My Lebanese grandparents were visiting from Toledo that summer. My grandmother was a saint—but I didn't like my grandfather. He was kind of mean, and I was scared of him. I can still feel the sting on my legs where he swatted me with a pussy willow branch because I was playing with a dog in his tomato garden.

Our dinner table was always a raucous affair, with everyone speaking over everyone else, telling stories and laughing. It was obvious that Grandpa didn't like this kind of commotion at the table. He preferred kids to be seen and not heard.

One night, I was pushing my food around the plate, as always, so it would look like I had eaten most of my meal. I was a terrible eater.

"Finish your vegetables," my father admonished.

I didn't.

"I see your children don't listen to you," my grandfather muttered under his breath.

Embarrassed in front of his father, Dad pushed his chair back with a loud scraping noise and stood up, looking as if he was going to spank me. I jumped up, shocked and frightened, and ran from the table.

"You're being disobedient, young lady!" Dad yelled as he chased me around the room.

I ran right into the corner. He was coming at me. I was terrified.

Suddenly, I stopped, spun around, waved my hands in the air and yelled in my best Hungarian accent, "Cut! Print it! Very good! We try it again!"

My father literally fell over laughing. My grandfather was disgusted with all of us. And I had learned a good lesson: Laughter is the best way to get out of a corner.

CHAPTER 3

The Boys

What fun they all had together. Milton, Sid, Jan, George, Phil, Red, Joey, Harry. They just loved to laugh—and to make each other laugh. Our dinner table was like a writers' roundtable, with each of my father's pals taking his turn trying to top the others. They were always attentive, and never heckled one another as each one "took the floor." Some jokes were told, but many of the biggest laughs came when they made fun of themselves.

It was a known fact that no one was funnier "in a room" than Jan Murray—and my dad was a sucker for him. One night, Jan told a story about trying to get Frank Sinatra's autograph for his son's admission counselor at Northwestern University. He felt like an idiot asking one of the guys for an autograph, but the counselor wanted it, and Jan wanted his kid to get into the college.

The way the story went, all the boys were at a casino in Miami. Jan walked up to Frank with a little piece of paper and asked him to sign it. But Frank brushed the paper aside and said that if it meant getting Jan's son into Northwestern, he'd send the man one of his albums. Jan said, no, that wasn't necessary. The guy just wanted an autograph.

"Nah, it's no trouble," Frank said. "I'll send him an album and a signed photograph."

But Jan was fixated on just getting that autograph. He followed Sinatra around the whole weekend, toting this little scrap of paper—sidling up to Frank at the gambling table, slipping it under his stall in the men's room, pushing it on him while he was schmoozing some blonde in the lounge. The whole weekend—Jan flapping his paper, Frank pushing it away.

I remember watching Jan tell this story one night at our house, wringing the absurdity out of each beat, building the frustration and idiocy of the situation to such a height that he had my father so convulsed with laughter that Dad was lying on the floor in total surrender, howling.

You'd think that Jan would let up, having gotten him to the floor— but, no, now he really had him. Jan stood over my father's prone body, legs straddling him, as he dug even deeper into Dad's funny bone. My father was laughing so hard he screamed, "Stop! Stop!" afraid he would actually die of laughing.

In the real world, the guy laughing that hard is having the most fun. In this world, the guy *getting* the laugh is getting what he lives for.

They were called "The Boys," and like all boys, they had a clubhouse. It was the Hillcrest Country Club, and that's where they spent their afternoons playing golf and cards. Hillcrest sat on a sprawling property in a beautiful setting just south of Beverly Hills. Its famous, rolling green golf course ran along Pico Boulevard, across the street from 20th Century Fox Studios.

Hillcrest had a terrific brunch on Sundays, and it was a great place to throw a party. The only problem—it was restricted. Jews only. This was because the Jews had been kept out of every other club in the city—the Bel Air Country Club, the Los Angeles Country Club—so in the 1920s, they built their own.

"The Boys" celebrating Dad's seventieth birthday at Hillcrest.
BACK ROW, LEFT TO RIGHT: Art Linkletter, Milton Berle,
Don Rickles, Steve Landesberg, Bob Newhart, Morey
Amsterdam, Bob Hope, Jack Carter, Joey Bishop, Carl Reiner,
(honorary "Boy") Phyllis Diller, Sid Caesar;
FRONT ROW: Jan Murray, George Burns, Dad, Red Buttons
and Buddy Hackett.

All of my dad's pals belonged to Hillcrest, but since he was a Lebanese Catholic, he wasn't permitted to join. He'd spent so much time there, however, that the boys decided they should find a way to make him a member, even if he was just an honorary member.

Of course, such a big decision had to be voted on by the board. Groucho Marx had the most memorable comment at the meeting.

"I don't mind making a non-Jew an honorary member," Groucho said, "but couldn't we at least pick a guy who doesn't look Jewish?"

Dad got in. And Groucho got his laugh.

George Burns was also a club member. He didn't play golf, but he loved to play cards. George would go to Hillcrest in the late morning, then spend the rest of the afternoon there, smoking cigars, having lunch and playing bridge with his cronies. He was such a darling, funny man. And a modest one. One day during a card game, he made a remark that broke up everyone at the table. I never knew what he said. I only heard the story of how he got such a big laugh he couldn't wait to use it again. But George, being George, decided to attribute it to someone else—Georgie Jessel—so he could retell it without sounding like he was bragging.

Everywhere he went, George would say, "Did you hear that great thing Jessel said at Hillcrest?"—and, sure enough, he'd get the laugh. This went on for a few weeks. Finally, Jessel ran into George at a party.

"Hey, George," Jessel said, "did you hear that great thing I said at Hillcrest?"

That story went around and got an even bigger laugh than the first one.

All of the boys took pride in coming up with the killer line, and if there's one thing they had in common, it was how quick they were. But Dad always said that the quickest of them all was Joey Bishop.

Joey and Sammy Davis were once driving from Los Angeles to Las Vegas. The route is 270 miles of flat highway through the desert, and everyone speeds like a demon through it. Sammy was going about 90 miles an hour, and, of course, he got pulled over. The cop asked to see his license.

"Do you know how fast you were going?" he demanded of Sammy.

"Around 70," Sammy said innocently.

"Seventy?" the cop said. "You were way over that. You were going at least 90."

Joey leaned his head toward the window.

"Officer," he said, "the man has one eye. Do you want him to look at the road or at the speedometer?"

Most people would think of a line like that three days later and say, "You know what I shoulda said?" These guys said it on the spot.

Sometimes the boys would travel in a pack, and one of their favorite pack nights was a trip to a club where Henny Youngman was playing. If ever a comedian was a joke machine, it was Henny. He was the kind of comic who built his entire act around a string of one-liners, bouncing from one joke to the next without any segues. He'd make a crack about his wife, then without the slightest concern for any semblance of a connection, talk about the snow outside.

The boys, all of whom painstakingly constructed their own acts, found this hilarious—and audacious. So they'd sit in the back of the club and yell out, "Hey, Henny, what about your wife?" Or, "Hey, Henny, get back to the snow!" Henny loved it, of course, and would heckle them right back.

Like everything else the boys did, it was all about having fun and getting laughs. That's what they knew. That's what made them the most comfortable.

But the toughest hecklers of all were the kids Milton Berle faced when he did card tricks at our backyard birthday parties. He wasn't the world's smoothest magician, and the kids called him on it.

"I saw what you did with that card!" they would holler. "Cheater!"

But nothing fazed Milton—or stopped him. He was *on,* and that was just where he wanted to be.

Years later, when I was doing my television series, *That Girl,* Milton appeared as our guest star one week. I had never worked with him—I only knew him as one of my dad's pals. But he was different on the set. Difficult, really. He'd roam around the soundstage in his big, white terry-cloth bathrobe, with a towel wrapped around his neck, like he'd just gone six rounds with Ali—constantly complaining. It was too cold in his dressing room. It was also too small. He'd been kept waiting too long. He wasn't feeling well. He had to get home. On and on and on.

Milton was driving everyone so crazy that our assistant director begged me to do something. Desperate, I called my father.

"Dad," I said, "Milton is behaving impossibly and I don't know how to deal with him. What should I do?"

Without a pause, my father said, "Ask him to spell words that begin with R."

"What?" I said. "Ask him to spell words that start with R?! What are you talking about?"

"Just do it," Dad said.

I walked back to the stage baffled, and spotted Milton, who by now was coughing and hacking and whining about how sick he was to anyone who would listen.

"Hey, Milton," I yelled, "how do you spell *recluse?*"

Milton snapped his head toward me.

"R-E-C-Q-U-L-S-E," he shot back, feet pointing inward.

Everyone laughed.

Then I yelled out, "How do you spell *remember?*"

"R-E-M-M-M-E-M-M-M-B-M-M-E-R-M."

Another big laugh from the crew.

That was it. Milton just wanted to feel comfortable. And he felt comfortable when people were laughing. Now he could go to work.

Kind of touching, really. I loved those guys.

P.S. Jan never got Frank's autograph.

DID YA HEAR THE ONE ABOUT . . .

An old man and his wife die and go to heaven.

They're sitting at a table having iced tea, with little umbrellas in their drinks. They're looking out at the lush hills and valleys, birds are fluttering about and the beautiful aroma of lilac trees is wafting over their table. Everything is perfect. Even no waiting at the tees.

After a while, the wife turns to her husband. "Darling," she says, "isn't heaven wonderful?"

"Yeah," he says, "and if it hadn't been for your goddamn Oat Bran we would have been here ten years ago."

CHAPTER 4

Socks and Moxie

Like the comics I grew up with, Jerry Seinfeld has a genuine need to perform. No matter his success or the fortune he has made from it, Jerry is still out there on the road, building an act—story by story, joke by joke, laugh by laugh. In 2002, he produced and appeared in the documentary The Comedian, *which trailed him as he traveled the country, determined to try out untested material one small club at a time, motivated only by the sheer challenge and his love of the craft. It was a brave and humbling adventure, and I found it touching to see into the heart and mind of a comedian who, like the legends before him, takes very seriously the art of being funny.* —M.T.

JERRY
SEINFELD

Marlo: Your generation of comedians is not all that different from "The Boys" I grew up with. No matter which generation, there's never a formula, but always a wide range of styles. And they each have their own loyal following.

Jerry: I was just saying to someone this morning that comedy is like smells. It's like a cologne counter at a department store. People just pick up the little tester bottles and say, "I hate this one, I love this one . . ." There's really no rhyme or reason to any of it.

Marlo: Did you ever doubt that you could make people laugh?

Jerry: Oh, always.

Marlo: Always?

Jerry: Sure. Still do. I think that's been the key to my success. I've never been overconfident.

Marlo: So where do you get the guts to say, "Okay, I'm going to do it anyway?"

Jerry: It's a very funny little mixture of humility and outrageous egomania. That's what makes a good comedian.

Marlo: So when it gets down to it, laughter—

Jerry: . . . is the greatest thing there is. I mean it. Even if you're not a comedian, if you say something funny or tell a joke and make somebody laugh, it's a moment of pure joy, one of the best things I know. It's cultural, it's genetic.

Marlo: You once said that stand-up comedy doesn't belong on the arts pages, it belongs on the sports pages. What do you mean?

Jerry: One of the things that drew me to comedy was that it's a simple world. It doesn't require the interpretation of any critic to tell you whether something is good or not good. If the audience is laughing, the guy's good. If they're not laughing, he's not good. Period. And that's the analogy to sports: You can talk all you want about how two teams played in a game. But we all know who won at the end. There's no debate. It doesn't require any perception.

That's where comedy is different from the other arts. Stand-up comedy doesn't require value judgments. If you get laughs, you work; if you don't get laughs, you don't work. It's all about the score.

Put it this way. When you do a play, your friends come backstage afterwards and say, "You were great," right?

Marlo: Right.

Jerry: And you say, "Really! Was I?" And they say, "Yes!" But all along you're wondering, *Are they telling me the truth?*

Marlo: Right.

Jerry: Well, I don't have to do that. No one has to tell me after a stand-up show whether I did well or not. It's quite clear to everyone what happened.

Marlo: Okay, so running with your analogy, does comedy take the same kind of training as sports?

Jerry: Oh, definitely. I was recently talking to a baseball player who played third base, but his natural position—the one he grew up playing—was shortstop. So I said to him, "If you wanted to switch back to shortstop now, how long would it take you to get comfortable there again?" And he said, "Six months to a year," because there are so many subtleties to playing that position.

Same thing with comedy. Stand-up has nothing to do with anything but stand-up. If you can do stand-up, that doesn't mean you can do anything else. And if you can do anything else, that doesn't mean you can do stand-up.

Marlo: Were there funny people in your childhood?

Jerry: Well, I think all kids are funny. But what was different in my life was how I valued it.

Marlo: I know exactly what you mean.

Jerry: Yeah, I'll bet you do. So I thought being funny and making other kids laugh was the greatest thing in the world. Then again, I recently read that the average child laughs something like 75 times a day . . .

Marlo: Really?

Jerry: Yeah. And the average adult laughs like 12 times a day. So I think as I grew up, I wanted to maintain that 75 figure into adulthood. It was always the most valuable thing to me, so I developed it. I worked on it. I was completely focused on what was funny.

Marlo: So were you the class clown?

Jerry: Not really. I could make other kids laugh, but I didn't think I had any real talent until I started doing stand-up in my early twenties. Any kid can make his friends laugh. That's just being a kid. But could I make strangers laugh? *That* was the question.

Marlo: Who was funny in your life when you were a kid?

Jerry: My dad was a hugely funny guy—unbelievably funny.

Marlo: Really? In what way?

Jerry: Just by being silly and singing funny songs. When he was in the army, he used to collect jokes in a file. He was stationed in the Pacific, in the Philippines, and I remember him telling me that he had all these jokes stored away. He was a great joke teller.

Marlo: Do you remember any of them?

Jerry: Oh, sure. One that I loved was about a guy who somehow falls out of a building window and lands on the pavement. Everyone runs over, saying, "What happened? What happened?" And the guy looks up and says, "I don't know. I just got here myself."

Marlo: That's a good joke. Your father sounds adorable.

Jerry: He was.

Marlo: Did your mother laugh at your dad's jokes?

Jerry: My mother was a good laugher. She always said that she married my father because he was so funny and the life of the party. But then once they got married, he wasn't so funny around the house. I think my wife has discovered the same thing about me. Comedians are not that upbeat in their private world, you know.

Marlo: Yeah, my dad worried a lot about his act. But he sure was funny at the dinner table.

Jerry: The dinner table is a good stage.

Marlo: Yup. And my father loved listening to his children tell jokes. Were your parents the same way?

Jerry: I was never funny around my parents.

Marlo: Really?

Jerry: Yeah. I was too shy.

Marlo: Did your father eventually see you in a club?

Jerry: Yes. And he'd say, "If I'd had some place where I could have gotten on stage, I would have wanted to do the same thing."

Marlo: If you were never funny at home, your parents must have been very surprised to see you perform.

Jerry: Oh, my God. My first *Tonight Show*? I'm telling you, I have never been more nervous about anything. Having my parents in the audience used to just terrify me.

Marlo: Really? Why?

Jerry: Because I was showing them this side of me that they had no idea about. Like, when I first told them I wanted to be a comedian—I was about 19 or 20—they said, "Really? But we've never seen you do funny things."

Marlo: That's a riot. So you were like this little closet comedian.

Jerry: Yes, yes—I was much more the closet comedian than the class clown.

Marlo: How did you do that night on *The Tonight Show*?

Jerry: I did well. But I wasn't that happy with it. I thought I could have done better.

Marlo: You were probably still nervous. Back then, *The Tonight Show* was like the holy grail for comedians. What does that feel like for a young comic?

Jerry: It feels like, like the stomach flu, you know? Except it's in your whole body. You can't eat, you feel sick. Those first couple of years, every time I did *The Tonight Show*, it was such a gigantic event in my life. I'd be up all night the night before, and so sick the day of the taping. I remember one time asking myself, *Why do I do this? Why would anyone put themselves through this?*

Marlo: And your answer was . . .

Jerry: Because if anyone can, we can. And that's why we do it. The only reason anyone would go through this hell is because they love it.

Marlo: Exactly. What about bombing? Do you remember one particularly awful bomb? Because, sorry to say, nothing makes me laugh more than flops.

Jerry: Well, I remember once doing a club where the waitress had to step on stage in front of you to get to her section.

Marlo: Oh, my God.

Jerry: And so all throughout my sketch, she would get up on stage and walk in front of me, with the drinks and the tray—back and forth, back and forth. Just awful.

Marlo: That must have been great for your timing. Tell me the anatomy of a Jerry Seinfeld joke. Like your famous missing sock routine, where you try to understand why there's always an odd, partnerless sock when you pull your clothes out of the dryer. And you theorize that the missing sock is actually a fugitive on the run. That joke's a classic. How did it come about? Were you actually folding your laundry one day when the idea hit you? How does a piece like this evolve?

Jerry: Well, first, there's *always* the missing sock.

Marlo: Right.

Jerry: And I can't remember how I hit upon the idea that they want to escape, but once you get your hook, you try to do what we might call a "switch piece," where you take everything that fits that scenario and apply it to the joke. Okay, so we have an escaped convict scenario. Now you find all the pieces that match up. You have the sock hiding inside the wall of the dryer, preparing for its getaway . . .

Marlo: [*Laughs*] Right.

Jerry: You have the sock out on the street that's gotten a few blocks . . .

Marlo: [*Laughs*] Right.

Jerry: Then you try to figure out the reason they would want to escape in the first place. Maybe it's because of their horrible life in the shoes, with the smelly feet . . .

Marlo: Right, right!

Jerry: And if you can come up with enough examples, what you've done is taken an absurd idea, then laid it out, proving it with rock-solid logic. That's the formula for that kind of joke. That's what audiences love.

Here's another one that I do in my act now. It's about the piñata at children's birthday parties. I explain how the piñata works, then say, "And then the parents tell the kids, 'And after we're done beating this animal senseless, we're going to put a picture of his brother on the wall, and everyone's going to get a pin and we're going to nail his ass!' " So I'm basically creating this whole idea about some kind of donkey hostility at children's birthday parties.

Marlo: That is *so* great.

Jerry: And, of course, everybody knows these two things—the piñata and Pin the Tail on the Donkey—but they've never put together the thought that they're both donkeys, you know?

Marlo: Right, I never thought of it, either.

Jerry: In the end, you're creating a false logic for fun.

Marlo: Most people credit you with doing "observational humor."

Jerry: I think "observational humor" is a completely meaningless term. There's no humor—no *anything*—that's not based on some kind of observation. Every movie, every poem, every book—it's all observation. And observing is nothing. The trick is, you have to know *what* to observe and how to present it. People also say, "Jerry Seinfeld just talks about real things." Well, if I just talked about real things, believe me, I'd be still living in that studio apartment.

Marlo: Sometimes when I'm watching you, I think, if somebody else was delivering this material, it just wouldn't work as well.

Jerry: But you could say that about any comedian.

Marlo: I'm not so sure. I don't think that about every comedian, but it's so apparent with you.

Jerry: I guess that's because the audiences teach you what's funny about you. One of the things that's most important to learn as a comedian is to remember whatever you did that made them laugh one night, then replicate it the next night—*exactly*. Whether it's some look, a hand gesture, a vocal inflection. It's the audience that shapes all of these things.

Marlo: Are there things you've discovered you shouldn't do? Do you have any rules you follow?

Jerry: Well, I do work clean. I don't like to use curse words because it's just not my technique. And not using them makes me create better things.

Marlo: The comics I grew up with used to say, "Anybody can get a laugh using a dirty word."

Jerry: Yeah. And I always say, "I don't want that bullshit in my bullshit."

Marlo: You were born in Brooklyn, as were many comedy legends— Jackie Gleason, Jimmy Durante, Buddy Hackett, Mel Brooks, Phil Silvers. Obviously, your brand of comedy is a lot different from the rat-a-tat style of those guys. What's in you that was in them?

Jerry: That's a great question. For lack of a better answer, I'm going to have to say there's a certain moxie. A sense that I belong up there. You know, you have to be born with that; and I think it's, in many ways, kind of an ethnic, New Yorkish thing—this whole idea that I should be telling you what I think, and that you should all listen. I feel that connection with those guys.

Marlo: When George Carlin died, you spoke publicly about your admiration of him.

Jerry: Yeah, George had this amazing kind of jeweler's acuity with an idea, the way he would dismantle a concept from so many angles. I learned a lot about precision from watching him. For example, we were talking about the sock thing. Two jokes is okay. But if you can get *eight* jokes out of it, well, now you're really taking it apart and creating something that can go for a long time. That's what George would do. To me, that's a big accomplishment in the writing part of it.

Marlo: What about women in the comedy business? Did you ever date funny girls?

Jerry: When I was young, I was very interested in funny girls because it seemed like the ultimate thing: someone of the opposite sex who was also funny. To me, that seemed to be everything you could want.

Marlo: It would seem to be . . .

Jerry: But, you know, girls in the comedy business, there's something about it that's a little . . . homoerotic. I eventually decided I didn't want to be in a relationship with someone who thinks being funny is as important as I do. That's not so good.

Marlo: Is your wife the laugher in your relationship, or does she make you laugh?

Jerry: Both—she's funny and she laughs. But, you know, it's not like one of us says something funny, and then we look at each other and say, "Are you going to use that? Because I could use that."

Marlo: When I told my father I wanted to be an actress, he said to me, "If you wanted to be a performer, I'd really encourage you, but being an actress you need too many people." He said, "Me, I don't need anybody. I go out there and all I need is the mike. I don't wear funny hats. I don't bring things on the stage. And because I don't need anybody, I can always do what I love." As a solo performer, do you feel the same way?

Jerry: Yes. I remember when I started doing some acting in college—which was the only acting that I had ever done—a director saying to me, "You're making this part too funny. It's not really supposed to be funny." And I remember thinking to myself, *You know, I think if I could get a little less help I might be able to get somewhere in this business.*

Marlo: Exactly.

Jerry: And it's still the same. I don't know what it is with comedians, but there's this conflicted thing of misanthropy and philanthropy: You hate people, but you'll do anything to please them.

Marlo: Given how tough the comedy business is, would you want your kids to be a part of it?

Jerry: I don't think I have a choice. My daughter, who's eight years old—and who I don't think really knows what I do—walks around the house with this joke book that's two inches thick. It's called *Joke-a-pedia*.

Marlo: Really?

Jerry: Yeah, she just carries it around. So maybe there's something genetic there.

Marlo: Ya think?

Jerry: Probably, yeah. A couple of years ago, she said to me, "Dad, I really like making people laugh."

Marlo: Oh, how great. And what did you say?

Jerry: I said, "Yeah, I know the feeling."

CHAPTER 5

The Wives

My mother, Rosie, was a band singer. So was Dolores Hope, Bob's wife. Like their husbands, a lot of the comedians' wives had worked in nightclubs.

The curvaceous Margie Durante had been a cigarette girl at the Copa in New York. Moving among the patrons in her glorious décolletage, she caught Jimmy's eye.

Toni Murray, married to Jan, worked on stage as a "Copa Girl." You could see why—she was a gorgeous redhead.

I once asked Toni if she sang, too.

"I couldn't even dance," she said in her usual deadpan delivery.

Toni was what they called in nightclub lingo a "show horse." Those were the tall girls who just walked across the stage looking luscious, wearing feathered, three-foot headdresses—and not a whole lot else. The dancers were smaller and called "ponies." I always wanted to be a pony. They looked like they had the most fun. As a kid, I used to love hanging backstage with them in their big dressing room when they were getting into their spangly outfits. They were young, loud and full of life. It was like being in a sorority dorm. With sequins.

But none of the boys' wives worked after they got married. They all had kids, ran big houses and took care of their husbands. And the latter was a full-time job. For all their brash hilarity and guts on stage, the boys needed a great deal of care. If your emotional equilibrium is so dependent every night on pleasing a group of strangers, you need a lot of salve on your ragged ego when you close the door at the end of the night.

There was a well-known adage that described the two kinds of comics' wives: "She put him up to it" or "She'll calm him down." But whichever one they were, they all had one thing in common. They were their husbands' greatest audience. They laughed at all their jokes, no matter how many times they had heard them. And whenever their husbands were on stage, they were there, standing in the wings when the show was over, to tell them they had "killed the people."

Most of the wives knew how to have fun—well, they were clubbers at heart. They loved to get dressed up, have cocktails and champagne and stay out late, laughing and telling jokes. They needed to be a part of the scene they had given up when they got married, and most of them probably liked it a whole lot better than staying back home with the kids. Especially with all those cute ponies swishing their tails around.

They were a lot alike, these women. Most had come from poor neighborhoods and had only high school educations. After dinner at our house, they'd all hang out together in the den talking about their kids and their parties while their husbands sat in the living room telling jokes and sharing on-the-road war stories. (That was the room I always wanted to be in.) One or two of the wives would get a swelled head and become a bit pretentious. I remember Red Buttons was married for a while to a woman who was taking French lessons. Soon after, she started calling Red "Rouge." Poor Rouge—the boys had a field day with that one.

But most of the wives understood the game. I think that was their bond.

Except for one. The dreaded wicked witch, Sylvia Fine, Danny Kaye's wife. From the time I was a little kid, I had always heard the women talking about what a "ballbuster" Sylvia was—she didn't even take his last name. And "poor Danny"—how she humiliated him, spoke for him, wore the pants and all that. I always felt so sorry for Danny Kaye. He was a cute and funny man who, unlike the other guys, was saddled with this terrible wife.

Decades went by, and I hadn't thought about Danny or Sylvia for what must have been thirty years. Then one night I was at a big dinner event in New York. Danny Kaye was long gone, and I spotted Sylvia from across the room.

Suddenly, this strange feeling came over me. It was like the melting of ice off a very old structure. Seeing Sylvia there made everything I had learned about women in the past decades flash before me:

Women who didn't play by the house rules were called "man-haters."

Women who took charge were called "bitches" (while men who took charge were "leaders").

Women who wanted to have their writing taken seriously used their initials to hide their gender.

I was now looking at a woman who had been far ahead of her time. She was her husband's manager and writer, both for his nightclub act and many of his movies. She had written some of his most successful songs, which had earned her Oscar and Emmy nominations. She wore the pants all right—if wearing pants meant having talent. That was her crime.

I got up and walked over to where Sylvia was sitting. I had no idea what I was going to say to her. I was even surprised to be walking toward her.

When I got to her table, she looked at me and stood up. I put my arms around her and whispered in her ear.

"I grew up thinking you were the most awful woman," I said. "But I just realized tonight what a gifted, unusual woman you have always been. And you took a lot of grief for it. So I just wanted to apologize."

Sylvia hugged me back and smiled. She knew. She'd lived through it and had taken it all. But no one had stopped her from her work. And in the end, it was better than standing in the wings.

In 2005, the American Film Institute nominated the 400 most memorable lines from motion pictures for its "100 Years, 100 Movie Quotes" list. Sylvia's line from her husband's film *The Court Jester* was included among the nominees.

"The pellet with the poison's in the vessel with the pestle, the chalice from the palace has the brew that is true."

It was the only quote from a Danny Kaye movie to make the nomination list.

TAKE MY WIFE . . .
AND HUSBAND, PLEASE!

If a man speaks in a forest and no woman
can hear him, is he still wrong?

•

My wife and I went back to the hotel where we
spent our wedding night—only this time,
I stayed in the bathroom and cried.

•

What are three words a woman never wants to hear
when she's making love? "Honey, I'm home!"

•

I just got back from a pleasure trip.
I took my mother-in-law to the airport.

•

I never knew what real happiness was until I
got married—and by then, it was too late.

•

A Woman's Prayer:
"Dear Lord, I pray for the wisdom to understand my
husband, the love to forgive him, and the patience for his
moods. Because, Lord, if I pray for strength,
I'll just beat him to death."

Stirring the Sauce with Joy Behar

*In a field that is predominantly male, mostly Jewish,
with a few Irish thrown in, there is but one Italian,
Catholic dame. I've been interviewed by Joy Behar on
The View and on her own show, and I've seen her
socially, as well. She bubbles with outspokenness
and delights in her one-line zingers as
much as you do. That's what makes any
outrageous thing she says acceptable. And
funny. When you look at Joy, you can
almost see the mischievous child in her
eyes. As another daughter of an Italian
mother, I understand the extended family
in which she was brought up. Joy would
have fit right in at the dinner table of my
grandma, the drummer.*
—M.T.

JOY
BEHAR

Joy: We are very Italian. Calabrese.

Marlo: My mother was Sicilian.

Joy: Calabrese, Sicilian—same thing. My uncle Joe used to carry a picture of Mussolini in his wallet. He'd tell us, "Mussolini wassa notta bad. Hitler wassa bad. Mussolini wassa nice."

Marlo: Oh, that's really funny. My father's nickname for my mother was Mussolini. I'm curious, how does your family react when you take on the Church? I read something you said—that "there are no saints anymore because of modern medication."

Joy: Well, that's true, isn't it? They were hearing voices, all those saints. They were psychotic. If they'd had a little Prozac, we wouldn't have had any of these saints. I got in trouble with the Catholic Church for that.

Marlo: I'll bet.

Joy: My aunt Joan called me from Pennsylvania to reprimand me. "How could you say that about the saints?"—you know, as if she's the guardian of the saints!

Marlo: You've also spoken out against Medicare coverage for Viagra.

Joy: No, they misinterpreted that. What I said was that birth control doesn't get any kind of health-care funding, but Viagra does. I said, "It's the crack-cocaine of the nursing homes."

Marlo: That's great. I love that.

Joy: Because the old men there are all over everybody. What—are we going to be faking orgasms into our golden years now? How many more years do I have to do that?

Marlo: I talked with Jerry Seinfeld about why so many comedians come from Brooklyn. You do, too.

Joy: I don't think it's about Brooklyn, per se. I think it's that many of us came from humble backgrounds and needed a way out. We needed a way to deal with the world and have some kind of power in it. You know, you feel powerless in Brooklyn. You're not in Manhattan.

Marlo: Right, right.

Joy: It's like growing up a beautiful woman. If you're a really beautiful woman, you don't have to develop a sense of humor. That's why most women comedians are not beauties. Same with guys. If you walk into a room and everybody drops dead from your gorgeousness, why do you need to be funny?

Marlo: Right. A lot of comics have told me they grew up not liking their looks.

Joy: Everybody has that story. For me it was kinky, curly hair.

Marlo: You had hair like that?

Joy: I still do. My fifth grade teacher called me "Brillo Head."

Marlo: Oh, how awful!

Joy: What a jerk he was.

Marlo: What did you say back to him?

Joy: I was in the fifth grade, his name was Mr. Frischer, and all I could come up with was to call him "Mr. Fish Cakes." That was it—but I *did* answer him back. *I'm* the first one to make a joke about my hair—not *you*.

Marlo: Your hair doesn't look like Brillo now.

Joy: That's because I didn't have a hairdresser in the fifth grade.

Marlo: Do you remember your grandmother and grandfather? Were they from the old country?

Joy: Yes, they all came from Calabria—which was a really rough ride for them. They came here right after a horrible earthquake. So they were very poor.

Marlo: Did they live with you? Did you see them a lot?

Joy: I grew up in a tenement in Brooklyn, one of those apartment buildings with fire escapes. My mother and father and I were on the fifth floor; my grandmother and her children were on the third floor, as was my aunt, her husband and mother-in-law—who was a witch. So I'd just go up and down in the building, and do shtick for them all day long.

Marlo: So you were the funny one. Were your mom and dad funny, too?

Joy: My father had a little bit of a streak . . .

Marlo: And your mother?

Joy: I think if you talk to a lot of women comics, you'll find that they had mothers who were sort of depressed.

Marlo: Oh, really.

Joy: Yeah, a little depressed. And because they were not actualized, they could have used some medication. "Hello. A little Zoloft for the ladies?" That generation was stuck at home. And my mother was not a housewife. She couldn't afford to be because she was married to a gambler.

Marlo: Wow.

Joy: So she had to work—she was long-suffering, the poor thing. And so I found that my escape from all of that was to make fun of everything. I got a lot of material just watching my mother and trying to make her laugh.

I think I had some kind of a funny gene, even as a little ten-year-old kid. I have recollections of how I was always performing. We'd go to wakes, and when we'd come home, I would make fun of everybody who was at the wake. And I liked acting crazy—like Jerry Lewis. Just being a little whack-job. My aunts and uncles on my mother's side were like a built-in audience. Then I'd go up to Springfield, Massachusetts, where we had other relatives. I would just kill in these places as a kid.

Marlo: That's a riot. You'd just kill . . . at *ten*!

Joy: They were like sitting ducks for me, you know? The problem—and this is an interesting point, I think—the problem was that I got so much attention and response from my family, that when I went into the real world of show business—where people don't know or care about you—I wasn't getting that kind of reaction. So I thought I wasn't good enough. The truth of it was, I had to win them over just like I had done as a child. I mean, I *worked* at it.

Marlo: Right, of course. You knew the room.

Joy: I knew the room. It's just that when I got a bigger room, I had to start from scratch in a way, and it took me a while.

Marlo: Were you funny in school?

Joy: I was always funny in school. I would get myself out of jams by being funny.

Marlo: Were you like you are on *The View*, with a strong point of view and not afraid to speak up?

Joy: Yes, I think I was always like that. And I really do credit my family for that. They never, ever told me to shut up.

Marlo: You started late as a stand-up, right?

Joy: Yeah, I was about thirty-eight.

Marlo: What were you doing up until then?

Joy: I was a high school English teacher.

Marlo: You must have been very funny as a teacher.

Joy: I was in some classes—if they were bright. If they weren't, I couldn't do it. I had to be strict.

Marlo: What other kind of jobs did you have?

Joy: I worked in a mental hospital—which prepared me for *The View.* I worked at an employment service. I did a lot of different little jobs, and then got a job at *Good Morning America* as a receptionist.

Marlo: How was that?

Joy: Good. Then I was fired.

Marlo: You're kidding.

Joy: Well, you know what they do in television. If the ratings go down, they fire the receptionist.

Marlo: That's smart. "It's her fault!" At some point, you made a turn and your humor became more political.

Joy: Yeah, I'm kind of like Bill Maher in that way. I call myself a "fundit."

Marlo: I love that term. And the fundits are taken seriously.

Joy: Well, yeah, because they have a lot to say about issues, especially during elections. Jon Stewart, Stephen Colbert.

Marlo: I've talked to both of them. They're great. They have bowling-ball balls, these guys.

Joy: I know.

Marlo: But so do you.

Joy: I know I do. We're all fundits. You know, I ran into Joe Biden one time, and he told me that he's more scared to go on Jon Stewart than on *Meet the Press.*

Marlo: Really? Why?

Joy: Because he knows Stewart'll get him.

Marlo: And he doesn't know how to manipulate that.

Joy: Right—it's harder.

Marlo: And because comedians don't have to be polite, there are no rules.

Joy: Yes, and there's an audience there.

Marlo: And if there's an audience there, the comedian will go for the laugh.

Joy: That's right, and they'll get the laugh at their guest's expense, if you let them.

Marlo: Right.

Joy: And remember, fundits are citizens.

Marlo: Of course.

Joy: Citizens with a big, big mouth.

Marlo: That's great, Joy. That's just great.

Joy: You're a good audience, Marlo.

Marlo: There's a good reason.

Hotels

Most people are disoriented when they stay at a hotel. Not me. I lived in hotels a lot when I was a kid, so they feel familiar, a little bit like home—with the added delight of room service.

On school holidays, my mother, brother, sister and I would travel from sunny L.A. to sunnier Florida or snowy Chicago to be with Dad. The nuns at school appreciated that my mother was trying to keep our family intact, and during the school year they were good about giving us Mondays and Fridays off so we could be together for long weekends.

Our family always stayed in the extravagant suites that were set aside for the headliner of the club—roomy enough for an entourage and perfect for a family of five. They had big dining tables, several bedrooms, spiral staircases, terraces, and even gardens. I was eighteen before I realized every hotel room didn't have a piano in it.

My father was always thrilled when we joined him. He was especially happy to have my mother back with him, and always made a lot of preparations for her arrival: champagne, red roses, a new negligee in a pretty wrapped box. Dad was a true romantic.

One year, we had barely opened our suitcases in our part of the suite when it became obvious that Tony, who was just four years old, had a very bad cold. Mom was the old-fashioned type who liked to be close by when any of her kids was sick. At home, our bedrooms had twin beds, and when one of us wasn't well, Mom would stay in the other bed until she was sure we were out of the woods.

When Dad finished his show that night, he came back to the suite expecting to find his negligee-clad wife as eager to spend the rest of the evening with him as he was with her. But instead, he found Mom in a bulky terry robe, ushering him away and shushing him not to make noise, as she'd just gotten Tony to sleep.

Mom explained to Dad how sorry she was that she couldn't be with him, but Tony had a fever, and she'd have to sleep in his room to keep an eye on him. And with that, she sent Dad off to their part of the suite.

This went on for a couple of nights, and Terre and I could hear our parents' angry whispers.

"When will he be better, already?" Dad asked in desperation. "You haven't slept in our room the entire trip!"

"Sssshhh! You'll wake him up!" Mom said.

On the morning of the third day, we were all having breakfast—there's nothing better than waffles and hot chocolate from room service. Tony was on the floor of the terrace, playing with a little pail of sand and a shovel. Without warning, he decided to toss the pail, then watched with a smile as it made the twelve-story plunge.

My father was frightened and furious. He picked Tony up.

"Bad boy!" he scolded. "Don't you know you could have hurt someone by throwing that bucket off the terrace? Now go to your room and be quiet until I tell you to come out!"

Tony started for his room, then turned around and looked at Dad.

"Just for that," he said, "tonight she sleeps with me."

Dad roared with laughter, then picked up little Tony and gave him a great big hug.

Four years old and the kid's timing was impeccable.

Tony and Dad. The kid didn't get the nose—
but he got the timing.

DID YA HEAR THE ONE ABOUT . . .

Two friends meet on the street.

One says, "I haven't heard from you in so long.
What happened?"

The other says, "Well, frankly you've become
a bit pretentious."

The other guy says, *"Moi?"*

Comedy Begins
at Home

*When it comes to comedians, I'm a sucker audience.
I laugh hard and I laugh a lot. But there are only a few
comics who can make me cry, too—and I did plenty
of that when I watched Billy Crystal perform 700
Sundays, his one-man Broadway show about growing
up in Long Beach, New York. Unlike
with most comedians, Billy's family
members (and there were a flock of them)
recognized his natural comic gift and
encouraged it. They were his first
adoring audience, and even supplied
props to help him develop his childhood
antics. This may be why there is such an
ease about Billy when he performs for us. We seem
like his family—laughing, clapping, adoring. As
Billy recalled for me, it all started with his dad . . .*
—M.T.

BILLY
CRYSTAL

*"Dad started taking the time to show us
the really funny people on television, to inspire us . . ."*
—Billy Crystal, *700 Sundays*

Billy: In the early days of television, the characters that the comics created made you feel: *These are my uncles, these are my aunts, these are the same people I know.* And if you wanted to be funny—if you wanted to *grow up* funny—this was the best time. Sid Caesar. Ernie Kovacs. Mel Brooks and Carl Reiner doing *The 2000 Year Old Man.* This was the time.

These comedians had a way of being Jewish, but without doing an accent or talking about stereotypical things. They just broke it all down.

So, for me, this was where it all started, with these visual, funny guys.

I very clearly remember watching Sid Caesar's spoof of *The King and I.* At the time, *The King and I* was huge, and Yul Brynner had suddenly become the biggest star in the world. So Sid played him just like in the movie. Bald. Wearing capri pants. And, of course, barefoot. He makes his entrance, then he hits that famous pose. And suddenly he screams and grabs his foot!

"Who's smokin' in the palace? There's no smokin' in the palace!" He's obviously stepped on a red hot cigarette.

Well, I'm watching this on TV—I must have been four or five—and that immediately became my thing. *"Who's smokin' in the palace?"*

So, of course, Dad brought home a bald wig—and now it became a real thing for me.

*" 'Pop, listen,' I said. 'I want to be a comedian. Is that crazy?'
'Billy, it's not crazy,' Dad said, 'because I think
you can be one. And I'm going to help you.'"*
—Billy Crystal, *700 Sundays*

Then there was Sid's "Uncle Goopy Sketch," which was probably the greatest sketch they ever did. It was a spoof on Ralph Edwards's show, *This Is Your Life*, where they'd bring on someone famous and honor their life with people from their past. Sid's sketch was based on a real *This Is Your Life* episode with broadcaster Lowell Thomas—who obviously did *not* want to be interviewed by Ralph Edwards. He was terribly disagreeable throughout the whole show.

Edwards would say, "Lowell, this is a voice from the past!" and he'd say, "I don't care." Edwards said, "We'll see everybody at the party at the Hollywood Roosevelt Hotel afterwards!" And Thomas said, "I'm not going."

Well, in his spoof, Sid played the reluctant *This Is Your Life* recipient, and Howard Morris played his Uncle Goopy. And there's this moment when they bring out Uncle Goopy, and he and Sid see each other, and they just both start weeping—I mean, really funny weeping.

And Howard was this little guy, and he'd jump up on Sid, and Sid would carry him all around the stage. Then they'd be separated, and Howard would start grabbing onto Sid's leg. And then they'd cry even more.

But the way Howard kept leaping on Sid like a little monkey was absolutely hilarious.

So that's how I started going off to bed: I'd jump on my father's back, then he'd set me down and I'd grab his leg. Then he'd drag me into bed. That started me thinking that someday, maybe, I could be funny.

"The older relatives weren't as much fun.
They always looked miserable. Always with a frown.
I called them the upside-down people, because if you
put them upside-down, they would look so happy."
—Billy Crystal, *700 Sundays*

Just like Sid Caesar, I started doing fake accents and gibberish with my grandmother. She spoke Yiddish and Russian, and whenever she would talk about something that she didn't want us to understand, she'd switch from English to Russian or Yiddish. So I would start doing my version of Sid to her—in Russian. She'd just look at me, trying to understand, then she'd say, "You're a crazy man."

I first started doing funny stuff in school as a little guy. Steve Allen was a huge influence on me. I loved his "Man on the Street" segments, and all of those great characters—Tom Poston, Louis Nye, Jose Jimenez. My friends and I would improvise bits from the show, then my brothers and I started doing the Nairobi Trio from *The Ernie Kovacs Show*. And when the comedians put out record albums, my dad would bring them home from his store, the Commodore Music Shop. We'd memorize them in a split second, then do the routines for the relatives. We were taught very young how to steal from the best.

Pretty soon Jonathan Winters became my favorite guy. My father had great taste in comedy, and he'd let us stay up late to watch the best ones on Jack Paar's *Tonight* show. And if Jonathan Winters was on the show? Oh, my God. It was like going to the playground for us. Or like watching sports. Getting to stay up late to watch Jack Paar!

You know what I would do sometimes when I watched Jack Paar? I would take my chair and put it next to the TV set, so that it looked like I was Jack's next guest. I was about seven.

And I knew my family was watching me—and laughing. I was always on. My family loved to laugh and would always encourage us to get up and do it. That's where it starts—by making your folks laugh. And we had such a big family—with cousins and aunts and uncles—that there was always a big room to play to. I mean, I've played smaller crowds now than I did as a kid on Passover.

And, of course, there was my Uncle Berns. What a funny man. He was very much like Sid Caesar—he had those same skills. Sid was a great physical mime, and Berns had the same kind of ability, being a clown master. For us he was *the magic man*. And he would encourage us to be funny in any situation. He was dangerous and bawdy, the uncle you could play with.

He was also the one you could actually perform with. He was a big guy—like six-four—and I was a little guy. He'd walk in and—boom!—I'd be up on his shoulders, and we'd put a top coat around us, so that I looked like I was an eight-foot man! Or we'd do fake operas, where we'd all pick a language and . . . just do it.

He was like a big kid—God bless him.

"Uncle Berns was a true eccentric—bigger than life.
He taught us about color and expression. He equated
comedy and art. 'Who's funnier than Picasso?' he'd say.
'Everyone has three eyes and six tits!'"
—Billy Crystal, *700 Sundays*

On the Road

Not too long ago, I found an old childhood diary of mine. The little burgundy leather book with the gold lock, the key long lost, had been my loyal friend from the time I was 8 until I was about 11. I dusted off the cover and there was the name I'd been born with, Margaret, embossed on the front in shiny block letters. I'd been nicknamed Margo, which I couldn't pronounce—it came out Marlo. And that's what I've been called ever since.

I opened the diary and leafed through the pages. I was amazed. I had forgotten how much turmoil there had been in our young lives.

On every few pages were casual entries about the departure and return of our parents.

"Dear Diary, Mommie left today to go to Chicago to see Daddy."

"Dear Diary, Daddy came home today and we watched *Miracle of Morgan's Creek* after dinner."

"Dear Diary, Daddy left for Florida today. Mommie doesn't go away till Friday."

We were kids, so we adapted to this kind of life, even though when my parents went away, it was like the circus had left town. The parties, the laughter and the music went with them.

And the house got darker. My parents' room was on the second floor, and the living room—where all the action took place—was on the first floor just below it, on the left side of the house. That meant that when Mom and Dad were gone, all of the lights were off on that entire side of the house. It was gloomy, ghostly and very lonely.

I didn't like coming home after school through the front door, because it was right in the middle of the house, and you could really sense the dark chill of their absence. So I used the back door, walking through the kitchen and up the back stairs to the kids' rooms, on the other side of the house.

To this day, I hate a dark house. Wherever I live is lit up like a Christmas tree. The lights are on in every room.

Whenever Dad was away and Mom was home, we'd take turns sleeping in bed with her. Some nights we'd all sleep with her. She liked that—she was lonely, too. When it was time for her to join Dad on the road, we would cry and beg her not to leave.

"Why do you have to go?" we'd wail. Mom had the most brilliant and practical explanation.

"Daddy has to go away so he can work," she'd say, "so we can buy all the nice things we have and live in our pretty house. And poor Daddy gets lonely for his girls. So one of us has to go and keep him company. And since you have school, I'm the one who has to go."

That always settled it. The only thing was, whenever we would visit "poor Daddy" on the road and go to one of his shows, he never seemed all that sad. On stage, his eyes would be glistening like they were dancing, and he'd have that same mischievous look on his face that he had at home when he would tease us about something. He was never happier than when he was working in front of an audience, making people laugh. You could see it.

When my parents were on the road, we were left in the care of Melanie and Anderson, the couple who had been with us all our young lives, and

All aboard—again.

who we dearly loved. My parents also made sure there was always family in the house, like an aunt or an uncle. Some we loved, others we didn't even like. And, of course, there was the ever-rotating nanny.

My dad once told us a joke about a man who goes to Russia, and warns his wife that they censor your mail there. So they come up with a plan: If what he writes in his letter is true, he'll use blue ink. If it's false, he'll write in red ink.

His first letter arrives. It's in blue ink, and it says: "Russia is one of the most beautiful places I have ever seen. The people are happy and friendly. There is plenty to eat, the food is wonderful, and there are lovely shops everywhere. In fact, they have everything here in Russia that we have in America. Everything but red ink."

This became my family's code for how we felt about who was taking care of us when they went out of town. My parents would call and ask, "So, how do you like Gert?"—referring to our new nurse, the one who'd surely been trained by the Nazis.

"We love her," we'd say. "She's great. Red ink! Red ink!"

Mother would be home on the next plane.

The week leading up to my parents' return was always exciting. Terre and I would write songs, poems and skits to welcome them back. We'd hang a sign on the front door that read, "WELCOME HOME MOM & DAD!" then make pom-poms and write little cheers.

"You are the best mom and dad in the land . . . !"

The day our parents were to arrive, we'd watch excitedly through the front window to see when their car was approaching. Then we'd sprint out the front door and go into our routine. They would barely be out of the car, and we were all over them like puppies—hugging and squealing and looking for our presents. The circus was back.

WHEN I WAS TWELVE, I wrote an essay in school called "Viva Today." It was about how everyone was so busy working for tomorrow, that they sometimes forgot about living their lives today. I used my father as an example.

"He's always away, working hard to make a better tomorrow for his children," I wrote, "but when he finally comes home for good, we'll probably be grown and gone." And I ended with the words, "So, I say, *Viva Today!*"

A few nights later, our parents made their daily call to us from the road. Every night, they would make the call person-to-person to a different child, giving each of us our own turn.

"Long distance, calling Miss Marlo Thomas." It was very exciting. Then we'd all get on the phone, one by one, and tell them about our day and what we did in school.

On that particular night, I proudly told Dad that I had gotten an A on my school essay, so he asked me to read it to him. I did. When I was done, there was a silence on the other end. Finally, he said softly, "That's beautiful, Mugs. Daddy needs to think about that."

Years later, I would learn that soon after he called Uncle Abe (Abe Lastfogel, his agent, mentor and surrogate father) and told him he wanted to get off the road. Could Abe get him a TV series? That set the wheels in motion. Dad spitballed with his writers, and they came up with the premise for the show—about a nightclub entertainer who is always on the road and desperately trying to have a family life. They got their title from what Mom used to say whenever my father was coming home from the road and she threw us out of her bed.

"We have to make room for Daddy."

ABOUT A YEAR after my father died, I went on the road with the national company of John Guare's *Six Degrees of Separation*. It was an eight-month separation from my husband and home. At the time, Phil was taping *Donahue* five days a week, and I was working six days a week in the play. So we took turns visiting each other, finding as many ways as we could to be together on our days off.

Opening in a new city every month, traveling and then promoting the show on your one day off is hard work. But *Six Degrees* is a wonderful play with a terrific part, and I loved performing it.

At night I'd get back to the hotel feeling exhilarated by that evening's performance—all the laughs, applause and affection of the audience. I'd have my nightcap of an Amstel Light and a Snickers from the minibar, look out the window at another strange skyline, and think, *Is this what it was like for you, Dad? Loving the few hours of getting laughs and being appreciated by an audience, then facing a night alone away from home? You didn't have the circus either, did you?*

DID YA HEAR THE ONE ABOUT . . .

A Russian and an American were arguing about
whose country had the most freedom.

The American said, "We're so free in America,
if I want to, I can piss on the President's car."

"Big deal," replied the Russian. "We're so free in
Russia, if I want to, I can take a crap in Red Square."

The American, feeling a twinge of guilt, confessed,
"Well, I have to admit. It's true, I *can* piss on
the President's car. But not while he's in it."

"Well, since you're being honest," said the
Russian, "I will be honest, too. I *can* take a crap in
Red Square, provided I don't take my pants off."

The First Laugh

If comic talent could be converted to nuclear energy,
Robin Williams could fuel his own personal power plant.
Ever alert, lightning-quick and practically possessed by an
enormous cast of characters and voices, the man can't help
but be funny. And we can't help but be drawn to him
and his obvious joy in entertaining us.
I worked with Robin on one of my TV
specials, and he spent as much time cracking
up the crew as he did performing on camera.
I have gotten to know Robin over the years,
so I've had the chance to discover the warm
heart at the center of all this hilarious chaos.
I was excited to sit down with him to find out how
he grew up laughing, and early in our conversation,
I asked him if he had a favorite joke. As you'll see,
he had many. But he started by talking about where
all the laughter began . . .
—M.T.

ROBIN
WILLIAMS

Robin: The first laugh is always the one that gets you hooked. And it's usually from a mother or a father. For me, it was my mother. I was always trying to make her laugh.

My mother was the funny one. My father had a good sense of humor, but it was dry. Both of my parents grew up in the Depression, but they came at life in different ways. Hers was extreme optimism; his was extreme realism.

My mother was outrageous funny—the only woman who ever rendered Joan Rivers speechless. Mom was once standing next to Carol Channing—who had a frozen smile that looked like Dr. Caligari's—and cracked, "Whatever you do, Carol, never get plastic surgery." Mom would say anything.

I used to love making my mother laugh. She was the comic influence in my life. My dad was more concerned with the acting thing. He had this great advice for me: "You want to be an actor? Then you should have a backup profession. Like welding."

Mom would also recite these sly verses. Not the "old man from Nantucket" kind, but stuff like "I love you in blue, I love you in red, but most of all . . . I love you in blue."

She wasn't afraid of the physical stuff, either. She had this bit where she'd pull a rubber band out of her nose. She also wasn't averse to taking the occasional fashion risk. She'd put on hot pants and a Harpo wig if the mood was right. The cowboy hat and evening gown was not out of her repertoire, either. She had this leopard muff—literally made from a real leopard—and a hat made from the same fur. At least, I think it was the same animal. I'm hoping they didn't get the whole family. One time she wanted to wear these furs to a zoo benefit. I said, "Jeez, Mom, that's like wearing a Gestapo uniform to a B'nai B'rith event. It's gonna be a hard night, you know?"

So, yes, if you grew up with that, pretty much anything is possible.

***Quick joke.** How do you get an eighty-year-old woman to say "fuck"? Yell "Bingo!" before her.*

I was born in Chicago, went to a private high school in Detroit, and lived in California for a while. My father was in the automobile industry, so we moved around a lot. Some comics grew up in tough neighborhoods, but not me. Where I grew up, people had their lawyers beat up someone else's lawyer. And the neighborhood kids had imaginary agents.

But I started noticing comedians very early on. Jonathan Winters was my favorite. He could even make my father laugh. As a boy, I realized, "Wow, that's a tough gig."

And I've always admired a fast mind. I remember hearing this great story about Elaine May. She was walking across the campus at the University of Chicago, and the wind was blowing her hair straight up into a big mess. This guy walks by and says, "Hey, Elaine, where's your broomstick?" And she says, "Why, do you need something to shove up your ass?"

***Quick joke.** Two old Jews are sent to kill Hitler. They're sitting in an alleyway with grenades, rifles and bombs, and they're all ready. Hitler's supposed to walk by at two o'clock—but at two, he doesn't arrive. Two-fifteen, no Hitler. Two-thirty, no Hitler. Three o'clock, no Hitler. Finally, one Jew turns to the other and says, "My God, I hope nothing happened to him."*

I was very quiet in high school. I went to an all-boys school for three years (*that'll* keep you quiet). But what started it all for me was when I took an improvisational theatre class in college. After that, all bets were off—for two reasons: The teacher was a gorgeous woman who was about twenty-five years old, and all the guys were taking the class basically for her. But I also started getting laughs on stuff that I improvised. And that became addictive.

Comedians are an interesting breed of animal. We have this very bizarre combination of masochism and exhibitionism that goes way beyond acting. I suppose it's a kind of legalized insanity, in which you're allowed to do things that, if you did them in any other venue, you'd get arrested.

Quick joke. A guy picks up a hooker. She takes him upstairs to her room and asks him what he wants. The guy says, "Oral sex." The hooker says, "Okay, and I want you to know I'm one of the best at that. Look at my wrist. You see that lovely diamond bracelet? Well, that's how I got it." The guy says, "Really?"

And the hooker says, "Sure, see for yourself." So the hooker gives the man oral sex, and afterwards he says, "Wow, you were right. I can see how you earned that diamond bracelet." And the hooker says, "Yeah, and if I had a vagina I'd own this town."

When I left school, I couldn't find any acting work. So I wound up in the basement of one of those tiny little music clubs and coffeehouses, which were trying out stand-up comedy as kind of a spacer. I thought, "Okay, I'll try it. It's like improvising—but all alone." Before long, the music scene died out and comedy became more popular.

Quick joke. Guy buys a parrot that is constantly using foul language. Really horrible stuff. Finally the guy gets fed up and throws the parrot in the freezer to punish him. After about an hour, he hears a faint tapping sound from inside the freezer and opens the door. There's the parrot, wings wrapped around himself, shivering. He says, "I swear, I'll never, ever curse again. But can I ask you a question? What did the chicken do?"

But the funniest person in my life was my mother. Big time. I had a pillow that I kept on my couch that had this quote on it, supposedly from Sigmund Freud. It said, "If it's not one thing, it's your mother." Mom looked at that pillow and said, "What does *that* mean?" I said, "Sorry, Mom, I can't explain it to you without a therapist in the room." It's like that old saying, "Your mother pushes your buttons because she installed them."

My mother died in 2001, a week before September 11th. That was probably good, in a way. The events of that day would have really shocked her. They would have upset her worldview that everything is wonderful.

CHAPTER II

The Funny Barber

Harry Gelbart was my dad's barber. He was a small man with a full head of black, curly hair, a thick mustache and twinkly eyes. He and my dad adored each other, and while he cut my father's hair, they loved to tell jokes. They probably spent as much time telling stories as they did on the haircut.

I always knew when Harry was over—you could hear their howling laughter all through the house. It was irresistible. I would stop whatever I was doing and run to my father's dressing room to be with them. I'd sit on the edge of the tub and listen to the jokes they'd tell. Harry was a great storyteller, and my dad was a great audience. So was I.

Harry had a sixteen-year-old son who wanted to be a comedy writer, and one day he asked Dad if he could help his son break into the business. My father told him to send the kid over to the studio, and he'd give him a chance to write a few gags.

Harry's son started by hanging around the writers' room and throwing out a few lines. Dad was impressed and began using some of his jokes. That was the beginning of a wonderful career. Larry Gelbart would go on to become a legend in the business, writing such classic comedies as *M*A*S*H*, *Oh, God!* and *A Funny Thing Happened on the Way to the Forum*.

Some of Harry's stories were so good they would end up in Dad's act. Of course, Harry would tell his version in a few minutes. But my father would take the spine of the story and make a twenty-minute routine out of it. That was his trademark. And he always gave Harry credit.

One of those stories became a Danny Thomas classic. It was about an old

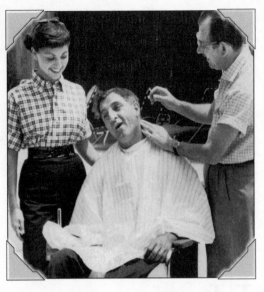

Harry cutting Dad's hair.
As usual, I was right there for the laughs.

man and a parrot that could speak Hebrew. When I told Larry that I wanted to write about our dads' friendship—and the way my dad used to tell his father's stories—he said he'd once written about it, too, and emailed me his favorite part:

> My father, that inveterate joke teller (not too hard to get laughs when you're wielding a straight razor) told Thomas about a man who takes his parrot, one that happens to be a brilliant linguist, to synagogue with him on Rosh Hashanah and wagers with members of the congregation that the bird can conduct the High Holiday service better than the temple's cantor. When the big moment comes, the parrot remains silent. Later, about to be punished by his outraged owner for the costly silence, the only thing that saves the bird's life is when he opens his beak and snaps: 'Schmuck. Think of the odds we'll get on Yom Kippur!' "

A funny joke, to be sure. But my dad was a *storyteller,* and in his hands, it became a small play, complete with the *Kol Nidre,* a chanted prayer of the Jewish High Holy Days (which he had learned when he played the son of a rabbi in the 1952 remake of the movie *The Jazz Singer*). Here's what his audience heard at the Sands Hotel in Las Vegas—music, dialects, and all . . .

Danny: This is a story about a little man, whom I ask you now to picture in your mind's eye—a middle-aged man on the healthy side of the financial ledger, walking in the business district of his hometown on a balmy summer's evening. And he happens to be passing a pet shop.

Dad was never happier than when he was on stage.
Look at those shining eyes.

It's a warm night, and the pet shop door is wide open, and through that open door, over the yelping of little canines and the screeching of the canaries, there comes to this man's ears a most familiar strain of music. And he slackens his pace and he listens. And he hears:

[*Slowly chants*] *"Kol, Kol, Kol nidre . . ."*

This man stands cemented in his tracks, for this is the music of his faith. The chanting continues, and the man walks into that little pet shop as though hypnotized. He gets inside and stands in complete awe and amazement at what he sees and what he hears. And he hears:

[*Continues chant*] *"Veesore vacharom . . ."*

"Ve'esarei, Vacharamei, Vekonamei, Vechinuyei . . ."

. . . coming from *a parrot*! But there it was, unbelievable though it may be, this little parrot on its perch, chanting away the sacred and semi-sacred Hebraic hymns! And a costly bird it was. But no matter what its price, the man had to buy it—and buy it he did. And every night he would sit in his favorite rocking chair, and the parrot would chant to him, oftentimes simple little Sabbath hymns like . . .

"L'cha dodi likrat kala

"P'nei shabbat n'kabla . . ."

The man was so happy with life, he could hardly wait for the High Holy Days to come.

Finally the week of Rosh Hashanah rolled around—Rosh Hashanah, taken from the ancient Aramaic, *rosh hashshanah*. It means the head of the year, the new year. A very happy holiday.

Off the old man goes to a tailor shop and has a *tallis* made for the parrot. That's a prayer shawl. Also a little *yarmulke*. That's a black skullcap. He has the same outfit made for himself, and they walk out of the tailor shop, father and parrot.

Now it's the day of Rosh Hashanah, and off they go to the synagogue—the old man sprightly running up the steps with the parrot following closely behind. They get to the front door—there's a fellow there called the *shamos*, like a sexton. Takes care of the synagogue. Also takes tickets on High Holidays.

And the shamos says, "Vait! Vere you going vith da boid? Vat you tink we're running here, a zoo?"

And the old man says, "Don't be so smart. Dat boid—*dat boid*—could chant better from you, da cantor, da rabbi and me put togeddah."

Naturally, from the shamos, comes the inevitable of all clichés: "Put da money vare da mouth is."

So they make a slight wager. While they're betting, other members of the congregation come up the steps, get into the argument, and before you know it there's $4800 bet. On a handshake, of course. They do *not* carry money on this day.

Now there is $4800 bet! And the old man looks at the fellas and says, "You're crazy! You lost already da money. Vait till you hear dat boid."

[*To bird*] "Okay, darling, make a chant. [*Pause*] Sveetheart, ve're vaiting—go ahead, make a chant. Don't be noivous. Could be something simple, like . . ."

[*Hums a little Hebrew melody*]

Nothing comes out of the bird. Not a peep. Not even "Polly wants a matzoh!" Nothing! One hour—begging, pleading, prodding, pushing—nothing comes outa the bird! And he loses the bet. He blows $4800!

Now he's incensed. He grabs the parrot by the throat, runs home and throws it on the floor. Goes into the kitchen, begins to cry for what he's gonna do. Gets the biggest butcher knife he can find, and he starts to sharpen it.

In comes the parrot. Looks up at the old man and says, "*Nu?* Vat are you doing?"

And the old man says, "You got a mouth now, huh? You're talking. Forty-eight-hundred you cost me—vouldn't make one chant! I'm gonna take that knife and cut off your head!"

The parrot says, "Vait! Vait! Don't be such a dummy. Vait for Yom Kippur—ve'll get bigger odds!"

My barber, Harry Gelbart, told me that story. I gotta go back and get another haircut, real soon . . .

DID YA HEAR THE ONE ABOUT . . .

A man was getting a haircut prior to a trip to Rome.

"Rome?" the barber asks. "Why would anyone want to go there? It's crowded, dirty and full of Italians. You're crazy to go there. What airline are you taking?"

"United," the guys says.

"United?" says the barber. "Terrible airline! The planes are old, the flight attendants are rude, and they're always late. Where are you staying in Rome?"

"The International Marriott," the guy says.

"That dump?" says the barber. "Worst hotel in the city. Overpriced, small rooms and lousy service. So whatcha doing when you get there?"

"We're going to the Vatican. We hope to see the Pope."

"That's rich," laughed the barber. "You and a million other people. He'll look the size of an ant. Good luck on this lousy trip of yours. You're going to need it."

A month later, the man returns for his regular haircut. The barber asked him about his trip to Rome.

"It was wonderful," the man says. "The planes were on time and we even got bumped up to first class. The hotel was gorgeous but overbooked, so they apologized and gave us the presidential suite— at no extra charge! And the food was incredible."

"Well," muttered the barber, "I know you didn't get to see the Pope."

"Actually," the man says, "we were quite lucky. As we toured the Vatican, a guard tapped me on the shoulder and explained that the Pope likes to personally meet some of the visitors, then took me to the Pope's private chamber. The door opens, the Pope walks in and I nearly fainted. I knelt down and he spoke to me."

"My God!" said the amazed barber. "What did he say?"

"He said, 'Where'd you get the lousy haircut?'"

He Said/He Said

*Ben Stiller grew up a lot like I did—only harder.
Both of his parents were performers—the popular comedy
team of Jerry Stiller and Anne Meara—and like all comics,
they frequently went on the road. Ben likes to tell stories of
how, when his parents were home, he and his sister Amy
would perform for them. Maybe all showbiz kids do this.
Terre and I were always putting on shows—from our
closet. It had a sliding door, which one of us
would pull back so that the other could pop
out and do her bit. We even had theme
songs. Children everywhere imitate the
grown-ups in their lives—showbiz kids just
have more material to work with. In the
1970s, Stiller and Meara were regular
guests on a popular game show called*
Tattletales, *in which celebrity couples had to answer
questions about each other—separately. So that's
how I decided to talk to Ben and Jerry—
first Ben, then Jerry.*
—M.T.

BEN & JERRY STILLER

Rehearsing at Home

Ben: When my parents weren't on the road, they were always writing their act together at home, and my sister Amy and I could hear them. There was this one routine they did called "The Hate Sketch," about a married couple and how much they hated each other. They would just go off: "I hate you," "I hate you so much," "I have such a big hate for you." We'd hear them yelling and we weren't sure if they were rehearsing or fighting. To my sister and me, this was what we were living with, and we didn't realize till later how funny that was.

Jerry: Our apartment wasn't very big—maybe five rooms—so Anne and I would rehearse in the living room. We'd turn on a tape recorder and write our act. So one day we're practicing "The Hate Sketch"—screaming at each other—and Amy walks in. She couldn't have been more than three years old and she was crying. She said, "Mommy and Daddy fight?" I said, "No, no, honey, Mommy and Daddy rehearse!" Two weeks later, Anne and I were having an argument, and Amy comes in and gives this big smile and says, "Mommy and Daddy rehearse!" I said, "No, no, honey, Mommy and Daddy fight."

Getting the *Shpilkes*

Ben: My parents did everything from nightclubs and summer stock to TV shows and game shows. I remember the game shows the best. There was this one show called *Tattletales* that was like a celebrity *Newlywed Game,* and Amy and I would watch it from backstage. There was definitely a stress level watching my parents perform. I wanted people to laugh and enjoy them.

Jerry: Amy and Ben would be in the green room when we were doing *Tattletales.* The idea of the show was that one spouse would tell a story about themselves and the other spouse would try to match it. But any time Anne and I screwed up, the kids would scream at us. "Don't you guys remember what you did? Why didn't you get that right?!" We tried to tell them, "Look, it doesn't matter—people came, they laughed, they had a good time." But the kids were still mad at us. They took the show very, very seriously.

Ben's Little Secret

Ben: When I was little, I wanted to be a spy. So I'd sneak a tape recorder into my parents' room and tape them. I think they knew what was going on, but they would play along. They were very encouraging of our playfulness.

Jerry: He put a tape recorder in our bedroom? That's what Ben said? I had no idea—I can't believe it. Oh, my God.

Parties at the House

Ben: My parents would throw parties—Thanksgiving, New Year's, even Passover Seders—and all these comedians would come over. Rodney Dangerfield, Andy Kaufman, Henny Youngman. My sister and I grew up around comedians and actors hanging out on late nights at our house. I really loved being around them. They were fun and funny and over-the-top.

Jerry: Everybody showed up. Henny, Jimmy Coco, Bill Hurt, Kevin Spacey. Actors love to come to a party, you know.

And we had a few Seders with Rodney. But he'd always have to leave early to keep an eye on his comedy club on First Avenue. He was the boss. He'd joke, "I don't even know why I'm here tonight. I don't play on Passover." Henny was funny, too. He'd sit in a chair and tell one joke after another, and everyone would be convulsing. He loved any kind of audience. But he always had the same line whenever I'd invite him to a party: "Over six people, and they pay."

Going to Work with Mom and Dad

Ben: I remember when they opened in the Persian Room at the Plaza. They were performing with Lola Falana. I was six or seven and I got to hang backstage in Lola's dressing room, which was really exotic. I also remember going to Vegas and Reno with them when they played the hotels out there. That was the best thing ever.

Jerry: Anne and I would schlep out to Vegas or Tahoe, and in summer we'd take the kids with us. We had a nanny who looked after them while we worked. One time, Gladys Knight and the Pips were staying at our hotel, so while Anne and I rehearsed, the kids would play in the pool with the Pips. We also put the kids into a day school. Later we found out they weren't going to the school. They were going to Circus Circus and playing the slots.

Following in Their Footsteps. Or Not.

Ben: You know I resisted it for a long time. I didn't think I wanted to be in show business, partly because my parents did it, and I wanted to do my own thing.

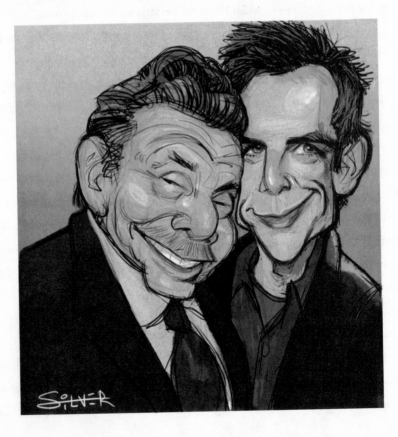

Jerry: Anne and I were once guest-hosting *The Mike Douglas Show*, and the talent coordinator says, "You've got to bring your kids on the show." Anne says to me, "No we are *not* going to bring the kids on"—she was vehement about this. But they kept pushing us. *"Come on, they'll have a little fun."* I finally said okay. The talent coordinator asks me, "So what do they do?" I say, "What do you mean what do they do? They're kids. It's not like they do impressions. They don't do anything!" Finally I tell him, "Well, they *are* taking violin lessons." "Great," the talent coordinator says, "let's have them play the violin." I say, "But they're *terrible*."

So they bring Amy and Ben on anyway, and they play "Chopsticks" on the violin—and they're really horrible. The audience was nice, but Amy and Ben were humiliated. Ben said to me, "You know, Dad, the kids in school are going to give it to us good for being so bad." And we did get a couple of cards from people saying, "How could you bring such terribly untalented children on television?"

Learning the Craft

Ben: Both of my parents were actors first, so I learned from them that you don't approach comedy any differently than you approach drama. If the material is funny, you don't need to play it up. You make your acting choice, and it just happens to be the more comedic one. That's what I always saw my parents do.

Jerry: I remember when Ben and Amy were about ten or eleven, they created this pretend acting class. Ben played the teacher, and I was the student coming in to take acting lessons. I started to do my first line, and Ben stopped me in the middle and tore me apart. He'd given me a name—"Bernard"—and he said, "Bernard, why don't you start the scene again, and this time think a little more about where you were *before* you came on stage." I tried again, but Ben wasn't very encouraging. He said, "Bernard, do not go into this business. It will only bring you heartbreak. You will bring humiliation upon yourself." It was a riot.

Using the Craft—and Embarrassing Your Parents

Ben: The masturbation scene in *There's Something About Mary*—yeah, I remember that day. That was a lonely scene. The directors, everybody, just sort of disappeared. Honestly, that was one of those things that, as an actor, I thought was very funny. I thought the movie was funny. And I was happy to have the job.

Jerry: When we got into the theatre, Ben was sitting about three rows in front of us, and he turned around and he said, "Dad, Mom, I hope you don't get embarrassed by what you're going to see." He was very serious. So the movie starts, and . . . I never laughed so hard in my life. Ben kept turning around and looking at us to be sure that we were not embarrassed, but all he saw was me laughing. As for that scene, what can I say? That's Ben. He really throws himself into a part.

Stillers: The Next Generation

Ben: I think what you learn when you have kids is that they come with their own personalities. My kids are so ridiculously funny to me. They love to do little characters. It's like they channel it from somewhere, and it makes you realize that they're born with it.

Jerry: Well, like all grandchildren, there's something special about them, and you never know what's going to happen. But I hope to God—and I really mean this—that they don't go into this business. They'd have to live up to two generations already! If they do, I hope they can navigate through it all, which is not easy.

My father was a bus driver, the funniest bus driver in New York. He would have gotten me a job—he had seniority and all of that—but I said no, and went off to be a comedian. He never really thought much of my work. He wanted to be a comedian himself.

But, God Almighty, was he funny . . .

THE DANGERFIELD ZONE
Remembering Rodney

"My wife only has sex with me for a purpose.
Last night she used me to time an egg."

"I was making love to this girl and she started crying.
I said, 'Are you going to hate yourself in the morning?'
She said, 'No, I hate myself now.'"

"Last night my wife met me at the front door.
She was wearing a sexy negligee.
The only trouble was, she was coming home."

"If it weren't for pickpockets, I'd have no sex life at all."

"My wife is such a bad cook, if we leave dental floss
in the kitchen the roaches hang themselves."

"My wife likes to talk on the phone during sex—
she called me from Chicago last night."

aka Orson

Where do you get your sense of humor from?

"I don't think you can learn to be funny," Larry Gelbart told me, "but you can grow up in an environment where you appreciate the surprise in a joke. You can develop a sense of humor."

You know the old saying, there are two kinds of people—those who see the glass half-empty, and those who see it half-full? Well, there are *three* kinds of people when it comes to seeing the funny in something— those who don't see it for years until they look back at it, those who will never see it, and those who see it as it's happening.

I remember one night my mother and father were bickering about something at the dinner table. The words flew back and forth, things escalated, and Dad angrily got up and left the table.

We all watched wide-eyed as my father stormed across the marble floor of our entry hall to the bottom of the long, winding staircase. Placing his hand on the carved oak banister, with the Viennese chandelier hanging overhead, he turned in fury to us and bellowed:

"Rose Marie, I cannot live like this!"

Then he doubled over in laughter. We all did. As angry as he was, he suddenly saw himself—a man standing in his opulent Beverly Hills stairwell announcing he couldn't live like this anymore. It took about a second for him to recognize the absurdity of it.

Where did he get this ability to instantly see the funny? Certainly not from his stern father, my scary Lebanese grandpa. My grandparents were very poor. They had ten kids—nine boys and a girl—and little else. And as in all of the immigrant families in their neighborhood, my grandmother was cook, laundress and nanny for the entire family. But after giving birth to her fifth son, my father, she became too ill to care for him, so for a while he lived with Grandma's brother, Tony, and his wife, Julia. They couldn't have children of their own, so for them this was a true blessing.

Uncle Tony was what the family called "a real card." He saw the humor in just about everything. My father once told me that he was so funny, he was barred from family funerals. (Years later, Uncle Tony would be personified as Uncle Tonoose on Dad's TV show, *Make Room for Daddy*.)

Dad and Aunt Julia,
his "second mom."

Uncle Tony—
the real Uncle Tonoose.

Uncle Tony and Aunt Julia not only gave my father a roof over his head and a lot of love and warmth, Uncle Tony also gave Dad the gift of laughter—a flair for the comedic in everything he did, including his parenting.

Dad's sense of drama, he must have picked up on his own. When I was in high school, I was supposed to be home at midnight on date nights. And my father was strict. When he said midnight, that meant 12:00 A.M., not 12:05. When we were teenagers, most of our dates took us to the movies. Afterward, we'd all go to Webb's, a drive-in restaurant on Linden and Wilshire, for a hamburger and fries. Everyone else was carefree, but I was constantly looking at the clock. The car radio was always tuned to our favorite show, which at midnight played "Goodnight, Sweetheart." That was a song I really didn't want to hear when I was still at Webb's, because that would mean I was past my curfew.

One night, we were all munching burgers, laughing and having a grand old teenage time. My date was so cute—tall, blond, all-American. He'd been voted Best Looking Boy at Beverly Hills High, and his name was all-American, too—Johnnie Anderson.

Suddenly the first strains of "Goodnight, Sweetheart" began to play on the radio.

"Oh, my God!" I screeched. "I've gotta go!"

Johnnie and I raced up to my house on the corner of Elm and Elevado. It was now 12:15, and my father was standing out in our driveway, wearing a black coat and a black hat—with a big black cigar in his mouth and a shotgun in his hand. Oh, the drama. We used to call him "Orson" (as in Welles) because he reveled in the dramatic.

Johnnie Anderson was a real WASP. He wasn't used to the histrionics of Middle Eastern fathers. We got out of the car. Orson just stood there, shotgun in hand.

"Young man, what time were you supposed to bring my daughter home?" Orson asked.

"Midnight, sir," Johnnie said quietly, terrified.

"And what time is it, young man?"

"12:15, sir."

"Well, then you're late, aren't you?" Orson said.

You could barely hear Johnnie's "yes" as he ran back to his car and drove off.

I was furious. "God, Daddy, how embarrassing," I said. "No one will ever ask me out if you keep acting like this."

"Wow, I really scared him," Dad said, then he burst out laughing. So did I. I could have killed him, but it *was* funny.

Orson's drama also had a musical side to it. One night I was with my boyfriend and it was late. We were in the den on the comfy sofa, doing what teenagers do—lights low, music softly playing. Suddenly a John Philip Sousa march blasted through the speakers. Nothing kills the mood like Sousa. Orson's message to my date was clear: "March!"

As if my father's late-night deejaying wasn't anecdotal enough for my date, my lunatic family had one more surprise. When we turned on the lights, there was Terre, crouched, hiding under the pool table with our cocker spaniel, Muggins, spying on us to see what the big kids do.

"Who's she?" my date asked, as he frantically looked for his jacket.

"I'm her sister," Terre snapped, "and you have no idea how hard it is to lie there keeping this dog quiet, with his awful dog breath in my face!"

Another boy who never called me again.

Testifying with Chris Rock

With all the breakthroughs in television, seven words are still verboten on the networks—and Chris Rock says most of them in his cable specials. My dad's generation called this "working blue," and Chris has clearly made that his color palette. Although I had seen all of his specials, I decided to watch them again, back to back, before sitting down to talk with him. The one thing that stood out far stronger than the forbidden language was his preacher-like message: Be responsible for your kids. Don't cheat. Pay attention to what your government is doing. Get a job. Stay in school. Treat women with respect. It's all there, woven in with the outrageous language and his larger-than-life energy. When I told Chris that I thought he was really a preacher at heart, his answer surprised me. "My grandfather and great-grandfather were preachers," he said. I guess it's not just comedy that's in our DNA.

—M.T.

CHRIS ROCK

Marlo: To be a successful nightclub comic, you have to have a lot of energy. But you have more energy than almost anyone I've ever seen. Most guys stay pretty close to the mike. You pace wildly back and forth, stalking the audience like a caged tiger. Why is that? *What* is that?

Chris: Basically I'm trying to be a good director.

Marlo: Meaning?

Chris: Meaning, if you're standing in one place, a person can turn away from you to say something to their friend, and then when they turn back you're right where they left you. But if you're walking around, they can't say anything to their friend. They have to pay attention.

Marlo: That's really interesting.

Chris: Yeah. I think [Eddie] Murphy was the one who told me that.

Marlo: And when you stop, we really pay attention.

Chris: Right. You stop on the punch line—and pow! It's walk-walk, plant, deliver punch line.

Marlo: Have you always moved back and forth like that?

Chris: You know, it's one of those things that, once I figured it out, it catapulted me. You learn a lot doing stand-up. First, you think it's all just about jokes. "All I need is jokes. If I have the best ones, this will work." Then if you're in it long enough, you realize that the guys who are actually the best performers go the furthest.

Marlo: And the guys with the best jokes?

Chris: They write for other people.

Marlo: Right.

Chris: So, you watch. And you get passed by some guys, and you learn from them. My friend Paul always says, "Competition keeps you in condition."

Marlo: That's right.

Chris: I remember before I cracked, I went to see Martin Lawrence at Radio City. And, you know, that was something—seeing somebody at Radio City who's your age, who started the same time as you, and he's playing in front of six thousand people while you're still playing in front of three hundred. You can be bitter and think there's some conspiracy against you, or you can sit there and *learn*.

Marlo: You're often compared to Eddie Murphy and Richard Pryor. That's a tough standard to live up to.

Chris: But those guys are better performers than me. They really are. They've got these great voices, great characters, and then they put jokes *around* those characters, where I just kind of start with the joke. But that doesn't faze me. I remember seeing Cosby one time and it was, like, one of the best shows I'd ever seen. It made me mad, like, "Uch, God, what am I doing with my life? How could this guy be so good?" And I said that to him when I went backstage after the show. And he said, "Well, of course I'm better than you. I've been doing this thirty years longer than you. What do you expect?"

Marlo: In Jerry Seinfeld's documentary, *The Comedian,* you come backstage and talk to Jerry about that. In the film, Jerry has been putting his act together, beat by beat, joke by joke, and you tell him you just saw two hours straight of Cosby, with all new material.

Chris: All new. All great. Confident.

Marlo: Right. And Seinfeld's face just falls. At this point, he has six minutes of new material, and that's all. We know exactly how he feels. But you not only keep coming up with new material, you also have something different from Pryor and Murphy. What do you think that is?

Chris: I guess just a different set of experiences. I didn't spend that much time on the chitlin circuit, so as a comic, I'm kind of raised by Jews, essentially. I was around guys like Robert Klein and David Brenner. I'm one of the rare black comics who got to spend a lot of time with Jewish comics. And because of that, I can perform just about anywhere.

Marlo: Like a lot of black comedians, you take white people to task. But you spend equal time taking black people to task.

Chris: I take *everybody* to task.

Marlo: Right. When I watch you on stage, I think there's got to be a preacher in your family somewhere because . . .

Chris: Oh, yeah—my grandfather.

Marlo: You're kidding me!

Chris: My grandfather and my great-grandfather.

Marlo: That's so funny. I was actually joking—but when I watch you, I think, *My God, this guy is sermonizing to people.* "Don't drop out of school. Get a job. Be responsible for your kids. Don't hit women." I mean, there's a whole moral code there, just like with preachers.

Chris: I like preachers. They're essentially doing the same kind of gig as me, just not trying to get a laugh. And we're both trying to hold people's attention.

Marlo: Right, and to lead them.

Chris: And to lead them. One of these days I want to do one big sermon as a TV special. A sermon can be about one topic for an hour and ten minutes. I would love to try to pull that off as a comedian. Literally talk about just one thing.

Marlo: I'm sure you could pull it off. You obviously picked up a lot from your grandfather.

Chris: Well, I spent a lot of time with him when he was preaching. He was like one of my best friends. He had tons of talent and used to preach on the weekends. He'd drive a cab during the week, and I'd sit with him in the front of the cab. And he would never write the sermon—he would just write the bullet points, then kind of rip the sermon. And I write my jokes in the same way. The important thing is what I want to talk about. *We'll figure out how to make this funny later, but right now, the most important thing is the topic.*

Marlo: Exactly. Like your jokes about our having so much food in our country, that we have the luxury of being allergic to it. You say, "There's no dairy intolerance in Africa." That's such a great observation. Was your grandfather also funny?

Chris: Oh, he was hysterical, hysterical. Some people are just accidentally funny, but he loved being funny.

Marlo: In his sermons?

Chris: A little bit in his sermons, but mostly in his life. He was kind of a Mr. Magoo, and full of contradictions— he was a reverend, he went to jail, he cheated on my grandmother constantly, just loved the ladies. One of those complete guys.

Marlo: Did he get to see you be funny on stage?

Chris: A little bit, but he never got to come to a big house. He was gone before I bought the big house.

Marlo: Did he tell you jokes?

Chris: No, he never told me jokes. My whole family's humor was mostly about how bad they were going to kick somebody's ass that day.

Marlo: Like?

Chris: Like, my brother once told a guy, "I'm going to beat you so bad you'll be the only guy in heaven in a wheelchair"—and you knew he meant it. He wasn't telling a joke.

Marlo: Beat-up humor. That's a new one.

Chris: Yeah. My family never, never ran out of ass-kick metaphors.

Marlo: Tell me about your dad. You revealed a little bit about your relationship with him in your TV show, *Everybody Hates Chris.*

Chris: Yeah, same thing as my grandfather—he liked being funny. But my father was a straight guy. He didn't chase women. He was his own guy. I don't know how to explain my father. He was a teamster and the person they would always send somewhere to be the first black guy to work at that place. Because he could take it.

Marlo: Take what?

Chris: The abuse.

Marlo: Physical abuse?

Chris: Sometimes physical. Sometimes verbal. He was the first black driver at Rangel Brewery, the first one at the *Daily News* . . .

Marlo: A stand-up guy.

Chris: A real stand-up guy—and they knew he could take it. Long story short: At any factory job or wherever, somebody always sells coke. Somebody is always in charge of drugs. It's their territory and nobody else is allowed to sell them. Well, my father's friends were selling coke at the *Daily News,* and my father was the one guy who decided that he wasn't going to do it. And these were all guys I grew up with—I called them "Uncle." And they ended up going to jail. But not my dad—he was home.

Marlo: That takes a lot of nerve. Was he a big guy physically?

Chris: Yeah, he was pretty big. But everybody's dad is big to them.

Marlo: What I mean is, he was the guy you knew could take care of himself in a fight.

Chris: Yeah, but to "take it" meant, if somebody hit you, you didn't do anything back. That's what they meant by "take it." They wanted the guy who wasn't going to get in a riot, or end up getting killed.

Marlo: He must have had a big influence on you.

Chris: Yeah, it rubs off. I can definitely "take" show business. My God, what the hell. If you can't deal with "no," if you can't deal with abuse, you know you're in the wrong business.

Marlo: And what was your mom like?

Chris: My mom is funny—she's still funny. Well, not as funny now because she's trying to get into heaven.

Marlo: You mean she used to be dirty funny?

Chris: Yeah, but not sexual dirty. My mother used to curse up a storm. But if you mention that to her now, she's like, "What are you talking about? I never cursed."

Marlo: That's so funny. You know, something you do that I find really charming—and I haven't seen any other comedian do this except Red Skelton: You're often delighted with your own joke. Red would laugh after he said something funny, and you do that, too, sometimes.

Chris: But you know what? I'm laughing with the audience. I just like to see them laugh, especially those people who haven't laughed in a while—and you can spot them because they're laughing so hard. I like shocking a crowd. I like it when the wife hits the husband because he's laughing that shame laugh. That *I can't believe he said that!* laugh.

Marlo: All of the man-woman stuff you do is wonderful. Like when you say, "You ladies, you know your man better than he knows himself. You *know* what kind of man you have." You can just see the women in the audience loving it.

Chris: Because it's true! "You knew that if you didn't sleep with him for a month, something was bound to happen. You knew this wasn't the guy to go on strike with. But you did it anyway!"

Marlo: Just great. Your act is beautifully crafted. You know, when I was a kid, I was fascinated by watching how my father crafted his material. I always thought of him as a cross between an orchestra conductor and a bullfighter.

Chris: Yeah, well, you won't get bloody, but you can get hurt up there.

Marlo: Do you map out everything ahead of time, or do you figure it out on your feet?

Chris: It evolves. The average HBO special that you watch, that guy has probably done that material in 30 concerts. For every special I've done, I must have done at least 120 shows.

Marlo: So you know what works.

Chris: I know what works, but I play with it, too. I don't lock in on show number 30 and do the same thing. I play with the order. "Okay, I'm going to do all the relationship stuff first tonight." Or, "Okay, I'm not going to curse tonight." I just play with all of it and see how the act works inside and out. You've got to make it like a movie, especially when you play the big houses. Your mentality has to be a little different.

Marlo: In what way?

Chris: When you're in a club, you can do a quilt of jokes and get away with it. You can go from joke to joke to joke, and do that for fifty minutes—people are pretty impressed by that, and it's a fine feat. But if you're at Radio City Music Hall or Madison Square Garden, you have to have a *show*.

Marlo: Right.

Chris: You're standing in the same spot Prince was two nights earlier. And your ticket price isn't that much different from his. So it can't just be joke, joke, joke, joke, joke, joke, joke, joke. I mean, you have to get the laughs from the joke, joke, joke, but it's got to be more like a movie. And the houses help. I mean, you're not competing with a waitress, and it's all set up for you. So you should take that extra time and really use it to get that extra laugh.

Marlo: In a way, you're a lot like Lenny Bruce. He was very shocking at the time, mostly because of his language. But when you look back at it now, what he was basically saying to people was: "Wake up! Look at what's going on in this country and in this world." You do that, too.

Chris: I try. I've seen Lenny Bruce. This YouTube invention is the greatest thing of all time—punch up any comedian you want. Sometimes I'll sit for hours, just watching comics.

Marlo: What do you learn from them?

Chris: That the times can dictate a comedian's impact—that the years in which someone is doing comedy can help the comedian as much as anything else. Richard Pryor is great, don't get me wrong, but the times he was performing in—my God! How could you mess up in that era? Look at what the country was going through then. How could you not be great during segregation? Then you've got a guy like Eddie Murphy, who's great, but it wasn't really a deep time when he was on stage. By the eighties, the struggle was over for the most part, you know what I mean? It was a different time. Lenny Bruce was part of such a great time. Probably no comedian has been of a better time, really.

Marlo: You seem to have no trouble finding social issues to talk about, either. I laughed hard at your piece about blacks and Jews, where you say that blacks don't hate Jews, they hate *white people*. You talk about not putting everyone in little categories, which allows us to laugh at our own prejudices. That's a very brave and honest thing to say, and it helps to bang down doors. You also did a very strong piece about "blacks versus niggers," which you've since retired. Why?

Chris: I'm always retiring stuff. That's the downside of the YouTube era; people can watch your act at any moment, and you can't be up there doing old stuff. You used to be able to write an act then ride that act for twenty years.

Marlo: That's what my dad and all those guys of his era did. Tell me about school. Were you the funny kid?

Chris: No, I barely spoke. I was bused to school, and was the only black boy in my grade for five or six years—there were two girls. It was scary, but that's what was going on in '73. You could still be the first black kid somewhere, even in the seventies.

Marlo: So if you weren't funny at school, when did you start figuring out you could make people laugh?

Chris: I was always interested in being funny. I was a weird kid. I remember I could watch any TV show and tell you exactly what the next joke was.

Marlo: Really?

Chris: Really. Even when I was eight years old, I would watch a brand-new show and say, "Okay, now they're going to say this . . ." And I always loved comedians. I couldn't wait to see *The Dean Martin Roast*. What kid wants to watch a Dean Martin roast? Couldn't wait. And I loved Alan King. Black kid in Bed Stuy worshipping Alan King.

Marlo: What about your uncles? You once said that uncles prepare you for life.

Chris: They do.

Marlo: That there's the alcoholic uncle, and the gay uncle, and the stealing uncle. Did you observe this in your own family?

Chris: Yeah, all those uncles. I have an uncle who's a surgeon, too, but, you know, that's not funny. He always gets left out.

Marlo: You talk a lot about men and women on stage. You say, "When you meet somebody, you're actually only meeting their *representative*, because all men lie, and all women have hair extensions, makeup, and heels." That kind of comment could be offensive, especially to women, but the women in your audiences really seem to love it. How do you do that?

Chris: You've got to include the women in on the joke.

Marlo: Meaning?

Chris: Meaning, when I'm on stage doing relationship stuff, I'm essentially a woman comedian.

Marlo: Ah-hah.

Chris: There are very few jokes I do on relationships that a woman couldn't do. I remember Martin Lawrence once telling me that, unless you're AC/DC, there's always going to be more women in the crowd.

Marlo: Really?

Chris: Yeah. And so you want jokes that get the hard laughs, not just the cute laughs—because most humor that's directed towards women is kind of cutesy. Some comedians assume that the women at their shows were dragged there by men, but I approach the women in my audiences as if they actually came to see me. Because women like to laugh hard, too.

Marlo: We sure do. In watching your concerts, what I found most shocking was your take on O. J. Simpson. You actually make the argument that you understood why he may have committed murder. You run through the whole thing—he's paying twenty-five thousand a month in alimony, another guy is driving his car, he's paying the mortgage and the guy is coming to his house. You say, "He shouldn't have killed her—but I understand." I was floored by that. Weren't you afraid people would stone you for saying a thing like that?

Chris: It's funny, I never had any problems with that joke. With lots of jokes, it's like, "Oh, man, I've got to figure out how to get this one right." Like the niggers and black thing. When you don't have that joke right, it's the worst joke ever. I was dying every night. People were walking out, cursing me out. But never with the O.J. joke. Everybody laughs at it. And the important thing is, even *women* laugh at it because . . .

Marlo: Because they understand jealousy?

Chris: Yeah, and let's not kid ourselves here. We're not supposed to murder, but let's not act like none of us ever thought about killing somebody. I mean, most of us have a switch that says *you can't do that.* O.J.'s switch did not go off that day.

Marlo: So, in a way, that gives you the license to do a joke like that.
Chris: Right.

Marlo: Which a lot of other comedians might shy away from.

Chris: Look, when you listen to the news, you realize that it's so much easier to report things as black or white. But the world is not black and white. The world is grey.

CHAPTER 15

Beverly Hills,
My Neighborhood

T he words *Beverly Hills* conjure up Rodeo Drive, Hollywood and glamour. But for the kids who grew up there, it was just our neighborhood.

Well, maybe it *was* an odd hood to grow up in. Louella Parsons, the famous gossip columnist who, like all gossips, was known to write (make up?) items that could be hurtful—personally and professionally—lived across our alley on Maple Drive. She and her assistant, Dorothy, would take a walk around the block every afternoon at about five. My mother did not want to have any interaction with Louella, for fear of giving her something to *misinterpret.* So the minute she saw them approaching, she would quickly dart inside. We kids even avoided Louella's house on Halloween. In our neighborhood, she was the all-year-round witch.

But that didn't stop us from going to all the other houses on our street. We'd dress up in our costumes, many borrowed from studio wardrobe, and toddle up and down Elm Drive, clutching our little bags with dreams of candy apples in our heads.

Some of our neighbors didn't quite have the Halloween spirit. At Robert Young's house, we were given autographed 8×10 glossy pictures of him—and that's all. So, of course, we did what any group of right-minded, candy-deprived American kids would do—we soaped his windows.

Edward G. Robinson always had all his lights off, and never answered the door. But we knew he was home—we could see a TV flickering in a back room—so we soaped his windows, too (and anything else soap would stick to).

Elizabeth Taylor's mom was nice, and she gave out good cookies. They lived just three doors up from our corner house on Elm, on the opposite side of the street. So we had a good view of Elizabeth as she came out the door, looking so beautiful, on the day she married Nicky Hilton at Good Shepherd Church.

Good Shepherd was where everything took place for the Catholics in our neighborhood. We made our First Communions there, we were confirmed there, my sister and brother both had their weddings there, and we had the funeral Masses for Mom and Dad there. My father and Ricardo Montalban used to pass the donation basket, pew by pew, to the congregation every Sunday. For all of its legendary status, it really was a neighborhood.

At Christmastime our house became the place where everyone brought their children to look at the Nativity scene on our front lawn. This was Dad's creation, and he loved putting it together, with Tony as his loyal sidekick. It was their annual project and every year they would enhance it in some way. They were relentless, those two. They even found hay in Beverly Hills.

The crèche was beautiful, with detailed carvings of Mary, Joseph and the Baby Jesus; the stable with the hay; the Three Kings, bearing their gifts; and all the familiar animals. Then Dad added music—"Silent Night"— playing so low that you could only hear it when you got real close. It was magical.

One year, Dad was playing at the Sands in Las Vegas just before the holidays, and they'd put a huge star of lights on top of the hotel sign. Dad took one look at it, loaded it in his car and brought it home to put on top of his stable. It was quite a sight, and the neighborhood families loved the addition.

Except for Aaron Spelling, who was one of my dad's partners. Aaron thought my father's Nativity scene was quite lovely, but just a tad too Christian for the neighborhood. So one year he organized a special procession

Dad with his crèche (ABOVE) and with Aaron and his camel (BELOW).
That Christmas in Beverly Hills, there was something for everyone.

that marched down the street to our house. At the front of the parade, Aaron led a very large—and very real—camel that was wearing a horse blanket emblazoned with the Jewish star on both sides. It was an incredible sight. Dad—all of us—erupted in laughter. Aaron had put almost as much work into his prank as Dad had put into his biblical tableau. Aaron wasn't one of "The Boys," but he had pulled off a gag worthy of the best of them.

Today, Beverly Hills is an ultra-chic shopping extravaganza. But when we were growing up, it was simply "The Village."

"I'm going into The Village," Mom would say. "Anyone want to come?" Terre and I would run to go with her. Tony would hide—in a closet, under the pool table, wherever he'd fit. He once told me that when he was a boy, his definition of hell was going shopping with Mom, and sitting for hours while she tried on clothes and had them fitted.

The Village's hot spot was Nate 'n Al's, the terrific New York–style deli on Beverly Drive. That's where Dad, Harry and the guys would meet for lunch and laughs, and where our family often went on Sundays after Mass. Next door was Beverly Stationers, and across the street was the Beverly Camera Shop, Beverly Cheese Shop, Jurgensen's Market and Pioneer Hardware. These weren't chains. They were mom-and-pop stores, owned and run by the people who worked in them. We knew them by name and they looked out for us—for all the kids and their families.

The friends we made there would last a lifetime. We all lived just blocks apart from each other amid the swaying palm trees—Camille Cannan on Walden, Barry Diller on Linden, Gary Tobey on Rexford. We grew up rooting for one another, and still do to this day. But back then, we'd ride our bikes to Whelan Drugs on the corner of Beverly Drive for a lime rickey, or to J.J. Newberry's, where you could buy items for just a dollar then sit at the soda fountain and have a peanut butter and jelly sandwich and a cherry Coke, or down to Will Wright's on South Beverly for the best hot fudge sundae ever made.

And then there was Livingstone's, a sweet, one-story fabric and clothing shop for the whole family. I remember the day Mom and Grandma took me there to buy my first bra. It didn't have cups—just two triangles—but I was thrilled. In many ways, my everyday childhood memories aren't really that different from kids in other neighborhoods of that era.

Except maybe for the time we had an Arabian prince over for lunch.

I'm not sure how it happened, but my parents were asked to host a luncheon for a crown prince of Arabia on his visit to Hollywood. I guess the planners felt that because Dad was Lebanese, we were close enough. The prince wanted to meet the A-list of Hollywood—like Cary Grant, Frank Sinatra and Gregory Peck—and my mother couldn't wait to start planning the lunch. Mom, who was a great hostess, was about to climb the Mt. Everest of parties.

Through the years, Mother had collected many pieces of real beauty for the house, especially for the dining table—some antiquities, some modern, and all exquisite. She even had a gorgeous set of 14-karat gold flatware that she had bought at auction. All of this finery came out of boxes, out of cabinets, out of the basement, as Mom began to envision the great table at which she would receive the prince and the distinguished guests. You couldn't get her attention for weeks before the event. She was completely obsessed.

As for Terre, Tony and me, this was one of the few parties we were definitely not invited to. But I will always remember what the table looked like. It was so beautiful as to be on fire. The lace cloth, the goldware, the antiques, the flowers. The prince would surely feel at home. It would be like lunch at a palace.

Just before noon on the day of the luncheon, the cars began to line the street in front of our house on Elm Drive. Then the guests started streaming in, and they all swooned as they walked into the dining room. It was Mother's opening night and they had hung a star.

After everyone had taken their assigned seats, my father gave a toast welcoming the prince, his entourage and the guests. He looked out at the impressive array of extravagance, held his glass high and said, "Ladies and gentlemen, this is *not* an indication of my wealth. This is *it.*" And he sat down . . . to thunderous laughter.

But for all the glamour of Beverly Hills, there was a shadow side that made it different from other neighborhoods. There was a lot of loneliness and unwanted exposure. Most of the kids had high-powered, high-profile parents, many of them working on the road, or on movie locations.

Maria Cooper was in my class at Marymount. She was an absolutely beautiful girl with a disposition to match—an angel, really. I never met her father, Gary Cooper. He was always filming a movie somewhere, so he never made it to any of the Father-Daughter Days at our school. My dad didn't make so many of them either.

Maria's father had an affair with the actress Patricia Neal that made it into the press, and eventually led to her parents' scandalous breakup. As Pat Neal wrote in her memoir, she once ran into Maria, and the thirteen-year-old girl spit at her when she saw her. Beautiful, sweet Maria. What public humiliation and heartbreak can do to the spirit of even the most gracious.

Another schoolmate of mine at Marymount was Judy Lewis. Her mother, Loretta Young, was my godmother, and Judy was Loretta's adopted daughter. But all of our mothers knew the truth. Judy wasn't really adopted—she was the illegitimate child from an affair that Loretta had with Clark Gable. The women would always whisper about Judy's "Clark Gable ears," but all you had to do was look at her to see her strong resemblance to her gorgeous mother. And she had the same button nose as her cousin, Gretchen, who was also at our school. All the gossiping about her—I don't know how Judy stood it.

The four Crosby boys (Bing's sons) were also part of our teenage crowd. They went to Loyola, the Catholic boys' school, and they always hung out

With my godmother, Loretta Young.
She was ever beautiful.

together, with their nanny and guardian, Georgie, forever hovering nearby. Georgie was tough, the boss.

Gary and the twins, Dennis and Philip, were older, and Linny (Lindsay) was our age. He was the sweetest of the brothers. All four were fun to be with, always pulling pranks and laughing. But even as teens, they smoked and drank heavily. I didn't like going up to the Crosby house on Mapleton, and we didn't go often. Their mom, Dixie, was always in her room "resting." But everyone knew she had a drinking problem. And their dad was hardly ever there, but even when he was, he was gruff and not so nice.

The Crosby boys didn't really talk about it, but they sometimes let it slip that their father treated them roughly. He called them mean names and knocked them around. That made me especially sad, because they were such sweet and respectful boys.

I ran into the Crosby kids through the years, even after I left Beverly Hills, and they weren't faring well. They had tried show business, first singing as a quartet, then as a trio when Gary went out on his own. I cried the day I heard on the radio that Linny had killed himself, brutally, by putting a shotgun in his mouth. Sweet Linny. He was 52.

Some houses had glamour, some had laughs, some had secrets and some had the worst of it. A neighborhood.

Dancing with Linny Crosby at my eighth grade
graduation party. You can see how sweet he was.

DID YA HEAR THE ONE ABOUT . . .

Two Beverly Hills women are shopping on Rodeo
Drive when one of them notices a child in a baby carriage.

"Oh, look at that beautiful baby!" says the first woman.

"Aww, how adorable," says her friend.

Then the first woman gasps.

"Oh my God, that's *my* baby!"

"How do you know?"

"I recognize the nanny."

My Dad

He was an old-fashioned dad. For all the fame and money my father had earned, at his core he was a working-class guy, the middle son of a large family from Toledo, Ohio.

I've listened to many sad "dad tales" from some of my women friends—about their distracted, non-demonstrative or simply unloving fathers. These stories have always sounded so foreign. My father truly enjoyed the company of his children. He hugged and kissed us daily, he told us that he loved us, he was emotional. We used to kid him that he cried at basketball games.

Through the years, whenever I called home, it was always a boost. When he'd hear my voice, I could hear the pleasure in his. "How's my beauty?" he'd say. I once said something to him that I was sorry about later, and when I called to apologize, he said, "Mugs, you know you can do no wrong with me."

In 1965, Dad's pal, Joe Robbie, asked him to partner with him to buy the Miami Dolphins, the first expansion team of what was then the American Football League. Dad was a big sports fan, so this was an irresistible opportunity for him.

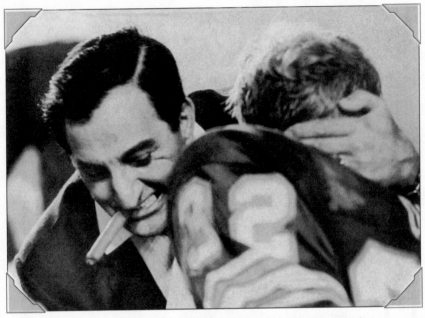

Dad greets Joe Auer in the end zone. They'd both run 95 yards,
Joe with the football, my father with the cigar.

In their first game, the Dolphins received the opening kickoff from the Oakland Raiders, and running back Joe Auer sprinted an amazing 95 yards for a touchdown. My dad was so excited that he jumped off the bench and ran along the sidelines the entire way with Auer, his cigar clenched in his teeth, his change falling out of his pockets, yelling "Go, baby, go!" When Auer finally crossed into the end zone, my father grabbed him and kissed him. He was a different kind of owner.

Dad brought that childlike enthusiasm to everything he did. When I was at USC, I got a 3.8 average one semester. He was so proud, he took my report card onto *The Tonight Show* with him, and boasted to Johnny Carson, "This is my kid—3.8! I have to talk to her through an interpreter." Dad was a frequent guest of Johnny's, and spoke to him like he was sitting next door with a friend. It was there that he made the announcement to Johnny (and America) that I had gotten my first bra, the audience howling at his vivid description of it. I didn't leave the house for a week.

But most of all he was a storyteller, and he found an audience to tell his stories to wherever he happened to be. I was on a plane once, going from Los Angeles to New York, and the flight attendant told me that she'd recently had my father on a flight, and what a delight he was. She said she saw him get up to stretch, then walk around and talk to a few people in their seats. Before long, he was enrapturing all of First Class with his tales, and they were howling. He had turned an American Airlines flight into his own personal dinner show. Most celebrities board a plane and try to hide themselves for a little privacy. Not my dad. Where else can you find a captive audience . . . for five hours?! He was in heaven.

And sometimes he couldn't let go of my boyfriends, even after I had. In college, I was pinned to a boy named Jimmy Pugh, a basketball player on a scholarship who was going into dental school. My father adored Jimmy and respected him for trying to make a better life for himself. I know in his heart, Dad had hoped I would marry Jimmy, but I was restless to get to New York and start studying acting. So that was the end of Jimmy and me. What I didn't know was that it wasn't the end of Jimmy and Dad.

After I had already moved east, Jimmy would still come to our house and have beers with Dad, and they'd talk for hours. After one of these visits, Dad walked Jimmy to his car—but it wasn't out front. Somewhat sheepishly, Jimmy explained that his car was such a "heap" that he'd parked it near the alley, rather than having it sit in front of our house. When Dad took one look at that awful jalopy, he exploded.

"You're going to be a dentist!" he said. "You can't let anything happen to your hands. You'll break every bone in your body in this wreck!"

Dad had just been sent a brand-new pickup truck from a company that he'd done a favor for, so he opened the garage and said to Jimmy, "Here, take this. I'll never drive it." I wouldn't learn about this until years later, after my father died, when Jimmy wrote me a condolence letter telling me the whole story.

"I was overwhelmed and reluctant to accept it," he wrote, "but your father got furious with me and made me drive it away on the spot."

I read the letter in awe, amazed that Dad had never mentioned this to me. But how typical of him—Jimmy may have lost the girl but he gained a V-8 engine with an automatic transmission.

WHEN I WAS AT Marymount High School, my best friend, Moya, and I were always up to some kind of mischief. We had to do something with all those unexpressed hormones. Not only was the school girls-only, but all of the teachers were nuns. There was hardly a male presence, except for the gardener—and the prettiest nun ran off with him. And there was the daily visit from FATHER from the nearby parish to say the Mass for us. The nuns were very respectful, adoring—and terrified—of FATHER.

"Oh yes, FATHER. Oh no, FATHER. Oh, thank you, FATHER."

In a regular church Mass, the priest is assisted by altar boys, who bring him the chalice of wine and place the bells. Back then, females were not permitted behind the altar rail. No female—not even a nun. So when Father came to say Mass at Marymount, he had to do it all on his own. God forbid any female should be let past that rail.

This really irked Moya and me. So one day, just before Mass, we decided to remove the altar bells. These bells are used at a very important part of the Mass. They are rung three times, one after each "Lord, I am not worthy."

The service began, and while all of the other girls were focused on the Mass as they should have been, Moya and I waited excitedly for the moment when Father would reach for the bells—which were always placed directly to his right. When the time finally came, we watched his hand reaching in vain, fumbling for the missing bells.

And then he did something that made us choke to keep from laughing. He called out in a loud voice, "Ding-a-ling-a-ling." We couldn't believe it. And then again, "Ding-a-ling-a-ling." And then a third time, "Ding-a-ling-a-ling."

The two thirteen-year-old girls doubled over in the back row were promptly suspended.

My father was summoned to a conference—"about your daughter"—with Reverend Mother Emmanuel. Unfortunately, I was invited, too. I was terrified of Reverend Mother. She was tough, no-nonsense. Her face squeezed by her binding, starched white habit, she looked out at you with severe green eyes.

On this particular day, that look was aimed at Mr. Thomas, as she told him in very strong words what a very bad girl I had been. She then rose proudly, determinedly, to her feet and pronounced her final sentence—the death sentence for Mr. Thomas's daughter.

"I'm afraid, Mr. Thomas, that Margaret does not have the poise for a Marymount girl."

Then my father rose. "I know, Reverend Mother," he said humbly. "That's why I've given her to you."

Check. I could see a glint in those severe green eyes. Reverend Mother knew she had met her match.

When we got in the car to drive home, I told my father how brilliant he was, and laughed at how he had checkmated Reverend Mother. But Dad didn't smile back. He looked at me sternly.

"I don't ever want to have to face off with that woman again," he said. "And I don't ever want to hear that you have done something unfitting at a Mass. Mass is not the place for jokes."

I felt awful. He was disappointed in me. We drove in silence for a few minutes, and then he said, "I was good though, wasn't I?" Then we laughed. It was good to have a dad on your side.

DID YA HEAR THE ONE ABOUT . . .

A Catholic teenage boy goes to confession, and confesses to a night of mortal sinning with a girl. The priest tells him that he can't be forgiven unless he reveals who the girl is.

"I promised not to tell anyone!" he says.

"Was it Mary Patricia, the butcher's daughter?" the priest asks.

"No," the boy says, "and I said I wouldn't tell."

"Was it Mary Elizabeth, the printer's daughter?"

"No, and I still won't tell!"

"Was it Mary Francis, the baker's daughter?"

"No!" says the boy.

"Well, son," says the priest, "say six Hail Marys and ask God's forgiveness."

Outside, the boy's friends ask him how it went.

"It went great," he says. "I got six Hail Marys and three good leads."

Harry and the Parakeet

There's an old joke that Harry Crane loved to tell us when we were kids.

A woman goes into a drugstore. She walks up to the salesman—an uptight, condescending sort—and asks him if they have any talcum powder. The salesman walks prissily in front of her and says, "Walk this way, madam." And the woman says, "If I could walk that way, I wouldn't need the talcum powder."

Terre, Tony and I loved that joke. The poor maître d' or hostess who led us into practically any dining room across America with the words "Walk this way" was always followed by giggles of laughter—and not just our giggles, but the giggles of the great instigator himself, Dad.

When I was just a little thing, I'd be in an elevator with my father, and I'd snuggle close to him.

"Please, madam," he'd say in a loud voice. "I'm a married man." Everyone in the elevator would laugh. The laughter made the world seem small and friendly.

Harry Crane was a wonderful comedy writer who worked with most of the boys, a lot for my dad. They were great pals. Harry had a very dry delivery, and he was fun to be around. Good thing, because he was always at our house for dinner.

Deadpan and sarcastic, Harry had a tender heart and I loved him dearly. He knew I wanted to be an actress from an early age, so when I was around twelve, he gave me a subscription to the Fireside Theatre book club for Christmas. Fireside sent a different play every month. I had never read plays before, but I immediately got hooked. Once I had read the first one, I couldn't wait for the next one to arrive. Odets, Hellman, Miller. Harry opened a whole new world of ideas and feelings for me.

He was also a true New Yorker, impatient and aggressive, and he'd never wait in line for anything. Once, Dad, Harry, and I were on a plane to Las Vegas when the pilot announced that the equipment had a problem and that we'd have to disembark and change planes. Our tickets were still usable, the pilot said, they just had to be stamped at the next gate.

All of the passengers rushed out to get in line for the other plane, but by the time we gathered our things, the line was quite long. Harry took one look at it and snapped into action. He grabbed the tickets out of our hands, marched to the front of the line and angrily approached the attendant.

"You didn't stamp these tickets!" he said to her accusingly.

The attendant, clearly contrite, apologized to Harry and immediately stamped the tickets. Then he turned around with that impish twinkle of his and walked back to us, his adoring audience. Pure Harry.

Even in the worst of circumstances, Harry was genetically incapable of resisting a punch line. He had hypoglycemia and often needed to get sugar into his system. One day, he was shopping in Beverly Hills, and feeling an urgent need for sugar, he ran into Nate 'n Al's deli and said to the guy behind the counter, "Quick, give me an orange!"

"We don't sell oranges here, sir," said the counter guy, who was too busy making pastrami double-deckers to help a man about to go into a serious swoon. "Have the hostess give you a table and your waitress will be right with you."

"Can't wait," Harry said frantically. "Please give me an orange right away!"

The counter guy stuck to his guns, but before he could even get out another word, Harry keeled over in a dead faint. He was rushed to the hospital in an ambulance.

Joey Bishop heard about the news and called Harry at the hospital.

Joey: "How are you feeling?"
Harry: "I'm fine now. Thanks for calling."
Joey: "Where are you?"
Harry: "You know where I am. You just called me here."
Joey: "No, no—I mean, how do I get there?"
Harry: "Just go to Nate 'n Al's and order an orange."

Harry also loved practical jokes. He and Jerry Lewis would concoct outrageous crank telephone schemes, tape the calls, then bring them over to our house for us to listen to. They'd go through the newspapers looking for ideas. The transcript that follows is from a call they made answering a classified ad placed by a guy who'd found a stray parakeet and wanted to locate the owner. In this one, Harry got to be the caller, while Jerry hung in the background, laughing and egging him on.

Most people get crank calls out of their system during adolescence. But The Boys were like big kids—they'd do anything to make each other laugh. And this is how they entertained themselves when they weren't entertaining an audience.

THE LOST PARAKEET

Guy on Phone: Hello?
Harry Crane: Hello. Did you advertise that you found a parakeet?
Guy: Yes, we did. It's a green bird.

Harry: That's right. How long have you had it?

Guy: We found it Monday, I believe.

Harry: Oh, you're so kind. What did it do, fly in the window?

Guy: No, my sister was out on the back porch and she saw it. Then my mother came out, and it jumped onto her finger and we brought it in.

Harry: Isn't that nice. I hope it's my bird.

Guy: I hope so, too.

Harry: Has it been talking?

Guy: No, it hasn't talked, but . . .

Harry: Is the bird there right now?

Guy: Yes.

Harry: Put the bird on so I can talk to him.

Guy: Well, I don't know if it'll talk on the telephone.

Harry: The bird will talk—if it's my bird.

Guy: Well, it's in a strange house. We had a bird that talked, too, and we lost it. It flew away and some people caught it, but they couldn't get it to talk.

Harry: I see. Well, can you have the bird fly over to my house tonight?

Guy: Well . . .

Harry: I'll tell you what to tell the bird. Do you have a pencil?

Guy: Yes, I do.

Harry: Tell the bird . . .

Guy: Yes.

Harry: To fly straight down Beverly Boulevard.

Guy: Fly down Beverly Boulevard.

Harry: Right. Go down Beverly Boulevard to La Cienega.

Guy: To La Cienega.

Harry: Yeah. And tell the bird not to go during rush hour. Then tell him to make a left turn on La Cienega . . .

Guy: Left on La Cienega.

Harry: Yes, to 1213 South La Cienega. He knows the apartment.

Guy: Oh.

Harry: And if you'll be so kind, can you tie a little birdseed to his leg? Because he's just a baby. Has he been crying?

Guy: No.

Harry: Has he been yelling "Nat?" That's my name, Nat.

Guy: Uh . . . no.

Harry: I'm heartbroken. You haven't hit him, have you?

Guy: No!

Harry: That's good.

Guy: Can we call you in case he seems reluctant about . . .

Harry: Flying here?

Guy: Yes, because it's a long ways, and he may not be up to flying back. It's a pretty hard flight. And there are cats around and such.

Harry: Well, I don't know. I mean, he's never soloed at night. But he'll do a day flight. If you let him fly at about four o'clock, he can make it in an hour.

Guy: But that'll be during rush hour.

Harry: He'll be fine if he doesn't stop to fool around or anything. My bird can go pretty good, you know. And if he gets lost, he can always call me.

Guy: Well, he hasn't asked to use the telephone yet, and we have some other people who think this bird belongs to them . . .

Harry: I'd like to see them take that bird.

Guy: Well, there's a lot of green birds and . . .

Harry: I'd like to see them take my bird.

Guy: Well, I can't say if it's your bird. What is the number on his band?

Harry: Does he have a band on?

Guy: Yes. Doesn't your bird have a band?

Harry: No.

Guy: Oh. This bird has a band.

Harry: Well, somebody put that band on, damn it!

Guy: Well, we talked to some bird owners down the street, and they say it's impossible to get a band on or off once the bird is grown.

Harry: No, that's not true. Look, if I give you my number, will you call me?

Guy: Yes.

Harry: At five o'clock sharp?

Guy: Uh-huh.

Harry: You sure?

Guy: Yes.

Harry: OK. I'm at Hollywood three . . .

Guy: Hollywood three . . .

Harry: . . . five, two, one, five.

Guy: . . . five, two, one, five.

Harry: Can you read that back to me?

Guy: Hollywood three, five, two, one, five?

Harry: No. It's Hollywood three, five, two, one, five. You'll call, right?

Guy: Yes.

Harry: At five.

Guy: I'll call at five.

Harry: You won't fail, no matter what?

Guy: No.

Harry: Because I'm so crazy about that bird.

Guy: Okay.

Harry: You won't let me down?

Guy: No.

Harry: Okay. [*Laughs*]

(Click.)

Angelo's Boy

*Jay Leno is TV royalty, having worked his way up from
the grungy comedy club circuit to the* Tonight Show *throne,
as the heir to the king of late night, Johnny Carson.
But his heart is always in the clubs. He plays more than
160 club dates a year—trying out new material, hunting
down the killer laugh, polishing his skills.
You would think that's the last thing he'd
need to do, but there's a reason for this—
and you can see it in his face the moment
you ask him about his work. He simply loves
what he does. To Jay, there's not some magic
component to telling a joke—there's the
right way, the wrong way, and the Leno way.
And the Leno way has made him a superstar.*

JAY LENO

*Most of the comedians I talked to demurred when
I asked them to tell me their favorite joke. Not
Jay—he had two. I'm sure he would have told
me more, but he had to get back to work . . .*
—M.T.

Jay: I grew up in a household with a dad who was very Italian and very loud, and a mom who was Scottish and timid. I was trapped between those two worlds, and that's where my humor comes from. It was a funny place to grow up.

My father was very outgoing. No matter what I was doing or who I was going to meet, he'd say to me, "Look, you make sure you tell them you're Angelo Leno's boy!" My mother was the exact opposite. To her, the worst thing you could do was call attention to yourself.

Here's the perfect example. When I made it in show business, I bought my dad a Cadillac—and because he's Italian, I made sure it was a *white* Cadillac, with red velour upholstery. For my mother, this was very embarrassing. They'd be in the car together and pull up to a light, and my mom would look over at the next car and say to these strangers, "You know, we're not really Cadillac people. Our son got us this." Then my father would start yelling. "What do you mean we're not Cadillac people? We got a goddamn Cadillac! *We're Cadillac people!*" My mom would sink down in the seat, out of sight, and my dad would keep screaming. Later that night I'd always hear from a friend who would say to me, "I saw your father today, driving down the street and yelling—but he was alone in the car. Is he okay?"

My mother would sometimes laugh this repressed kind of laugh, but for the most part she was quiet. She liked to say "Shhh" a lot. I remember when I played Carnegie Hall, my mom and dad were sitting about four rows back, dead center, and behind my mom were six or seven college kids who'd seen me on TV and knew my routine. So they're laughing hysterically at my jokes, and my mother turns around and says, "Shhh!"

So I stop the show and say, "Mom, you don't shush people at Carnegie Hall!" I mean, how can you not find humor with parents like this?

MY MOTHER CAME FROM SCOTLAND. When she was small, her mom ran off with a younger man, and there were so many kids in her family

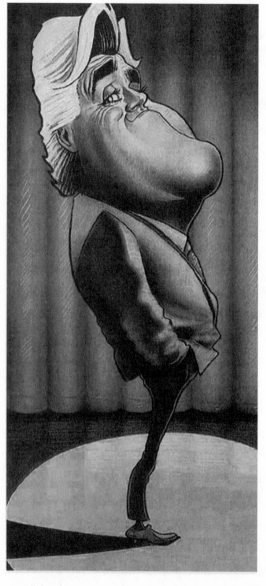

that my grandfather had to get rid of a few of them. He went door to door with my mother—*Anybody want a daughter?*—and eventually put my mom on a boat and sent her to America to live with her sister. She was eleven, and went to work in a factory.

So I always sensed a sadness in my mom, and I felt it was my duty to cheer her up or make her laugh. If I could do that, I'd get a great feeling of satisfaction.

But sometimes I went too far. When I was a kid, one of my favorite things to do was go to the supermarket with my mother. I would run away and go up to the manager and say, "I'm lost—could you page my mother?" And he'd get on the loudspeaker and say, "Would Mrs. Catherine Leno please come to the front of the store?" I knew there couldn't be anything more embarrassing for her, but I was a kid. I thought it was funny.

Even when I started appearing on TV, she'd say to me, "You know, nobody wants somebody who's funny all the time. If you want, tell a joke, sing a little song, do a little dance." I'd say, "Mom, I'm not going to sing and dance to get to tell a joke."

MY DAD HAD a real good sense of humor. He was a salesman who worked himself up to manager of the office, and once a month he would have to give a pep talk to the other salesmen. So he'd write a funny speech and practice it on me. "Hey, you think this is funny? You think the boys in the office will like this?" And I thought, *Oh boy, being an insurance salesman has got to be the best job in the world, because you get to tell funny stories!*

Dad also told me stories about the early days of selling insurance in Harlem. When he went to work for the insurance company, he asked, "What's the toughest route?" And people, being very racist in those days, would say, "Harlem. You can't sell insurance in Harlem." My dad said, "Well, everybody's got a family. Everybody wants insurance." So he sold nickel policies in Harlem.

When he died in the early nineties, I talked about this on *The Tonight Show,* and I got a letter from a lady in Harlem who said that when she was a little girl, there was a man named Angelo Leno who used to come around to collect on the nickel policy. She said he was the only white person who had ever had dinner in her home.

"Your father would always give me candy," she wrote, "and my opinion of white people was based on him." It was such a lovely letter. I called her up, and it was great to learn a little more about my dad from her.

I know that a lot of comics had unhappy childhoods, but I didn't. I had a wonderful childhood—and a wonderful family.

I NEVER WANTED TO BE A TV personality. I always kept my day job, thinking I would do this comedy thing until I had to get a real job. I'd put the money from my comedy job in one pocket and the money from my after-school job—working at a car dealership—in the other pocket. Then one day I realized that the comedy pocket was much bigger than the other pocket. So instead of quitting comedy, I quit the other job and went to L.A.

I like being a comedian because it's a trade—and when you have a trade, you can always make a living. That's the real key. I mean, doing TV is nice, but—as we know—they can tap you on the shoulder at any moment and say, "Okay, you're done." And there's nothing you can do about it.

But if you have a trade, you can always keep working. You can go to some small club. You can do a Christmas party. It's like going to a gym for an hour and a half and running up and down on a machine. The stage is not a normal place to be, and if you're not out there at least twice a week, it seems abnormal. But if you do it like clockwork, it becomes easier.

I have never touched a dime of my TV money, ever. It all goes in the bank, and I live on the money I make as a comic in the clubs. This way, I'm always hungry. I try to do a minimum of three gigs a week—about 160 dates a year. That's a lot of material.

But jokes are disposable. Here's my thing: write joke, tell joke, get check, go home. I mean, if you think it's anything more than that, you're mistaken. It's a disposable product—like a tissue. You use it and it's gone. You don't reuse it and say, "Oh, here's a tissue I blew my nose in two years ago." If you keep moving forward, you never have to go backwards.

Being a comedian is sort of like being a transmission specialist. There's always somebody with a broken car who needs their transmission fixed. Same thing with comedy. There's always someone who needs to laugh.

A JOKE FROM JAY . . .

A man is in a hospital, and he's hanging in traction.

He's been hanging for two years. Every bone is broken.

He's bandaged from head to toe, looks like a mummy—

except for one little opening near his left eye.

Everything else is bandaged, except for this one little slit.

Doctor walks in, looks him in the face and says,

"I don't like the look of that eye."

ANOTHER JOKE FROM JAY . . .

This man always wanted to meet the Pope; he's been making donations to the Catholic Church for years. Finally he gets invited to the Vatican, and he's so nervous. He's in a room with about fifty people also waiting to meet the Pope, and he's at the end of the line.

The Pope comes in and starts going down the line. There are kings and queens and senators and heads of state—and in the middle of the line, there's a homeless man in this long, filthy, raggedy coat. The Pope walks down the line and blesses each person, and when he comes to the homeless man in the raggedy coat, he puts his arms around him. Big hug. The American thinks, "That's unbelievable! Here are these kings and queens and senators, and they get a little papal blessing, and this homeless guy in a filthy coat gets a hug. I'd do anything to get a hug from the Pope."

So he steps out of line, goes up to the homeless guy, and says, "Look, give me that jacket!"

The guy says, "You don't want the jacket."

The American says, "Yes I do. I'll buy it. Here—I'll give you a thousand dollars. Give me that coat!"

So the homeless guy gives him the coat for a thousand dollars, the American puts it on, messes up his hair, and gets back in the line. The Pope walks by, sees the American, puts his arms around him and whispers into his ear:

"I thought I told you to get the hell out of here."

Miss Independence

When I was growing up, my nickname was "Miss Independence," and it fit. I was clearly of the *I can do it myself* persuasion, and though my dad had warned me that show business was a very difficult business—especially for women—I believed I could get where I wanted to go on my own. Still, the stories were legend, and scary, about how pretty young women were eaten alive at the hands of casting directors, directors and studio heads.

My desire to be an actress had always been a sore point with my father and me. He had come to see me in all of my school plays, and he always left worried.

"She's got 'the bug,'" he would say to Mom.

After two years of college, I was restless and told my parents I wanted to go to New York to study acting. "Finish college first," Dad said. "That way you'll have something to fall back on."

The day I graduated from USC as an English teacher, I handed him my diploma and said, "This is for you. Now I'm going to study acting."

I remember one night around that time, we were arguing about this during dinner. George Burns was at the table, and listening carefully to the back-and-forth. After a while, he took my side.

"What do you want her to be," he asked Dad, "a milliner?"

A milliner. What a choice. But it took the air out of the argument, and made us all laugh. Then George said something that I found touching and revealing.

"To tell you the truth, Danny," he said, "I feel sorry for anyone who isn't in show business."

And so I just kept on plugging. I studied, did workshops, appeared in plays (even got good reviews), auditioned for everything I could, took meetings, knocked on any door that I could find. And I was getting nowhere.

Finally, my father couldn't take watching my frustration any longer and begged me to let him help me by setting up a meeting with a producer friend of his, Mike Frankovich at Columbia Pictures. I immediately felt uncomfortable about the meeting, but I went anyway. I sat across from Mr. Frankovich at his big mahogany desk feeling both desperate and hopeful.

He began by telling me what a great guy my dad was—a brilliant performer, a terrific golfer. After a while, I tried to bring the conversation around to me and my work. Mr. Frankovich looked at me dismissively.

"Why would a lovely, educated, well-raised girl like you want to be in this lousy business? Why don't you marry your boyfriend, settle down and give your father some grandkids."

I was totally demoralized. I called my father, told him about the meeting and drew a very clear line.

"Please, Dad," I said. "Don't ever—ever—make any more calls on my behalf. I'm going to have to do this on my own."

But as I continued to try to make my way, it continued to eat at my father that I, his beloved daughter, was pounding the pavement in vain. So one night, he decided to talk to me about it.

"If you were a solo performer," he said, "like a singer or a comic, you'd always be able to find work, just like I always can. But actors are too dependent on others for a job. They need a writer, a director and other actors. Too many things have to fall into place."

And then he said in very plain language that he thought I should give it up—that it was a long shot that lightning would strike twice in the same family, and that I should rethink what I wanted to do with my life.

The more he spoke, the more upset and insistent he became.

"You're an educated young woman. You could be a senator, for God's sake! Why would you pick something at which you cannot succeed?"

I couldn't believe it. After all the years of unconditional love, of encouragement, of support in everything I did as a kid, he had withdrawn his belief in me.

I got up from the table and walked to the doorway. Then I turned back to him.

"Not only am I going to make it," I said in a fury, "but someday you and your partner, Sheldon Leonard, are going to want to hire me and you won't be able to fucking afford me!"

And I stormed out.

Later I learned that my mother had overheard it all, and had immediately gone to my father.

"Don't you think you were too tough on her?" she said. "Maybe you should go after her."

"No, let her be," Daddy said. "If she really wants it, she'll have to face a lot tougher rejection than this."

YEARS LATER, after I had my own television series, my father and I were standing together in the wings of a Las Vegas showroom, watching Terre at the microphone, singing her heart out to the crowd in one of her first professional engagements. Tapping her foot as she sang, she looked adorable and sounded great. She has the loveliest voice—a lot like my mother's—and as I watched her, I thought back to all the times when we were younger, when she would sing along to Doris Day records. My eyes filled with tears. I was so proud of her.

"Isn't she good?!" I said to Dad.

My opening night in a summer stock production of *Gigi*.
Dad didn't want me to be an actress. But he was there.

He stood there, his arms crossed, his unlit black cigar in his mouth.

"She's very good," he said. "But she'll never make it. She's not angry like you were."

We'd never know. Six months later, like Mom, Terre left singing behind, followed her heart and went home to raise a family.

My Big Brown Eyes

I guess it was inevitable that I'd go into the family business. I started by doing plays in little theatres in and around Los Angeles—Santa Barbara's Lobero Theatre, the playhouses at Laguna, Ojai, San Diego. Getting laughs from an audience clicked right into my DNA. The sound, the rhythm of the comedy, came out of me like a song that had been playing in my mind all my life. And I was never happier than when I got to sing it.

The one thing I wasn't ready for was that every review and interview compared me to my famous father. Would I be as good as Danny Thomas? As funny? Last as long? God, it was scary. Would I ever be able to get out from under his giant shadow? And be judged on my own? Would I ever be seen just for myself? I felt I had no place to hide, no place where I could fail unnoticed. And how do you learn if you can't fail?

But I just kept going, mostly in comedies—*Gigi, Two for the Seesaw, I Am a Camera, Blithe Spirit, Under the Yum Yum Tree*—and some *not* comedies—*Our Town, Glass Menagerie, View from the Bridge.* I had gone to USC for four years to become an English teacher, but I had studied for this all of my life.

One summer, I was doing a light comedy called *Sunday in New York* with John Aniston, Jennifer's father, at the Civic Playhouse in L.A., when David Dortort, the producer of the hit TV western *Bonanza,* knocked on my dressing room door. He asked me if I could do a Chinese accent. Silly question to ask an actress.

"Of course, I can do a Chinese accent!" I said.

"Great," he said. "I've got a wonderful part for you."

He needed to fill a guest role on the show that had been written especially for the actress Pat Suzuki, who had just scored a big success on Broadway in *Flower Drum Song.* The episode was to shoot the following week, but Pat had the flu and wouldn't be able to fly in from New York. David had been searching for another Asian actress with the same kind of "spitfire," as he called it, but was having no luck. That's when he got the bright idea that I could do it. All I needed was a little eye makeup and a decent accent (which I said I had) and he'd have his perfect Tai Li, a Chinese mail-order bride for the character of Hoss, played by Dan Blocker.

Once he left my room, I anxiously called Sandy Meisner, the great acting teacher, to find out how I could learn a Chinese accent in three days. I had studied with Sandy for a year in Los Angeles, when he took a hiatus from the Neighborhood Playhouse in New York to help 20th Century Fox build a new stable of stars from young hopefuls. It was a great idea for the studio, and a terrific opportunity for budding actors to study with a master—for free. I was one of the kids Sandy chose. It was an exciting year, and even though Fox didn't pick up the option on any of us, I had made a friend in Sandy.

When I reached him, he told me to go to Ah Fong's, a Chinese restaurant on Canon Drive in Beverly Hills, and hire one of the waitresses to come to my apartment to work with me. By spending time talking with her, Sandy said, and having her read my part on tape, I would easily pick up her accent.

Yup, that's me—as a Chinese mail-order bride
on the TV western *Bonanza.*

So I went to Ah Fong's, ordered dinner (Peking duck, always) and
tried to figure out how to propose this idea to the waitress without sounding like I was offering a different kind of proposition. But she was as
young as I was and happy to make the extra money. So we did what
Sandy suggested.

The next step was to look Chinese. I don't think David Dortort realized how hard that would be. They tried "applications"—tiny pieces of
rubber to make my very round eyes look oval-shaped. They tested me on
film with them, but I could barely see. I also kept blinking, like I had
something in my eye. Well, no wonder—I did. So that didn't work. Then
they tried creating the look just with makeup, and we tested that, too. Better, but my eyes were still too round.

Nothing was working, and time was running out, so they pulled a classic Hollywood maneuver: They wrote into the script that Tai Li had a Persian mother.

So with a cockamamie accent and not too oval eyes, I played the part of a Chinese mail-order bride (with a Persian mother) who turned out not to be the supplicant bride Hoss had hoped for, but, instead, a feisty revolutionary girl who was trying to unionize the Ponderosa.

Just as my character was becoming successful with her mission, Hoss was to pick me up angrily and throw me into a water trough. Dan Blocker weighed close to 300 pounds. He was huge. So when he threw my 98-pound body into that tiny, half-filled trough, I hit it with a thud. Tears poured down my face, but on film the splashing water hid them. So, thankfully, I didn't have to do the scene again.

I took away three things from that experience: (1) a bad back, (2) the realization that I was not a stuntwoman, and (3) the lesson that you should always politely ask the director to try not to kill you.

Funny about my eyes. When I was a little girl, my grandma, the Lebanese one, would take me to the grocery store with her. The man behind the counter would always give her a piece of candy for "your granddaughter with the big brown eyes." My grandmother would then spit on my head three times to shoo away the bad spirits who might have overheard him and be jealous.

When my agent sent me to meet the casting director for the detective series *77 Sunset Strip,* the first thing she told me when I arrived was how beautiful my big, brown eyes were. I was, of course, pleased. Then the director came in.

"Look at her eyes!" the casting woman said. "Aren't they great?" The director heartily agreed, so now I was really pleased. *Boy,* I thought, *my eyes are really going to do it for me.*

I was given a part and I was ecstatic—I didn't even have to read for them. The scene would take place in an operating room. The man lying on the table had a time-bomb planted in his stomach that was about to go off—it needed to be removed and defused in just seconds. I played the O.R. nurse and wore a surgical mask, so all you could see were my eyes. I was told to look from the patient to the clock at several intervals during the scene. Back and forth, forth and back, back and forth. The idea was that the ticking clock and my darting eyes would dramatically build the tension of the scene.

No wonder I didn't have to read for them. They only needed a pair of big brown eyes. Had I known, I would have spit on my head, turned around three times and headed for the door.

But I had lots of little jobs like that in the early days. No one was really paying any attention to me at the factory-like William Morris Agency, except for my childhood pal Barry Diller. Barry had been a close friend of Terre's since they were little kids, and was always at our house. He was family. So when he became the assistant to Marty Dubow, a big TV agent at William Morris, he also became my secret agent. Typically, assistants were only supposed to answer the phone. But Barry would sneak a peek at the casting breakdowns on his boss's desk and get me an audition for whatever small roles were available on TV. I'd land a part, get paid $400, and you'd have thought we'd robbed a bank. We were like Mickey and Judy, putting on a show in the barn.

Shortly after that, I was sent out on a call to read for Elizabeth Ashley's New York replacement in Neil Simon's comedy hit *Barefoot in the Park*. A chance to work on Broadway! I was so excited—and I was ready. The role of Corie Bratter was just the kind of part I had been playing for the past few years—vivacious, optimistic, funny.

When I got to the theatre, my heart sank. There was a very long line of young actors—male and female—waiting outside to audition for Mike Nichols, the director; Saint Suber, the producer; and Neil Simon. Then a man came out to the line and gave us each a number that signified who we would be reading with. My partner was Marty Milner. I didn't know him then, but years later he would have a successful TV series called *Route 66*.

But that day we were two little nobodys among hundreds of nobodys. We finally got in and read for Mike Nichols. He was extremely encouraging and kind. He laughed at what we did, and when we were finished he hopped onto the stage, gave us notes and asked us to do it again. That was a good sign.

The next day I got a call to come back. After reading for them just one more time, I was told I had the part. I was beyond thrilled—that is, until I found out that I hadn't been reading for the New York replacement after all. Penny Fuller, Ashley's understudy, had been promised that plum. Instead, I was being offered the year-long national touring company.

I turned it down. My agents were stunned and asked me why.

"I just cannot travel this country for a year being compared to my father," I said. "I'll go crazy giving interview after interview answering questions in every city, not about my work, but how it feels to be Danny Thomas's daughter. It will be a nightmare for me. It will kill my spirit."

My agents threatened that I would never again be taken seriously after turning down such a break. That stopped me.

"Let me ask you something," I said. "Who did the great Anne Bancroft part for the national company of *Two for the Seesaw?*"

Silence.

So I didn't do it.

Months later, I read that they were casting for the London company of *Barefoot*. I knew that would be just what my spirit and I needed—to get out of the country, go where my father wasn't so well known, and stand or fall on my own. I wanted to try out for it, but I was afraid my agents had had their fill of *Barefoot* and me and wouldn't be supportive.

I paced in front of a phone booth in Greenwich Village and finally got the guts to call Mike Nichols at his office at Warner Bros. I feared he wouldn't take the call—but he did. I asked him if he remembered me. He did. I asked him if there was a chance I could read for the part of Corie for the London company.

Silence.

"What a good idea," he said.

I don't know if it was the sweat from my hands or the tears from my eyes, but everything was so slippery that I actually dropped the phone. I got the part and went to London.

We had a terrific cast. English actor Dan Massey played the Robert Redford part, and Kurt Kaszner and Millie Natwick had come from the New York company to re-create their roles. We "toured the provinces," as they say, trying out the play in Bournemouth, Brighton and South Sea. They're summer resorts, really, so most everything was closed up, and our only entertainment was each other. So we all hung out together and became close friends. (Dan and I became even closer.)

Giving 'em hell as Corie in *Barefoot* in London.

I'll always remember the opening night at the Piccadilly Theatre in London. The audience laughed nonstop, but nothing was as funny as what happened just offstage. Dan was a terrific actor, but he had a hard time with the last moment of the play, when he had to laugh hysterically as he drunkenly headed for the door. Everything had gone so well up until then. We were on the five-yard line, and I remember thinking, *Go for it, Danny!* But that night when he opened the door, Kurt was standing on a chair—out of the audience's eyeshot—bent over, and all you could see was his bare butt with a daisy sticking out of it. Dan laughed hysterically all right. Only problem was, I had to chew off half my cheek not to laugh, too. God, it was a funny sight.

It was a great night. My parents had flown over for the opening, and it was a triumph—for Neil Simon and all of the actors. At the end, the ovations seemed to go on forever. My dear parents told me later that they had sat on their hands throughout the applause, so no one would think they had started it.

The excitement in my dressing room after the curtain came down was thrilling. My mother was ecstatic—everyone was happy and crying. Then I saw my father. He looked like he had just finished the triathalon. I knew he had lived through every moment of the play with me. And he was drained.

I'll never forget the look on his face. It wasn't joy, it wasn't pride. It was utter relief. I was going to be okay.

The next morning I received spectacular reviews, but none more liberating to me than the one that ended with "She's the daughter of an American comedian, I'm told."

In true form, Dad was funny about it all. One night I had forgotten my curlers at the hotel, and Dad ran over to the theatre with them in a paper bag. The old man at the stage door yelled down to my dressing room, "There's a dark-complexioned man here with a package for you." My very famous, very adorable father came down the stairs, handed me the bag of curlers and said, "I'm going back on American Airlines where they know who the hell I am!"

Killing and Dying

Alan Alda and I made a movie together in 1968 called
Jenny, and we've been friends ever since. He always makes
me laugh, and I love listening to him tell stories about his
childhood with his famous dad, the actor and musical
star Robert Alda.

Like me, Alan grew up surrounded by
comedians—in his case, burlesque comics.
He traveled with his parents and a troupe
of singers, chorus girls and comedians
to places like Buffalo, Pittsburgh and
Philadelphia. From the time he was two
years old, he'd stand in the wings,
watching very funny people perform about
five times a day. ("Sometimes, we'd stay up all
night drinking beer," he jokes. "I didn't drink
beer till I was three.") It's always good to catch up
with Alan, especially when we're talking about
our favorite topic: growing up with laughter.
—M.T.

ALAN
ALDA

Alan: Funny, I just saw you the other day. I was looking at pictures from my last birthday party, and there you were.

Marlo: There I was.

Alan: And you look good.

Marlo: You're sweet—you're no slouch yourself.

Alan: I don't look too bad in pictures. I've noticed that I never like any pictures of me when they're taken. I should put them in a drawer and wait three years—then I'll look sensational.

Marlo: I'm always glad to be there for your birthdays. It's great being old friends. My father used to say, "Never trade an old friend in for a new one."

Alan: My dad was like that, too. Even after he began making movies in Hollywood, he never abandoned his old pals. The burlesque comics would come over on Sundays and there would be, like, fifty people there. They'd fire up the barbecue and everybody would get up and do old sketches. They'd even let me join in with them. I was constantly in the midst of funny people.

Marlo: So your comic training started early. How old were you when you first realized you were funny?

Alan: About four.

Marlo: You're kidding! Four?

Alan: Four. And I remember exactly where I was. My parents were in bed, and I was in their bedroom, picking up newspapers from the floor. As soon as I picked one up, I'd immediately drop it—you know, like Buster Keaton. And each time I did it, my parents would laugh. Finally, my father said, "You're doing a bit, aren't you?" And that's when I realized I was deliberately going for the laugh. I think that may be the first time I thought I was funny.

Marlo: That's so cute. You were already honing your physical shtick. But I've always believed there's something more than just comic skill inside comedians. Do you agree?

Alan: Yes. I think it comes from the desire—the need—to please. And you can't ignore it. Comedians always talk about killing. In a sense, that's a very accurate term. When you make people laugh, you make them helpless. So, in a way, you *are* killing them.

Marlo: That's interesting—I never thought of it that way.

Alan: I think it's good for people to laugh together—which is why I always recommend to actors that they laugh with one another an hour before a show. Because then they'll be vulnerable and opened up to each other. You can't stay guarded while you're laughing. You can't be in your own world when you're on stage.

Marlo: When does a comic truly know he's killing?

With Alan on location for *Jenny*.
Were we really ever that young?

Alan: When he's got the whole room rocking with laughter. I remember I was once waiting to go on stage for some event and standing in the wings with Dan Rather. Alan King was on stage, and the place was his. I said to Rather, "Listen to him—listen to what he's done!" He'd been on stage only two minutes, and the audience was in his complete control. Everything he said—every syllable—caused this eruption of hilarity in the audience.

Marlo: What a great observation. What did Rather say?

Alan: He said, "Oh yeah . . . What do you mean?"

Marlo: That's so funny. What about actual comic delivery? It's a given among comedians that there are people who say funny things, and people who say things funny—like Jack Benny. He'd say one word—"Well!"— and it always brought the house down.

Alan: Right. A funny person doesn't need word-jokes or puns to get the laugh. A funny person doesn't need formulas—like that thing with *threes* that you always hear in every amateur joke-teller's joke. You know: "So this guy walks into the bar for the *third* time . . ." Whenever I hear the first thing, I think, *Oh, shit, now I have to sit through two more of these . . .*

Marlo: I know exactly what you mean. I love the stories you've told me about your childhood. When you were nine, your father took you with him to the Hollywood Canteen to entertain American troops. What do you remember about that?

Alan: We did Abbott and Costello's "Who's on First?" routine.

Marlo: Wow, really?

Alan: Yeah—I did Costello's part.

Marlo: That's the part that gets all the laughs. Were you nervous?

Alan: I was shaking with fear in the wings beforehand. But as I went out, I felt the warm spotlight on me, and within the first couple of lines, I heard this roar of laughter coming at me. It was such a feeling of power.

Soldiers, sailors on their way to the Pacific, and here I was this nine-year-old kid.

Marlo: Nine. That's amazing

Alan: And I could make them laugh.

Marlo: Isn't that great? It really says something that your father trusted you to come out there and do that routine with him, because if you weren't good you could have killed it. His faith in you must have been empowering.

Alan: It was. I remember the rehearsals. They were very loose, and he left a lot of the choices up to me. So the energy that came out of me was genuine.

Marlo: And alive.

Alan: Yes. And starting that way—planting my feet on the stage and feeling comfortable and confident that I could come up with that kind of energy—is what gave me the ability to go out there.

Marlo: Right. It made you fearless.

Alan: Yes, but there was also that sense of power. You know, people always talk about the dark spirit of comedians. Well, I think it comes from a deep feeling of powerlessness, a desire to score, to be there and to *deserve* to be there; and the feeling that, unless you control them, they'll control you. They'll kill you if you don't kill them first.

Marlo: What a combo—people you want to please and also want to kill. The language says it all. I can't count how many times I heard that as a kid—my dad or one of his comic friends talking about having a bad night on stage. And how did they describe it? "I died."

Alan: And there's nothing worse. Carol Burnett told me that when she was just starting out, she was once on stage in a nightclub and really bombing. After her act, she went backstage and was practically in tears. Suddenly this guy from the audience comes walking down the hallway, on his way to the bathroom. He says, "Hey, didn't I just see you in the show out there?" Carol says, "Yeah." And the guy says, "Jesus, you stink."

Marlo: Oh, God!

Alan: So, yes, they *will* kill you.

Marlo: But the best comedians always come bouncing back.

Alan: Right, and all because of that need to please. That urge. Funny people—really funny people—will be funny under any circumstances. Someone can just lift their eyebrow or make a little shift in their tone, or get a look in their eye, and you'll fall down laughing. And that's because they want to be in a pleasant frequency with you. It's like you're both tuned into the same thing, and you're dancing together. And through that funniness, the two of you can share a moment of pleasure that you can't get any other way. An intimacy.

Marlo: Intimacy. Dancing. Killing. A funny business, this comedy business.

Alan: You bet.

Comedians in Their Dressing Rooms

George Burns, Milton Berle, Sid Caesar—any of the nightclub comedians I grew up with—could be found before a show in his dressing room, waiting to go on, sitting in his starched, white tux shirt, black satin bow tie, and . . . a pair of shorts. They never put their pants on till the last minute. As my dad used to say, "People eating dinner don't want to look up at a guy with a crumpled crotch."

I loved that about those guys—such respect for the audience. And they all made it look so easy, as they'd stride out on stage to their theme songs, looking happy, snappy and eager to entertain you.

Well, it's not easy. That performance you're watching as you sip your cocktail or enjoy your meal has been carefully measured, honed, worked and reworked until it feels good enough to present to you.

Traveling around the country doing two shows a night, six nights a week, requires a huge amount of energy and Superman guts. You've *got* to have guts to go out there all alone, take a diverse group of strangers, spellbind them, and bring them together as *your* audience.

My father always reminded me of a matador. Often when he was telling a story, he would make a turn, spin off course and back himself into a corner—seemingly a dead end. I'd wonder how he'd ever get back, and then he'd masterfully whip the cape of his wit, make another turn and bring the house down.

I once had a pair of cuff links made for him with matadors on them, and on the back, I had engraved one word: "Olé."

One night at a party at our house, Bob Newhart told a story about a comedian in his dressing room, waiting to go on. He gets a knock on his door, and when he opens it, there's a lovely looking woman standing there. He can see she's a little nervous.

"I am so sorry to disturb you," she says, "but I just had to let you know that I saw your show last night, and I can't tell you how much you did for me."

The woman gulps a breath.

"You see, I lost my husband six months ago and I have been so blue ever since. I've really felt I had nothing to live for. But last night my friends dragged me out of the house, saying it would be good for me, and they brought me to see your show. Well, I laughed like I have never laughed before. Really, you were so wonderful, you took the sadness right out of me. And I just wanted to thank you from the bottom of my heart. You saved my life. So I just thought if there's anything I can do for you—I mean, I know you must be lonely on the road away from home. Well, I live nearby and I'd love to make you a home-cooked meal. I also have some very good wine. And, well, frankly, I'm a little lonely, too. So if you'd like to stay over, I have a beautiful negligee I could slip into. We could have a very lovely night together."

The comedian looks at her for a moment and then says, "Did you see the first show or the second show?"

A Phone Call
with Mr. Warmth

If there's one thing that proves how many generations of comedy Don Rickles's career has spanned, it's that he still wears a classic tuxedo on stage. When's the last time you saw that in a comedy club? I smile whenever I see Don, because he reminds me of all the comics I grew up with who thrived in the early days of Las Vegas. But Don was unique among them. He had chosen the most difficult and dangerous way of trying to make people laugh— by insulting them. And they loved it. They still do, tipping the maître d' to put them up close in hopes of being the subject of his outrageous barbs. In 2008, Don had a best-selling memoir and won an Emmy for a documentary about his career. At 85, he continues to storm the stage and pack the house, because we know that beneath all that blustery insult stuff, the man is an adorable softie.
—M.T.

DON
RICKLES

Marlo: Hello, Don?

Don: Yeah . . .

Marlo: Hi, it's Marlo Thomas.

Rickles: Hi Marlo. What are you doing in town?

Marlo: I'm not in town, actually. I'm in New York.

Rickles: Well, I'm not gonna do it.

Marlo: You're not going to do what?

Rickles: I thought you were going to ask me to do something for that hospital you raise money for. And I was going to say, no, I'm sick, I can't do it.

Marlo: [*Laughs*] Oh, Don, you make me laugh. Wait. You're not really sick, are you?

Rickles: Yes. A truck hit me about a week ago, but I know you've been busy. Don't worry about it.

Marlo: [*Laughs*] Well, if you *were* sick, you know that I know a lot of people in the medical field, so you can always call me . . .

Rickles: I'm too big now, Marlo. I can't even speak to you. You know, when you become an Emmy winner . . .

Marlo: I know. I watched the show, and it was quite a thrill to see you win.

Rickles: Oh, you saw it.

Marlo: Yes, Phil and I watched it together. It was great.

Rickles: Did Phil understand it?

Marlo: [*Laughs*] Yeah, he got it.

Rickles: Explain to Phil that I got bigger than him, and now I don't have to go to Cleveland to be on his Mickey Mouse show.

Marlo: Well, you'll be happy to know that he's not in Cleveland anymore.

Rickles: I know that, Marlo. I've been around.

Marlo: I'm calling you because I'm writing a book that has lots of stories about my dad . . .

Rickles: Who's your dad?

Marlo: Some old guy. I also read *your* book . . .

Rickles: Oh, did you?

Marlo: Yes.

Rickles: Did you enjoy it?

Marlo: Yes I did. I loved the stories about your mother and your relationship with Frank Sinatra. Great stuff.

Rickles: Well, thanks. You know, I have a new one out now.

Marlo: I know—the one with the letters to you. I read that, too. I thought it was fun.

Rickles: It's so funny. All of a sudden I've become the Jewish Mark Twain. Tell Phil I'm the Jewish Mark Twain.

Marlo: I will. He'll get that. He knows from Mark Twain.

Rickles: Okay.

Marlo: So, anyway, my book is about growing up with comedy, and I was wondering, was there somebody in your childhood who made you laugh? How did you become as funny as you are?

Rickles: It was always my personality. Even as a kid, my sarcastic humor and the insults, it was all just in me. It's not something you go to school for, though Milton Berle was my hero when I was growing up.

Marlo: You watched him on television?

Rickles: Yeah, Milton was one of the first guys I used to watch. His delivery was something else. Then as I got older, I realized I was wrong. Don't put that in the book.

Marlo: [*Laughs*] Too late—it's in.

Rickles: I think he would've gotten a kick out of that.

Marlo: Me, too. How about on the radio? Any heroes there?

Rickles: Jack Benny, Sid Caesar, and that whole group. Those were the guys I listened to.

Marlo: Were you funny in school? Did you make people laugh?

Rickles: Yeah, I was the president of the Dramatics Club in high school, and failing every subject.

Marlo: Because you were funny?

Rickles: Because I was always busy acting and never studying. Then the war came, and I went into the navy.

Marlo: I saw that picture of you in your book. You were handsome as a sailor.

Rickles: Handsome? You must have cataracts.

Marlo: Not yet, thank you. So when did you realize you could make people laugh? When you were a little boy, did you make your parents laugh?

Rickles: It wasn't like that. In my case, I never realized it. My mother would just say, "Get up there and do Uncle Jack—show everybody how he walks." So I'd make fun of my Uncle Jack. And my Aunt Dora. Then when I was about 12 and the holidays came around—Hanukkah or Christmas—I would get up in the synagogue and do impersonations of the rabbi, off the top of my head.

Marlo: So your mother knew you were funny.

Rickles: Yes, she knew I was funny, but believe it or not, she didn't believe in my humor.

Marlo: Meaning?

Rickles: Meaning, she'd laugh, but she'd say, "Why can't you be like Alan King?"

Marlo: That's funny.

Rickles: Used to break me up. But once my career took off and she started to get jewelry and a nice house, she said, "Okay. Your humor has some merit to it."

Marlo: Right. Let's get back to the synagogue. You'd actually get up and imitate the rabbi? That's pretty nervy.

Rickles: Oh, sure. But I've always had a way of doing things that were funny. Like at the Kennedy Center Awards. When Clint Eastwood received that honor, he invited Barbara and me to be there. A lot of stars were invited to speak, and everyone's saying, "Clint is a genius," "Clint is the greatest," "God bless Clint," and so on. And I get up and say, "Now, Clint I'm gonna be very honest with you—you're a lousy actor." And everybody falls down.

Marlo: That's great. You know, my dad used to take me to comedy clubs and I remember seeing you at a little place called—

Rickles: . . . the Slate Brothers. They'd line up around the block at this dumpy joint. I had no act, really. I'd just get up and make fun of people. Everyone showed up.

Marlo: Was this the act you wound up doing later, or were you doing something different?

Rickles: I was honing it. I developed a beginning, I developed a middle, and I developed an ending. And now, today, I got music and I'm a big star.

Marlo: You always end your act by confessing that your ribbing is just in fun, and that you really like people. Didn't my father tell you that you needed that little cutter at the end, just to let people know you're a good guy?

Rickles: Yes, and I still do that to this day, but in a much smaller way. If I'd left it up to your father, I'd be reading the Bible at the end of my act.

Marlo: That's funny, Don.

Rickles: But, yes, your dad was always full of advice about how to make a joke better.

Marlo: He was that way with me, too. I was on Letterman's show once, and he asked me to do a spit-take, because Dad was famous for spit-takes. Well, I'd never done a spit-take in my life, but I said to Letterman, "Okay, give me a glass of water." Then I whispered in Letterman's ear, "You've gotta say something to set this up. Say to me, 'Aren't you the girl who's married to Geraldo?'"

So Letterman says, "Oh, I love this—this is going to be fun!" So I lift the glass to my lips, Letterman says the line and I spit out the water. But the spit-take is terrible. The water just kind of dribbles out. Sure enough, that night I get a call from my father. He says to me, "You're supposed to *blow*, sweetheart. You don't spit, you blow." And I said, "Oh, okay, Daddy. I don't think I'll be doing a lot more of those; it's not really my thing. But if I do it again, I got it now. Blow, don't spit."

Rickles: Oh, that's funny.

Marlo: You mentioned before that when you were a kid, your mother made you do impersonations. In a way, are you still trying to perform for her?

Rickles: Well, if we get into the mental stuff, who knows? But I will say that if it wasn't for my mother, I'd probably still be a very shy kid living in a box. She always made me get up and entertain—and I would.

Marlo: You wanted to please her.

Rickles: Yeah. She was the driving force behind everything I did.

Marlo: And your dad? Was he funny?

Rickles: He wasn't a funny guy, but he was a kibitzer—and very warm. Nobody in my family was really funny. My mother was like a half-assed entertainer. She'd stand up and do an impression of Sophie Tucker. She loved to get up on the stage. She was a frustrated actress, I suppose, living her life through me, performing-wise. But her Sophie Tucker *was* pretty good.

Marlo: You make me laugh, Don. Okay, I'm going to let you go now. You've been wonderful.

Rickles: You, too, Marlo. And, listen, if you and Phil are in L.A.—and I mean this sincerely—we'd love to see you. Give us a call sometime.

Marlo: I'll do that.

Rickles: And could you please tell Phil something for me?

Marlo: Sure. What do you want me to say?

Rickles: Tell him I'm a star.

DID YA HEAR THE ONE ABOUT . . .

An old Jewish man is walking along the beach when he sees something glittering in the sand. He picks it up—it's a bottle. He brushes it off and a genie pops out.

"I will grant you one wish," the genie says.

"One wish?" the old man says. And from his back pocket, he takes out a crumpled old map.

"You see this?" he says to the genie. "This is a map of my homeland, Israel, and right next to it is Palestine. They are neighbors and yet for years and years they fight and kill each other. My wish is that you bring peace to my homeland and Palestine."

The genie says, "Oh, my, that is a very big wish you ask for. And though I am a very magical genie, I don't think even I can grant that wish. Do you have any other wish?"

The old man says, "Okay. How 'bout that my wife Sadie should like the oral sex?"

The genie thinks a moment and says, "Let me take another look at that map."

The Two Dannys

My father had a thing about fear. He hated it. He would get angry with Terre, Tony and me if he thought we were afraid. Then he'd talk admiringly of his father.

"Your grandfather was fearless," he'd tell us. "At funerals, he would kiss the corpse on the mouth!"

Why that was a good thing I never knew.

When Dad went to London to appear at the famed Palladium, it was a great test of his appeal. London audiences and critics were known for being very tough on performers, and though Dad was a household name in America, he wasn't known in England. He was coming in cold.

He was also following Danny Kaye, who the London press adored. One of the newspaper stories heralding Dad's arrival bore the headline "AMERICA HAS SENT US ANOTHER DANNY!"

The two Dannys couldn't have been further apart in what they did onstage. Kaye was a lighthearted, aristocratic elf; Dad told stories of the struggles of his immigrant neighborhood, with all the colorful accents he had picked up as a child. The comparison was not one that gave my father an edge with the London crowd.

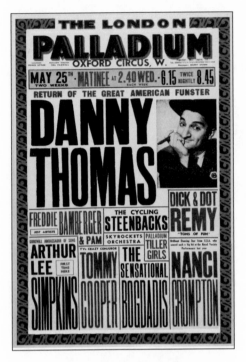

My friend Julian Schlossberg unearthed this treasure in a dusty little poster shop in London.

He'd had trepidation even before he left. He'd told Jack Benny that he was worried that the London audience might not get his material. Benny tried to put him at ease.

"You're a great storyteller," he said to Dad. "Just do your stuff and you'll be fine."

"But their humor is so different from ours," Dad said. "What if they don't understand me?"

"You're going to do your act in English aren't you?" Benny said.

"Of course," Dad said.

"Well, the language was born there," Benny said. "They'll understand you."

Dad said that on opening night, when he walked out on the Palladium stage, it was the first time he'd ever experienced that kind of fear. He actually felt his knees knocking together. He was terrified and he hated himself for it.

He looked up at the tiers of well-dressed, well-heeled Brits, and out of his mouth came words that were at once spontaneous and brilliant.

"I hear you're the toughest, most discriminating audience in the world for a performer," he said. "Well, I wouldn't be in your shoes tonight for all the money in the world." Olé.

The audience roared—he knew he had them.

My father told me later that he had no idea where that line came from—that it had sprung from a fight-or-flee situation. He had found himself cornered, then turned the dynamic around—which is crucial to a stand-up comic (or any stand-up person). He had taken the bully to the ground.

But no audience in the world was as appreciative of my father's craft as I was. When I was a teenager, and out on a date, I'd catch myself checking my watch. Even if I was having a good time, I'd want to get home to the dinner table—or coffee afterward in the living room—when all the guys would gather with Dad, smoking cigars and telling stories. My friends were great, and I was always crazy about some boy, but Sid Caesar, Phil Silvers and George Burns were at my house. The laughter would go on for hours. And I wanted to be there.

Some nights our living room would be filled with comedy writers, working on a TV special, Dad's act or one of his shows. They'd be throwing around ideas—"spitballing" they called it—and I'd laugh at something that one of the writers threw out.

"You like that?" Dad would ask me. "You think that's funny?"

He got a big kick out of his kids seeing the funny.

One night after the taping of one of Dad's specials, he and I were leaving the El Capitan, the grand old theatre palace on Hollywood Boulevard. As Dad and I hit the sidewalk, one of the people from the audience waiting outside called out to him.

"Hey, Danny," the guy shouted, "Jack Benny just about stole the show from you!"

"He'd better," Dad hollered back. "That's what he gets paid to do."

On the drive home, I asked my father what he thought about that man's comment.

"In any business, Mugs, you want the strongest people around you," he said. "It's not the strong ones that'll kill you. It's the weak ones."

Always a killing.

Turn-ons with
Conan O'Brien

Conan O'Brien is a genuine double-whammy. A lot of comedians write their own material; but rare is the comic who cuts his teeth writing for other hit comedy shows (Saturday Night Live *and* The Simpsons) *before becoming a star performer himself. Since 1993, Conan has been television's favorite goofy cut-up, and his unique blend of Harvard-boy charm and unapologetic nerdiness has earned him his own niche in the late-night TV galaxy. It also makes him terrific to talk to. I enjoyed spending time with both Conans—the clown and the intellectual.*
—M.T.

On ... the kitchen table

Conan: There's definitely a genetic component to comedy, and there's also a huge cultural part. My family is Irish-Catholic, and I'm one of six kids, the third boy from the top. My brothers were funny and my sisters were funny, and both of my parents had a really good sense of humor. So whenever anybody asks me how I got started in all of this, I tell them that I learned ninety-five percent of what I know at the kitchen table. We'd sit around that table and see who could make my dad laugh—and he had good taste. He wouldn't laugh at everything, so if he did laugh, you knew you had said something really funny.

Even at an early age, I remember thinking that all my brothers were good at things, but I didn't know what I was good at. Then I figured it out—this is what I do. I can really make people laugh.

On ... that magic moment

I want to do what that guy is doing. That's what I was thinking when my father took me to see Sid Caesar's *Your Show of Shows* in a movie theatre. I was ten years old and I distinctly remember watching that famous "This Is Your Life" sketch, when Carl Reiner goes into the audience to get Sid Caesar and bring him on stage. But Caesar runs away—and then everyone chases after him. That was a seminal moment for me. I literally remember thinking, *This is what I want to do.*

On ... those 10,000 hours

A lot has been written about how you need ten thousand hours of practice to get good at something, and comedy is no different. You have to put in a lot of time. Like the Beatles—before anybody knew who they were, they went to Germany and played clubs where their sets went on for ten or twelve hours, seven nights a week. So by the time they started recording, they'd already done their ten thousand hours. They really knew their stuff. I believe I got my thousands of hours, too.

On . . . the class clown

I was never the class clown. To me, the class clown is the kid who jumps up on the desk and sets the clock ahead an hour, the one who plays all the pranks. That kid usually doesn't end up too well. He winds up in some sort of motel shooting. I was the kid who did my work and kept to myself. And then, when I made close friends, they would say, "Hey, wait a minute—this guy's really funny . . ."

That's sort of been the way my careers have unfolded. When I was a writer, I would always show up in the writers' room and be quiet for a few days. But by the end, I was Morey Amsterdam—the one who was up on the table making everybody laugh. I need to get comfortable with people. When I first showed up on TV, people were like "Who *is* this guy?" They didn't get it right away. They had to get acquainted with me—and I had to get acquainted with them.

On . . . repression, sex and comedy

Growing up in a Catholic house, you learn that there's a lot you can't talk about. Like sex—no one talks about sex. But I think repression gets a bad rap in our society. Think about the way an engine works—you've got a confined space, you build up all this pressure, and it makes the car go ninety miles an hour. Same thing with growing up in a Catholic house. Our mother wanted us to behave. Manners were very important to her; no elbows on the table, get good grades in school, that sort of thing. And then you have all this stuff that you're taught through the Catholic Church about what you can't do and what you can't say.

So what happens is, comedy comes out of it. It's like a teakettle, where there's just this tiny little spout that steam can shoot out of. Comedy becomes the way that you can talk about things, and it's okay because you're being funny. It's like an escape from never having had the permission to really go for it.

I still feel that way when I do my show. The show is my hour where I'm allowed to do whatever I want to do—things I'd never do at a party or at a friend's house. I'm chronically polite and nonconfrontational, the kind of person who, if someone punches me in the face, I'll say, "Excuse me. I shouldn't have put my face there." But on my show, I have permission to be somebody else. And that's where a lot of really good comedy comes from. It's like a slingshot: You get pulled way back, then snap forward in the other direction.

On . . . the pluck of the Irish

I was at some event once, and looked around, and there were Rosie O'Donnell and Regis Philbin and me—and I remember thinking: *All Irish.* Oppressed cultures do well with comedy because it's all we had. You have no power over your life, you don't have a gun, you don't have a tank. So, instead, you mutter jokes under your breath, and make fun of everyone. It's been that way throughout history. The Irish were oppressed by the English. African-Americans were oppressed by the West. The Jews were oppressed by everybody. And now these are the really funny people.

On . . . being ridiculous

I've always, always been self-deprecating. And it's funny because it all comes out of something real.

When I was a kid, I wasn't good at sports. I also looked funny. I fell in the driveway when I was about two years old, and for a long time had two dead teeth in the front of my mouth. I had orange hair and freckles, and I was really skinny. So I felt like I had a lot to overcome.

So I would make fun of me. I'd find myself ridiculous because I couldn't go the other way—I couldn't really say, "Look at me, I'm the greatest!" Your core personality develops pretty early on, then you hone it, hone it, hone it. So this is the style I adopted as a kid. What's interesting is that some people now say to me, "You're six-four, not a bad-looking guy, have a beautiful wife and kids, and this big, successful career. Why do you still make fun of yourself?" And I think it's because that ship has already sailed. I'm still that kid who finds himself ridiculous. I could be made dictator of the world tomorrow, and I would still make fun of myself. My personality is my personality.

On . . . surrendering dignity

I love—absolutely love—silly stuff. To this day, I can be in a foul mood, but watching a *Pink Panther* movie with Peter Sellers still does it for me.

He's so outrageously committed to his comedy. And I still laugh at W. C. Fields in that famous clip of him playing ping-pong at a fancy party. I love it when people completely surrender their dignity. It all appeals to me on some sort of anarchic level.

And the Three Stooges! I'll never forget this one short they were in. They were all in the woods, hitting and yelling at each other, and then this bear steals their car and drives away. There's this long shot of the bear driving down the road, and at the last second you see the bear put his paw out the window to signal for a left turn. I'll be ninety years old and still think that's hilarious.

On . . . playing the room (*any* room)

I went to jury duty not long ago, and what happens is, when famous people show up, they're put in a separate room and told, "Look, you're not going to get on a jury because everyone knows who you are. But we'd like you to get up and speak to the bailiffs and court officers and the different people who work in the courthouse." So that's what they did with me, and I did really well. I remember turning to someone and saying, "I'm killing with these court officers." I'm sort of shameless that way.

But it doesn't matter where you are—you could be at a wedding, you could be waiting for a subway, you could be with a bunch of three-year-olds at a birthday party. You're always aware when you've got a good audience.

I got married in the Catholic Church, and my wife and I were up on the altar. It was a pretty formal ceremony, so we had to kneel. The priest, who was a friend of mine, was giving the sermon at the wedding Mass, and he started to joke around a little with the audience. All of my friends were laughing—and it was *hell* for me. I was kneeling up there thinking, *This is a great room and I'm forced to kneel here and not say a word.* It was like some kind of punishment in the afterlife.

On ... comedy snobs

My least favorite thing about comedy is the occasional snobbery. People often say they want their comedy to be meaningful and intelligent. But I say: Comedy is hard. And if you're really making people laugh, you're probably doing something good, so don't think about it too much.

When I first got my show and nobody knew me, people made assumptions about me. They'd look up my past and say, "Oh, he went to Harvard, so he's going to be a very erudite, serious, Dick Cavett kind of guy. He's going to do *intelligent* comedy." But why put labels on comedy? I like giant ostriches. I like absolute silliness. I love that almost cartoon childish sensibility. That stuff can be funny and still be smart.

My dad is the perfect example of this. When he was a resident in medical school, he always stayed up late. So he'd watch Steve Allen's *Tonight* show. Or Jack Paar. And he loved Johnny Carson. And what's funny is, my dad is this really brilliant guy—a highly intelligent scientist—but he's always just loved to laugh. And so I learned early on that being funny doesn't necessarily mean being stupid.

On ... coming home

My parents still live in the same house I grew up in, and they still have that same kitchen table we all used to sit around. Whenever I go home—and here I have a national television show, I've been around the block a few times—I'll sit at that table with my sisters and brothers and my parents and find myself trying to score again. It's like going home to that little court that you used to play on. You'd think I wouldn't need that anymore, but I do.

DID YA HEAR THE ONE ABOUT . . .

An old Irishman, Paddy, is about to go to his eternal reward.
He looks at his grieving friend, Mike, and says,
"I have one last request, Mike."

"Anything, Paddy," Mike says. "What is it?"

"In me kitchen pantry you'll find a 100-year-old bottle of
whiskey. When they put me in the ground will you
pour it over me grave?"

"I will, Paddy," Mike says. "But would you mind
if I passed it through me kidneys first?"

The Bow

Like many nightclub performers, my father would acknowledge the presence of a star in his audience. "Stand up and take a bow," he would say to the celebrity. I'd seen this ritual countless times since I was a child. In 1966, after I had become *That Girl*, I was in my father's audience at the Sands Hotel, when I heard him call out from the stage, "Ladies

and gentlemen, we have a special star in our audience tonight. Miss Marlo Thomas, please stand up and take a bow."

For the little girl who had watched her Daddy hone his act so many years before—and for the father who had hoped to spare his big girl the heartache of show business—it was a powerful moment for both of us.

Twenty Questions for Stephen Colbert

Of all the comedians I grew up with, there isn't one who reminds me of Stephen Colbert. He's from another planet of comedy. Maybe that's why he had his DNA shot into space.

In 2005, Colbert launched his late-night talk show, The Colbert Report, *after a winning run on* The Daily Show, *starring his friend Jon Stewart. Within three years, Colbert's character—an audacious, politically incorrect loudmouth—had run for president (in a campaign sponsored by Doritos), visited troops in Iraq (shaving his head on the air) and coined a word—"truthiness"—which serious journalists began using in their columns. He also began wearing a consciousness-raising bracelet in honor of his wrist, which he broke while cavorting around the stage.*

Not since Archie Bunker has there been a character that we so strongly disagree with— but laugh at anyway. And when he's out of character? The guy is wickedly smart . . .
—M.T.

Q1 You are so edgy-funny. And really fearless. Where did that come from?

I think it came from my mother. She would always say things like "In the light of eternity, none of this really matters." If anything bothered you or embarrassed you, if you suffered in any way, she'd say, "It's another jewel in your crown. Offer it up."

Q2 Oh, that is so funny. So Catholic. Are you surprised that you've become such a serious force?

I do not accept this "serious force" stuff . . .

Q3 Journalists constantly credit you with being a driving force in our popular and political culture. I'd call that serious.

Look, Marlo, I just wanted to make it to Christmas. We went on the air in October 2005, and got a 32-show buy. I told my producers, "Don't buy any nice furniture. Don't get me a desk—I'll just use that steel thing in the corner. Because we're not going to be here at Christmastime." And you know what? I'm still working on that idea—that by Christmas, we're all going to be looking for work.

Q4 When I first saw *The Colbert Report,* I thought, Wow, this is hilarious—but it's a three-week show. He'll never be able to sustain this character.

That's what my wife said! The thing about my character is, he is never wrong. What is factually accurate does not matter to him. What matters is how things *feel*. So in that way, my character is a little bit Zeitgeisty. He's all about what is valued and devalued in the country. Americans don't really value intellectualism. They value feeling over thinking. They'd rather feel things are the way they want them to be than examine the way they *should* be. And that aggressive, self-preservative ignorance is what my character is based upon. I have described him as—and the order of this is fairly important—a well-intentioned, poorly informed, high-status idiot.

Q5 What cracks you up personally?

I'm pretty omnivorous when it comes to that. I like all kinds of different things. When I was a kid, I loved Phil Silvers. And I really loved Steve Martin. I never did stand-up, so I don't necessarily have performance joke structure in my head. What I like is *behavior*. I learned to do comedy through character behavior in Second City. And that's what really appeals to me. I also like relationship humor, and I think my show has that—my relationship is with the audience. And with my guests.

Q6 I read that you once did a television show where the sponsors pulled out after one episode. True?

Yes, it was a sketch show starring Dana Carvey. I'd done television before that, but this was my big break. It was back in 1996, and at the time, the number one shows on TV were *Home Improvement*, with Tim Allen, and *Seinfeld*. They'd trade off week-to-week in the number one slot. We came on right after *Home Improvement* and had a 13-show guarantee.

In the very first show, Dana Carvey does an impression of Bill Clinton, talking about how he's going to get rid of Hillary because she's such a burden, and he'll be both father and mother to the nation because he can do anything. Then he opens his shirt and has these animal teats going down his chest, which had been rigged by a guy who worked for Henson MuppetWorks—so they actually lactated. And then he breast-fed puppies and kittens. Remember, this is right after *Home Improvement*, which is as gentle as comedy can get.

Q7 So what happened?

According to the minute-by-minute tracking, at 9:30, we had something like 25 million viewers. At 9:32, we had 12 million viewers.

We had lost, like, 13 million viewers in 30 seconds. And we never got them back. Our sponsors were six different Pepsi subsidiaries, and four of them pulled out. So after that we were sponsored by Diet Mug Root Beer or something like that. We were done.

Dana came into my office afterwards—Steve Carell and I were office mates—and said to us, "I'm sorry. I've ruined your careers." We said, "No, we're having fun!" He said, "No, guys, you don't realize—it's over."

Q8 You're the youngest of eleven children. Most people develop their sense of humor around the dinner table. How did you ever get a word in edgewise?

In my family, it was a *humorocracy*. The funny person in the room was king. So I learned to retell my brothers' and sisters' stories, emulate their styles. Like, my brother Jimmy has a rapier wit. He could cut you right down. And my brother Billy actually taught me jokes—like guy-walks-into-a-bar jokes. And Eddie was known as a storyteller. Other members of the family were more physical. Everyone had their specialty, and there was never a moment in which we didn't try to make each other laugh. We were constantly at it. One of my clearest memories was watching them and thinking, *I wish I had made that person laugh.* Or, *I wish I had made that joke right there.* Or, *I wish I could be like them.*

Q9 That's like growing up in a school for comedy. Were your mom and dad funny?

Yeah, they were. I don't remember much about my father—he died when I was young. But I've been told he was known for his sense of humor. Very funny, very dry. And my mother has a good sense of humor. She just loves to laugh. She's a big hugger, too. And for no reason. That was a rule—you never had to ask for a hug.

Q10 It's been said that your ancestry is both French and Irish. Which one is it?

We always thought we were French because we grew up hearing that Jean Baptist Colbert had been finance minister for Louise XIV, and was the Marquis de Seignelay. My father's family was too dirt-poor and uneducated to have made that stuff up. They wouldn't have known about that—they were, like, horse thieves from Illinois.

Q11&12 Didn't you have your DNA sequenced on your show?

Yes, and they told me that my DNA almost perfectly matches four people in the world—and all of them live in Ireland. They also said, "Your family evidently are very specific racists: They will only marry other Irish people."

Did you?

I have a mixed marriage. I married a Scots-Irish.

Q13 Tell me about your wife. Is she funny?

Yes, my wife's funny. But I had to teach her *silly*. I brought the silly to the marriage. She'll say to me, "Why did you just do that?" And I'll say, "Because it's ridiculous." So now there's a complete balance of humor in the family, but it took a little while.

Q14 What about when you were single? Did you date funny girls?

The thing about comedians is, they don't get groupies. That always bugged me when I was young and single. How come rock stars get groupies and comedians don't? When I was with Second City, we'd do two hours of sketch comedy, and afterwards, it would be like, "I just killed, man!"—but never, ever did anybody want to talk to us. I kissed a girl maybe once during the entire time. And, I mean, it was like a peck-on-the-check, let's-go-to-the-ice-cream-social kind of kiss, not like Sodom and Gomorrah.

Q15 You took on President Bush pretty fiercely when you hosted the 2006 Correspondents' Dinner. It was like a Friars Roast. Were you there to make him laugh, or were you there to skewer him? I mean, what were you thinking?

It was a little bit of both, I think. I actually thought he'd laugh more than he did. But I can't tell you how much he laughed because I've never watched the tape. On a certain level, I'm not interested in that evening.

I just went and did exactly what I wanted to do. I figured I'd get some laughs, and maybe there would be a slight hint of brimstone in the air, but no more than on my show. They'd invited me to come, and I just did my material.

Q16 What about the next generation of Colberts? Do your children have your family's sense of humor?

My daughter is very funny. When she was three, I heard her create her very first joke. We were walking down the street; she was on my shoulders and my son was in the old papoose on the wife's belly. And I said to my daughter, "What does the dog say?" And she said, "Ruff-ruff." And I said, "Right! Now what does the cow say?" And she said, "Ruff-ruff." And I said, "No, no—the cow doesn't say ruff-ruff!" And she said, "Yes, he does. He has a dog in his mouth!" And she knew it was a joke! I thought, *That's fantastic!* I had to tell Jon Stewart that story—proud papa, and all. And he says, "She's three, and she's writing *New Yorker* cartoons?"

Q17 Speaking of Stewart, is there anything you could teach him about the art of comedy? And, by the way, I'm going to ask him the same thing about you.

No, and I'll tell you why: I think I have a pretty good idea of what I'm doing, yet I've never had a discussion with Jon Stewart about an idea I wanted to go after, or the structure of a joke, or even the presentation of a joke, that I was not . . . "impressed" doesn't begin to capture how I feel about the clarity that he brings to it all. It's frightening.

Q18 Have you and Jon ever disagreed on how to make something funny?

I only went to the mat with Jon maybe four or five times in the entire time we worked together, and I was never right—and I don't like saying that because I have as big an ego as the next guy.

Q19 You lost your father and two of your brothers in a plane crash when you were ten. How difficult that must have been for you.

Yes, after they died, I became quiet, distant. A little bit of an outcast. In school, I didn't necessarily talk to other people from, like, fifth grade until my junior year. For six years I wasn't particularly a funny person. And then I started making people laugh. I started making the *popular* people laugh, if you know what I mean. I don't know what it was, but people started laughing at everything I did, and that sort of reintroduced me to the society of my school, you know? A year later I was voted wittiest in the school.

Q20 But what about at home? How did you all ever find laughter again?

We just did. I remember coming back from the funeral in the limo, and one of my sisters made another of my sisters laugh so hard that her drink came out of her nose. And the first sister actually got up in the back of the limo and started dancing for victory—celebrating that she'd been able to do that to the other sibling. It was as if we were sitting around the dinner table. And it was wonderful.

And I remember thinking, *I want that. I want to be able to do that.* Because we all felt wonderful—or at least relieved. At that moment, the coin of the realm for our family was making each other laugh.

CHAPTER 28

Dinner at the Goldbergs

The Jews and the Lebanese have a lot in common. The food they eat is just about the same, their music sounds the same and they have the same noses. So I guess it's no mystery why most people thought my dad was Jewish. And playing the cantor's son in *The Jazz Singer*—singing the Hebraic hymns with such ease in his throaty Middle Eastern tone—cemented the impression.

When I was going out with Leonard Goldberg, we were visiting New York during Passover, so he invited me to Seder dinner at his family's home in Brooklyn. I love Seders. We even had our own version of them at our house for Uncle Abe and Aunt Frances Lastfogel, since we were their adopted family. I love the ritual of the Four Questions—*Why is this night different from all other nights?* I love the songs, the prayers, the candles, hiding the matzoh and all of the food—everything but the gefilte fish. It's a smelly, gooey lump, an acquired taste that I never acquired.

The day of the dinner, Lenny and his dad were picking up items for the evening meal when Lenny pulled his father aside.

"Please tell Mom not to push the gefilte fish on Marlo," he said. "She doesn't like it. She's had it a few times, but she didn't grow up with it like we did."

Lenny's father looked at him in disbelief.

"What do you mean she didn't grow up with it? Danny Thomas isn't Jewish?"

"No," Lenny said. "They're Catholic."

Mr. Goldberg replied in a hushed tone. "Don't tell your mother. It will ruin her evening."

That night, Lenny hired a car and driver to take us out to Brooklyn, and on the way he told me about the conversation. I thought to myself, *I have to make it up to his mother for not being a Jew. I'll eat the damn gefilte fish.*

The dinner table was covered with every imaginable food for the holiday. I happily devoured the brisket and potato pancakes—and then, with a deep breath, stuffed in the dreaded fish, smothered with hot horseradish, and washed it down with an enormous glass of water.

Suddenly, Lenny's mother jumped up from the table, crying, and ran into the next room, slamming the door behind her. Her husband ran after her, but I could hear her through the wall.

"His children will come to my house wearing crosses!" she wailed.

It was a terrible moment. And I had already eaten the damn fish.

Lenny looked at me apologetically. Obviously, his father had tipped off his wife that I was a shiksa. Mrs. Goldberg came back to the table and tried to be gracious. But the elephant was in the room.

On the way home in the car, I vomited up the gefilte fish. (Who says I'm not a great date?) The next day, I called my mother and told her what happened.

"Good girl!" she said.

"Good girl *what*?!" I responded. "I vomited."

"It's the least you could have done for that poor woman."

They have a club, these women.

. . .

NOT LONG AFTER THAT, Lenny, who was the head of Screen Gems Television at the time, was having lunch with comedy writer Bernard Slade, and told him the story of "Marlo's Night at the Family Seder." Bernie screamed with laughter, and a few weeks later brought Lenny a pilot script for a TV comedy called *Bridget Loves Bernie,* about a Catholic girl and a Jewish boy who fall in love. In a pivotal scene in the script, Bernie takes Bridget home to his family for dinner, which turns out be disastrous.

Lenny gave me the script to read and there it all was—the gentile girl, the nervous glances at the gefilte fish, even the vomiting. But in the script, Bridget doesn't wait to get into the car. She jumps up from the table and runs to the bathroom.

Mrs. Goldberg's line about wearing crosses was there, too. But I asked Lenny to cut it. It would be too hurtful to his mother to use her feelings for a laugh. So Bernie took it out—well, he changed it to "His five children will come to my house, and three of them will be *nuns!*"

Mrs. Goldberg's line was better. But it didn't matter. Screen Gems and Bernie Slade got a show on the air that ran for a season. If only all of my relationships had proven to be so lucrative.

DID YA HEAR THE ONE ABOUT . . .

Short summary of every Jewish holiday:

They tried to kill us, we won, let's eat.

The Survivor

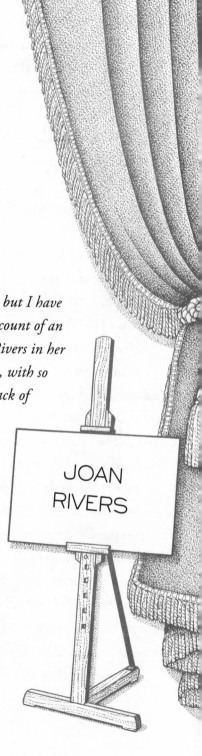

I've read many comedians' autobiographies, but I have never read a more honest and harrowing account of an uphill climb than the one written by Joan Rivers in her memoir, Enter Talking. *It amazed me how, with so many years of early failure and a constant lack of support, even from her family, she was unstoppable. What fuels such passion and perfectionism is that indefinable trait that separates the achiever from the also-ran. Joan has never looked away from the toughest parts of the human condition— even her own. She has the guts to confront them all dead-on, and somehow, miraculously, make them funny.*

—M.T.

JOAN
RIVERS

Marlo: I've got to tell you, your book *Enter Talking* was the most honest and unsettling account of becoming a comedian I have ever read. What amazed me was that, with all the failure you went through, you knew you were as good as you later proved to be. How did you know?

Joan: I didn't know. I was one of the lucky ones who had no choice. And I don't mean that melodramatically. But at this age you can look back and get it. I knew I wanted to be in the business and I knew that's where I was going.

Marlo: But you were failing everywhere—even your parents begged you to stop.

Joan: Yeah, I know, it's not rational. It was like drugs, and in my case, it's my drug of choice.

Marlo: When did you know you were funny?

Joan: I didn't know I was funny. I just knew I had to perform.

Marlo: Were your parents funny?

Joan: My whole family was funny. My father was very witty. He was a doctor, but he would tell great stories about his patients. I think it's all truly DNA. You don't just say, "Oh, gee, I'm going to become funny." You just see the world . . . *differently.*

Marlo: How about your mother?

Joan: She was the only one in my family who wasn't funny. She would always say—and it was so sweet—"I'm an appreciator."

Marlo: Did being an appreciator make her encourage you?

Joan: In comedy? Oh, God no! None of them did. They didn't want me in the business. They didn't want me to be an actress, and couldn't even say the word "comedian." To them it was the lowest rung on the show-biz ladder. Even when I was already hosting *The Tonight Show,* my mother would still say, "Joan is basically a writer."

Marlo: You often talk about comedy in such a violent way: *Comedy is a medium for revenge, humor is a gun.*

Joan: That's because comedy comes out of anger. Comedy comes out of "I'll show you." Comedy comes out of "You'll be sorry." The minute somebody is having a wonderful, soft life, they're not so funny anymore.

Marlo: You're still funny.

Joan: My life has always been rough.

Marlo: Even now?

Joan: Oh, absolutely. Always. Now I'm fighting the age barrier. They tell me, "You're great, but you're not the demographic." I think one of the reasons I did *Celebrity Apprentice* was to say, "I can still take you with one hand behind my back." And I was so glad to have won because of that. Literally to say, "Enough, stop writing people off!"

Marlo: You like to make fun of older women being with younger men.

Joan: Yeah, I do a lot of cougar jokes. I mean, what's with these older women? I don't want to wake up in the morning, look over and say, "Is this my date or did I give birth last night?" That's not what I'm looking for.

Marlo: You've referred to yourself as a lion tamer when you're on stage. More violence.

Joan: Absolutely. I think any actor or performer has to be in command. You have to be the strongest and they have to pay attention. You don't want an audience talking during you.

Marlo: I have this vision of you with a chair and a whip.

Joan: Just about. You have to say, "I'm here and we're all going to have a good time, but you will be quiet and listen to me."

Marlo: And why should we listen to you?

Joan: Because I'm the funniest, and because you paid your money to see me.

Marlo: Why do you say, "Never trust an audience"?

Joan: Because you can't. Bill Cosby told me this a long time ago. He said the audience decides collectively if they like you or don't like you, every time you walk on the stage. You must never think, *Oh they adore me, so they'll adore me tonight.* No, no, no, no. Bill said—and it's so smart—"If they don't know you, they give you three minutes. If they do know you, they give you five."

Marlo: How do you handle a heckler?

Joan: I saw Sinatra do something once, so I just copied him. Someone was heckling him— and yelling and talking during him—so he just walked over, gave the guy the microphone and said, "You think they'd rather hear you? Here—go do it. I'll be back." And he walked off stage.

Marlo: That's brilliant. You're known for saying very funny but insulting Don Rickles kinds of things . . .

Joan: But it's never directed at the audience. I have great respect for my audience. Nobody got all dressed up to have a bad time. They came to have fun. So I would never hurt them or intimidate them in any way. I go after the big guns.

Marlo: Like Elizabeth Taylor. What did this woman ever do to you?

Joan: I truly feel that a comedian is the one who says that the emperor is not wearing clothes. I succeed by saying what everybody else is thinking. I was the first to say that Elizabeth Taylor is . . . *huge*! Remember that picture of her getting out of a limousine with David Geffen and she couldn't fit through the door? That was my first Elizabeth Taylor joke. Then I just kept going: "She has more chins than a Chinese phone book." "I sit in McDonald's just to watch her eat and see the 'How Many Served' numbers change."

Marlo: And you never let up.

Joan: Oh, I let up. When she got in a wheelchair, I said, "Okay, let it go."

Marlo: I'm so impressed with your drive. You've never lost that, have you?

Joan: No, no, no, no, you don't. You can't.

Marlo: As harrowing as your survival stories are, they're also very touching. Like when you first appeared on *The Tonight Show* with Johnny Carson, you were so frightened and felt so unsupported, that you wrote "Break a leg" on one knee and "Good luck" on the other. They were covered by your dress, so you could touch them while you were on the air. That was so moving to me.

Joan: Yeah, well, you've got to bolster yourself. I had been brought up so many times for *The Tonight Show* and was always turned down. And, you know, the humiliation of getting up in front of a secretary . . .

Marlo: You auditioned for a secretary?

Joan: . . . who's eating a sandwich. And *she* rejects you! I wasn't brought on the show to anybody's expectations. I was just thrown on in the last ten minutes, the worst spot. And three weeks before, my agent had told me, "You're too old. If you were gonna make it, you'd have made it by now."

Marlo: That's nice—and that's your agent. So how did he get you on the show?

Joan: He didn't. I went on because Bill Cosby had been on the show with a comedian who was so bad, he said to the bookers, "You might as well use Joan Rivers. She can't be worse than that guy." And that's why they finally put me on.

Marlo: What a recommendation.

Joan: No one had faith in me. They didn't even think I was good enough to do stand-up, so they brought me out as "a girl writer."

Marlo: And it went great, right?

Joan: Yeah, I was funny out there—and Carson, right on the air, said, "You're going to be a star." But it wasn't until the next day, when every critic came out and said something wonderful, that the phones went off the hook. It was like an overnight sensation, really. Amazing.

Marlo: So you were on your way.

Joan: Not yet, because I knew one thing—and no one told me this, I just knew it was true: that it wasn't the first shot, it wasn't the second shot, it was the *third* shot that establishes you and proves you weren't a fluke.

Marlo: So how far apart were your three shows?

Joan: About six weeks—and, every night, I went to a club in the Village with my Wollensak tape recorder and continued to do exactly what I had been doing—working on the shots, working on the shots. That's all I did—I wanted to show them. Anyone can be funny once. We've all got seven good stories in us. But can you come up with 160 good stories?

Marlo: I love that you taped it. It's the craft.

Joan: Yeah, I still do that. Nothing has changed. I work in a place on Forty-second Street in New York every Wednesday night. I go in, ad-lib, and tape the whole thing.

Marlo: No kidding.

Joan: Nothing has changed—just the machine is smaller.

Marlo: Are you creating material to use on television?

Joan: To use on television, to use on a roast, to keep me relevant. Right now, I'm going over last night's transcript so I can pull stuff together for Vegas next week.

Marlo: What joke is in front of you right now?

Joan: My "Helen Keller Was My House Guest" routine.

Marlo: Tell it to me.

Joan: Oh, please.

Marlo: Come on, tell me!

Joan: It's still so new. Okay—here's one joke: Barbara Walters wrote in her book *The Art of Conversation* that if you're a house guest you have to have one good story at every meal.

Marlo: Okay . . .

Joan: So Helen Keller has one story: "I put my hand under the water and I went *wa-wa*." Which is good for Friday night—but come Sunday morning, it's like, "Okay, we heard it, Helen." You can't even tell her to shut up.

Marlo: You're vicious! Let's talk about marriage. I didn't realize that you were married before Edgar. How long did that last?

Joan: About seven months. As I've said, "Our marriage license turned out to be a learner's permit." It was all about *I don't think I have the courage to go on and do what I want to do.* I knew it was bad for me. While I was married to him, I wouldn't go to the theatre. I just couldn't bear to go and see live performing because I wanted it so much.

Marlo: How sad.

Joan: When it was finally over, it was truly like getting out of jail. Years later he called me up and wanted to meet me, and I took a vote. My entire body voted.

Marlo: And what was the verdict?

Joan: A hundred percent *no way.* "Come on, toes! Everyone's gotta vote here!"

Marlo: "Come on, toes"—that's funny. It's what you said—"Personal truth is the foundation of comedy."

Joan: Oh, it has to be. Comedy has got to come right from the gut. And that makes all the difference in the world.

Marlo: And what are you saying about age in your act now that's right from the gut?

Joan: How horrible it is. How I hate old people—especially old people who buy in bulk. "What are you doing with eighteen jars of mayonnaise at Costco? You're not even going to make it through the checkout line!"

Marlo: You're so funny.

Joan: As long as you talk about what you really experience, audiences know you're telling the truth.

Marlo: And how did you deal with that when you were coming back from losing Edgar?

Joan: Oh, I talked about it immediately—I had to. You can't come on stage with this elephant in the room and not mention that your husband has committed suicide.

Marlo: How did you?

Joan: I would come out and say, "I've had some year. You think you've had a year, don't start with me because I've had a worse year than you, okay? My husband committed suicide." My joke was "And it was my fault. While we were making love, I took the bag off my head."

Marlo: Oh, God . . .

Joan: But it gave them relief, you know what I'm saying? We all knew it. I knew *they* knew it. And we were able to go on from there. I work everything out on stage.

Marlo: Did your daughter, Melissa, ever get mad at you for making jokes about her in your act when she was younger?

Joan: She was never the butt of my jokes. Same with Edgar. I made myself the butt of *their* jokes.

Marlo: Like?

Joan: Like, "On my wedding night I came out of the bathroom and Edgar said, 'Let me help you with the buttons,' and I said, 'I'm naked.'" It always came back on me.

Marlo: Your whole career—your life—is about being a survivor.

Joan: It's mountain after mountain, Marlo. And the mountain at this moment is the age thing, and staying relevant.

Marlo: Do you think you'll do a book on aging now?

Joan: I don't know—I still don't feel old. But people say to me, "You should really think about selling your apartment." I say, "Are you crazy?" And then I think, *What would I tell a seventy-six-year-old woman? I would say, "Sell your apartment."*

Marlo: Will you?

Joan: Probably, because my life has changed.

Marlo: And will that new life sit well with Joan Rivers, lion tamer?

Joan: It will be fine. Cindy Adams, Barbara Walters and I have talked about this. We want to live at the Pierre Hotel, have three apartments on the same floor—and share one nurse. It's our dream.

Marlo: What a dream.

Joan: And we'll have one person to walk all of our dogs. We'll have a very good time.

Obsession

The saying goes, "Dying is easy, comedy is hard." I think that's what makes comedy such an obsession. And you have to be an obsessive to work in it. Fixing, honing, scratching out. You know it when you hear it. And until you can hear it, you can't stop.

I remember when we were shooting the pilot of *That Girl,* I was going over lines in the script, working through each scene to be sure we'd covered everything. Our director, Jerry Paris, looked at me, amused.

"What is it with you?" he said. "Every scene is opening night?"

"Yes," I said, incredulous. "Isn't it with you?"

But it *was* with Bill Persky, who was a co-creator of the series, along with his writing partner, Sam Denoff. As the Executive Producer I worked closely with both of them, but I had an immediate bond with Billy. He liked women, and was one of the first men I'd ever worked with who had no problem having a woman as a boss (even one in her twenties). There weren't a lot of guys who did. Lucille Ball was our landlord at Desilu Studios, where we rented our soundstage. She had real power—she owned the studio. Tony told me years later that, whenever someone was looking for me, the joke was "She's having a meeting in the men's room with Lucy." That was the climate in the late Sixties, which made Billy unusual. He really seemed to understand the feelings of a young woman. He had grown up with a sister and had three daughters. So he got it.

I depended on Billy a great deal during the first year of the show, and we quickly became friends. One day he developed serious muscle spasms in his neck—obsessiveness can do that to you—and was confined to his bed by his doctors. I was worried about him, and worried about how the show would proceed without him.

At the table with Billy Persky—on the same side, in more ways than one.

Billy loves to tell the story of my coming to his house to discuss some trouble we were having with the script we were about to shoot. There he was in traction, lying absolutely flat on his back with a nine-pound weight pulling on his head. He couldn't see anything but the ceiling, so he had to wear a special pair of glasses that were actually mirrored cubes, cut diagonally so that he could see down even though he was looking up—kind of like a periscope. But since he couldn't move his head, he could only see me when I was directly in front of him.

Undaunted, I paced back and forth at the foot of his bed, passionately laying out the script's problems, oblivious to the fact that he was flat on his back—and oblivious to the mirror's limited range of vision. Billy could barely move, but he desperately tried to follow me with his eyes as I darted back and forth in his mirrored glasses. At one point he moved his head to try to catch my fleeting image, and winced in pain. I felt terrible, so I sat on his bed to comfort him—which caused the mattress to depress and him along with it, as the weight stayed stationary, almost pulling his head off. Then we burst into uncontrollable giggling at the absurdity of the situation. We were obviously made for each other.

A few months later, I was in the makeup room at the studio, about to begin the day's work. I took a brush to my hair and, after a few strokes, I froze in pain. I couldn't get my arm to come down. I had my own muscle spasm, and ended up in a similar hospital bed and neck brace.

My father came to visit me. He walked into the room, stood at the foot of the bed and said, "If you live, you'll be a big star." Then he lectured me on pacing myself.

Now he tells me.

FOR THE SECOND YEAR of *That Girl*, we had the great fortune of getting Danny Arnold to produce the show. Danny had produced the first year of *Bewitched*, and would later create a hit show of his own, *Barney Miller*. He was superb at everything—writing, directing, editing, producing— and was the ultimate obsessive. I felt like I had died and gone to heaven. I would leave the studio at 9:30 P.M. after a day of shooting—having first arrived that morning at 5 A.M.—and I would see the lights on in the editing room and know Danny was still there. A man like that makes an obsessive like me sleep like a baby. Someone was minding the store.

Danny did so many great things for me. One of them was to bring in a female story editor, Ruth Brooks Flippen. Until Ruth joined our all-male staff, I had felt like a lonely voice in the wilderness, constantly explaining, *But a girl wouldn't say that to her father . . . or her boyfriend . . . or her best friend*... I had always known that, for a woman, there was safety in numbers. It's never wise to be the only female at the table. Experience had taught me: One is a pest, two is a team, three is a coalition. Now I had Ruth. We were only two but, together, we were like the Red Army.

I remember one late night we were leaving the office of one of our writers, who had been moaning about how hard we were being on him.

"Why do some men always make you feel like you've beaten them up just because you don't agree with their opinion?" I asked.

"I know what you mean," Ruth said. "All I've ever really wanted was a good cry, but my husband always beats me to it."

I loved her—she always nailed it.

And I was learning that, even for a woman with power, the path was dotted with land mines—*she's so ambitious, she's so aggressive, she's ruthless.* "Funny thing," I used to say, "a man has to be Joe McCarthy to be called ruthless... all a woman has to do is put you on hold."

After the series ended, I went to New York to study acting with Lee Strasberg, and learned a whole new way to work. It became my true obsession—I felt like I had found a home. Strasberg wanted all you had to give. He welcomed it.

When I had my first meeting with Lee, he asked me why I wanted to study with him after having had such success in television.

"Because I've gone a long way on charm and a natural comic ability," I said. "I want to learn how to work deeper."

"Don't look a gift horse in the mouth," Lee said. I loved him for that. I had heard he was a stern man, even mean, but that's not the man I met that day. I told him that I really loved comedy and wanted to work on a comedy scene in his class. He said no—no comedy scenes. I wouldn't understand why until much later. I would learn that the sense of truth that was at the heart of the dramatic work would *feed* the truth of the comedy.

My father teased me. "Call me when they have the class on comedy timing," he said. "I want to attend."

BUT I WAS still a bit intimidated by Lee because of his reputation, and I felt that everyone in the class knew the work—but me. I didn't want to make a fool of myself (*look who's a TV star!*), so it took me six months to stop hiding in the back row and come forward.

When I finally got up to do my first scene in front of the class, Lee's eyes twinkled.

"Well, welcome," he said, and then he announced the scene as he always did. "This scene is from *The Gentle People,* by Irwin Shaw." But I was so nervous that his voice sounded like it was coming from a great distance and through a filter. I thought, *How unfortunate to lose my hearing the day I do my first scene for Lee Strasberg.* Fear does play its tricks.

With Lee at a black tie gala. While everyone
hobnobbed, he hung out with the waiters. He could spot
from across the room that they were aspiring actors.

But once I got that first scary day behind me, I couldn't wait to do more. And I did *three years* more. I only wish Lee could have lived to see me portray a schizophrenic in *Nobody's Child*. I never would have gotten near playing that kind of part without Lee's exercises, and the subsequent work I did and continue to do with his primary disciple, the brilliant Sandra Seacat.

On the set of *Nobody's Child* with two of my favorite obsessives: Tom Case (my makeup artist of 40 years) and my acting coach Sandra Seacat (who was emoting).

Sometimes two obsessives don't make a right—and it didn't with me and my guy at the time, Herb Gardner. Herbie was a wonderful playwright, a funny man and a true original. But when it came to work, there was only one way—his. And there was no talking him out of his position.

Herbie wrote a play for me called *Thieves*. He even wrapped it in a box tied up with a ribbon and gave it to me for my birthday. What a deeply romantic and loving man he was. But when Herbie and I started to talk about the play, I questioned the ending, which I thought went awry. Herbie became furious. We argued so much about it that I finally said, "Let's not do this. It's going to be the play or us. We all won't survive."

So I backed away, and the part was given to Lily Tomlin. Soon after, Lily had a conflict and had to pull out, and Valerie Harper was cast, with Michael Bennett directing.

The play wasn't received well in its Boston tryout, and the producers canceled the New York opening. Herbie was heartbroken—three years of work, and it was over. Just like that. Welcome to show business.

A few nights after the opening, some good friends of Herbie's flew in to be with him in Boston. I had been on the road promoting *Free to Be . . . You and Me* and had flown in with Chuck Grodin. We were all at a restaurant after the show—producers Norman Lear and David Picker; Frank Yablans, the head of Paramount who was backing the play; Chuck and me. After a while, Frank came up with the idea that if I stepped into the lead role, and Chuck redirected the play, Paramount would put in some more cash, and maybe we'd all just pull it off. Herbie, Norman and David enthusiastically agreed. Chuck and I were stunned. We had just come to *see* the show. It felt like a set-up, but what could we do? We both loved Herbie and didn't want to see his work die in Boston. Only problem was, we'd have just four days in which to do it. The perfect scenario for a pack of obsessives.

I'll never forget that opening night. Herbie and Chuck came to my dressing room before the show to give me a pep talk and burst out laughing when they saw the expression on my face. I looked like a trapped rabbit. I wasn't entirely sure of my lines, and I had no idea where to make my entrances in the complicated, multilevel set. It was the classic actor's nightmare of being totally unprepared. Only it was really happening.

When the curtain went up, I was lying in a bed and I could feel my heart pounding. It felt like it was banging through the mattress.

Oh my God, I thought. *I'm going to have a heart attack on stage.*

Al Hirschfeld's wonderful drawing of the *Thieves* cast.
Richard Mulligan and I share the bed, and behind us are:
Irwin Corey (IN GLASSES), Haywood Nelson (WITH LAMP), Sudie Bond (IN HAT),
Bill Hickey, with arm draped around David Spielberg, Sammy Smith (DOORMAN),
and Pierre Epstein and Ann Wedgeworth (IN THE BALCONIES).

Herbie and Chuck happily burn the Boston closing notice.

But I didn't die—and neither did the play. We were re-reviewed and went on to New York to play for a year.

One of the sweetest memories I have of that run is of Herbie's pal, writer Paddy Chayefsky, sneaking into the Broadhurst Theatre on many nights to see the poignant final scene between me and my cabdriver father, Irwin Corey. I could always tell when Paddy was there because I'd see a little slice of light coming from the theatre's side door. He loved that scene, and it touched me so that he would often drop by just to watch it.

Then one night, Herbie pulled off another romantic surprise. We were seven months into the Broadway run and it was my birthday. Herbie slipped a flyer into the program that read, "When Ms. Thomas takes her bow and lowers her head, everyone please sing 'Happy Birthday.'"

And they did. Twelve hundred people burst into the birthday song when I took my bow. I lurched back in shock. The sound was so loud I thought I had been shot. Then I saw Herbie and his two best friends, Bobby Fosse and Paddy, coming down the aisles carrying birthday cakes. And the audience was invited on stage to have cake with us.

Bobby later said that Herbie had ruined it for all theatre guys ever after. No guy could ever top that gesture for a girlfriend in a show.

Herbie and Barry Diller:
Opening night of *Thieves* in New York.

DID YA HEAR THE ONE ABOUT . . .

The Broadway musical *My Fair Lady* was being packed up to go out on tour, and the producer went to the theatre to do one last check. He was surprised to see the huge crystal chandelier still hanging in the center of the stage.

"Why isn't this packed up?" he asked the stage manager.

"We thought it would be too much trouble to pack and unpack every time we move theatres," the stage manager replied, "so we decided to just pick one up in every city."

The producer bellowed, "*My Fair Lady* is the biggest moneymaking Broadway hit of all time! Maybe it's the pretty music. Maybe it's the great lyrics. And maybe it's the friggin' chandelier. Put it in the truck!"

Fall-Down Funny

My father used to tell us that when he was a little boy,
his family was so poor that he and his eight brothers had
to take baths together—and they all took turns being the
plug. We always laughed at these stories, but they also
gave us a feel for the early lives of the immigrant family
my grandparents raised in tough economic
times. I think that's why I felt such a warm
connection to George Lopez. Our ancestries
are different, but the old country influences
are much alike. Born and raised in Los
Angeles's Mission Hills district, George,
who is Mexican-American, survived a
childhood of poverty and an absent father,
and recast those experiences as the warm, beating
heart of his stand-up act and hit TV series. It was
good to talk to George about how it all began—
and to learn one of the most amazing things
I've ever heard about a basketball.
—M.T.

GEORGE
LOPEZ

**Your stand-up act, your TV show—it's all a comic reflection
on the history of your life, isn't it?**

Yes, it's like that reality show *Cops*. A lot of the stories on that show are
reenactments of real-life events. That's what I do in my comedy: I talk
about experiences from my life, and try to make them funny.

My life's never been easy, but I wouldn't have changed any of it, because when I do stand-up—and it's been almost thirty years now—it
serves me well. When I'm on stage, I feel like a five-star general, because
I've made it through all the other ranks.

You make a lot of jokes about growing up poor.

Right—and that stuff is still funny to me. Like going to the store and
having to put things back that we couldn't afford. For my family, shopping was like *The Price Is Right*. We'd go up to the counter and say, "How
much is all of this stuff together? Is it more than five dollars?" And the guy
would say, "No." And we'd say, "Okay—we'll buy it all!"

**You let us in on some pretty sobering memories,
but you have fun with it.**

Because there's humor in pain. For instance, I never had a jacket
when I was a kid. That's funny to me because, even now, I have a hundred jackets, and I'll still leave the house without one. I don't even *think*
about taking one. I was in Chicago once, it was cold, and I wasn't wearing a jacket. A homeless guy walked by me and said, "Boy, where's your
jacket?" Or I'll be golfing and it'll start to rain—and everyone will have
on the right clothes, and I won't. I am continually unprepared for things,
even when I have more than my share. This is a constant thread in my
life.

So, yeah, a lot of my comedy is about not having much, and learning
to deal with it. Like waiting for the sun to blow up my basketball because
we couldn't afford a pump. The heat of the sun actually expands the air—

so you just put the ball in the sun to get it to fill up. Those recollections can be funny, and at the same time remind you of times when things were more simple. A lot of people can relate to that. I'm sure poor kids everywhere put basketballs on top of their houses.

Where do you think you got your sense of humor?
Were your mom and dad funny?

I never knew my father, and my mom was more goofy than anything else. In my family nobody was funny without falling. If they fell down, my grandmother would laugh and say, "I wish I had my camera."

Someone once wrote that if it wasn't for your grandmother,
you wouldn't have a career in comedy.

Yes, and it took me a while to put that together. So much of my comedy comes from her. She was like a tragic clown, my grandma, because her life was so tough, but the ridiculousness of it all made it funny. Like, if I was crying, she'd say, "Why you cryin'?"—not "Why *are you* crying?" but "Why you cryin'?" I'd say, "Because I fell." And she'd say, "No you didn't— that was nothing." It's almost like I grew up with this whole idea of opposites. I never got congratulated for things that were good, but only for things that were bad. Like the time my grandmother co-signed on a car for me when I was eighteen. I crashed the car a month after I got it. So there it is, sitting in front of the house—it just got towed there, totally mangled— and my grandmother takes a look at it and says, "Congratulations, I'm so proud of you. I'm even prouder that I co-signed for it."

I can see why she made you laugh. Did you make *her* laugh?

Oh, sure, I would make her laugh. But I don't think she understood how difficult this business is. I had a cousin who got his life together and landed a job that had full benefits. I was doing stand-up at the time, and had just started taking off. I got on *Arsenio Hall* and *The Tonight Show,* and my grandmother says, "Yeah, but your cousin has full dental and medical." To her, that was more impressive than me being on TV.

Were you funny in school?

I wasn't like a class clown. The class clown is the guy who grabs a girl's sweater, puts it on his head and jumps around. I was more of a class *commentator*. I wasn't silly, but my words were funny.

I think a lot of it comes from the fact that I'm an only child, and I was very suppressed. So when I went to school, I felt free for the first time. I had some good friends in the neighborhood, and I would do impressions of their fathers' accents, or the way people in their families walked. But I wasn't like that at home. When someone would tell my family that I was funny, they'd say, "George? But he doesn't even talk!" It was only around my friends that I could be funny.

Was there ever a time in your life when laughter got you out of a jam?

Yes. In high school I had to retake an English class because I didn't get what they called "the requirements," so I had to write this paper in order to get my diploma and graduate with everyone else. I turned in the paper, but because my penmanship was so bad, the teacher couldn't read it. So she says, "I want you to read it to me." And as I'm reading it to her, I'm realizing that it wasn't a very good paper—so I added things to make it funnier. And that's how I got out of high school. I don't know where this ability came from. But I trust it now, because it's been with me forever.

What is it about your childhood memories that make them so accessible to an audience?

I think it's because it's real. It's the same reason that some films hold up. There's a certain humanity in them, a recollection of things that happened to all of us, regardless of what color we are. So if you can tap into that—if you can tap into the way your grandmother sounded, or the things that she said or the food that she made—you can make that connection with your audience.

And it's not just things from my past. I have a daughter who's twelve, and she's hilarious. She eats fruit roll-ups but won't eat a tortilla. I tell her, "Tortillas were my roll-ups—roll-ups with butter and salt!" Or she'll toss something next to the trash can instead of throwing it away, and I'll say to her, "Listen, my goal as a parent is to teach you to actually throw something *in* the trash." And she'll look at me and say, "Good luck with that." Or I'll say, "If you don't do good in class, you won't pass." And she'll say, "Why do you always have to be so negative?"

That's exactly like my grandmother. My daughter is so sharp—sharper than I was at her age. It's really kind of fun to see. I think that being funny is definitely in your genetic makeup, in your blood.

Time magazine once called you one of the most influential Hispanics in America. That's pretty impressive.

Yeah, pretty good for a kid who couldn't talk.

Tony's Pilot

I picked up the phone. It was Tony calling from L.A. His voice was filled with concern.

"What is it?" I asked.

"It's Dad," he said.

"What?! What's wrong?"

Tony explained that he and Paul (Paul Witt, his producing partner), were about to shoot a pilot for a new comedy show they had developed called *The Practice*. It was about an irascible neighborhood doctor, the last of a dying breed, who did house calls and took a personal interest in his patients and their families. Dad had read it and thought it would be perfect for him.

"Great," I said.

"Not great," Tony said. "NBC doesn't want him."

I was floored. My father had been a star on television for decades. The idea of a network turning him down seemed unthinkable.

"Why not?" I asked.

Tony sighed. I could hear the pain.

"Because they think he's too polished," he said. "They think of him as a performer. You know, the shiny black hair, the pressed tuxedo. They want a Spencer Tracy kind of guy—a rumpled, disgruntled, ashes-on-his-shirt type. They're talking about Art Carney."

"Wow," I said. "Well, if he really wants the part, he should make a test."

"A test?! Dad? He's not going to do that."

"But he has no choice if the network doesn't think he can do it. He has to show them."

Tony was in a tough spot. He and Paul were successful TV-movie producers with a decent track record (they'd go on to produce *Soap, Benson, Empty Nest* and *Golden Girls,* with their partner Susan Harris)—but they did not have that kind of clout yet. And without it, it is very difficult to get a network to cast who they don't want to cast. As a producer and (more important) as a son, Tony was stuck.

We knew what we had to do—we had to get Dad to make a test. So we strategized. Tony would call Dad and tell him the problem. (That would be hard enough.) Then after Dad had a chance to digest it, I'd call him with the hope of a solution.

Tony did his part. Then, after a little pacing, I made my call. I told Dad that I'd heard about the situation with the network. He was furious and devastated.

"Well," I said as carefully as I could, "why don't you test for it?"

I knew what was coming.

"Test?!" he bellowed. "I've been on television most of my life. What the hell do I have to prove to *anybody?*"

"Look, Pop. Marlon Brando tested for *The Godfather.* These people don't have any imagination. They saw what you did last and that's all they think you can do. Do you really believe you can play this part?"

"I know I can," Dad said.

"Then let's make a test and show them."

I convinced Dad to come to New York so I could produce it. I couldn't go to L.A. because I was still on Broadway in *Thieves.* Then I asked Chuck

Grodin to direct the test. In addition to *Thieves,* Chuck had directed me in my TV special *Acts of Love and Other Comedies,* and I knew he'd be perfect to direct my father. He was funny, sensitive, patient.

As Dad traveled to New York, Tony, Chuck and I got to work. We chose three scenes that would show different sides of the character—one in his office with a patient, one with his children (he was a widower), and one with a love interest. We talked Dad into dyeing his hair white and making it curly. Chuck put together a supporting cast and rehearsed them with care, as if the show were actually going into production. ABC, which was my network at the time, gave me a soundstage for the shoot, and we hired a crew. Everything was set.

The night before the filming I couldn't sleep. What was I doing? What if Dad couldn't pull it off? Wouldn't that be an even bigger heartbreak than if we had just let it go as a bad network decision? My father was trusting me. It would kill me if I hurt him.

Morning came; we held our breath and shot the test. Dad was remarkable—grumpy, rumpled, warm and funny. Like he always had, he stepped up to the plate.

Dad left for L.A. I called Tony—he hadn't had much sleep the night before, either—and told him what a great job Dad had done. Then Chuck and I went into edit. We stayed up all night putting the scenes together. At around 6:00 A.M., Chuck and I left the editing room. I was so grateful to him. He had put so much time into this, purely out of friendship. I hugged him tight and said, "I can never truly thank you for what you've done for my father." In true Grodin style, he said "*Your* father? I thought he was *my* father."

I took the edited tape with me and went to my apartment to shower. Then I called Marvin Antonofsky, head of programming for NBC. I asked him if I could come in to see him—right away. He said sure.

When I got to his office, we made the usual small talk for a few minutes. Then I casually segued to Tony's pilot.

"I read Tony's script for *The Practice*," I began, "and I like it a lot."

Marvin smiled. "We love it, too," he said. "The network is very high on it."

"You know," I said slowly, "my dad wants to play the doctor . . ."

Marvin was totally caught off guard. I could see how uncomfortable he was.

"Oh, Marlo," he said, "this part isn't right for your father at all." He then described the rumpled, disgruntled kind of guy they were looking for.

"My dad can do that," I said. "Let me show you."

And I pulled the tape out of my bag. I might as well have pulled a rubber chicken out of my bag. He had no idea what was happening, but what could he do? So he put the tape in his player and clicked it on. We watched it together.

It was even better than it was at 6:00 A.M. I kept looking at Marvin as we watched. There was no way to read him. (Network guys never show you what they're feeling.) When it was over, he leaned back in his chair.

"That's very good," he said. "I have to admit I'm surprised."

"Does that mean he can have the part? Who else has to decide on this?"

"Dave Tebet," Marvin said.

That was good news. Dave had always been a fan of Dad's. Marvin buzzed Dave and asked him to come to his office. We watched the tape again. Dave wasn't so easy to read either.

Twenty minutes later, with the tape in my bag, I went down in the elevator and thought of all the things my father had done for me, had taught me, had given me. And I thought about what an odd reversal of roles this was.

I guess we all do this with our parents in some way. I had never seen my dad as needing any help—certainly not from me. What could I have ever given him, anyway? Successful children give their parents a house, a new car, a trip to Tahiti. I could never give him any of those things. He had everything. But here was this one thing, out of the blue, that I could do for him.

I walked out of the building and looked for a phone booth. There was one on the corner. I was already starting to cry as I put the coins in the slot. I waited anxiously for him to answer. When he did, I could hear the apprehension in his voice. So I got to it quickly.

"Daddy," I said. "You got the part."

With Tony and Dad on the set of *The Practice*.
We rumpled him up pretty good, didn't we?

Oh, Donald

Anyone who works in comedy knows that, unless you're a solo performer, you're only as good as the guy who sets up the joke. Speaking about his wife and comedy partner Gracie Allen, George Burns once said, "Gracie and I worked together for four decades. We walked on stage, I said to Gracie, 'How is your brother?' and Gracie talked for the next forty years."

Gracie Allen was brilliant, no question, but George was one of the greatest straight men who ever lived. It takes perfect comic timing to be a good straight man. First you have to know how to lead into the joke, and then when to talk into the laugh—before it dies down—to lead into the next joke. And being a straight man takes generosity.

I was lucky to have had Ted Bessell as my straight man on *That Girl.* The story line of the series was constructed around the idea of Ann Marie being a free spirit, a force of nature who somehow always got herself into funny jams.

Not many actors with Teddy's comic abilities would have set Ann up so well, let her take the spotlight, and not been mowed down by her. As Ann's beleaguered boyfriend, Donald Hollinger, Teddy was the perfect foil. And he was pretty funny himself.

The girls who watched the show all had crushes on Donald Hollinger, and the guys wanted to be like him. But Teddy's most remarkable skill was being able to step aside from Ann—or be beside her—without diminishing any of his own strength or maleness. Quite an accomplishment. When I spoke to Jerry Seinfeld, he told me that he and a friend had been talking about how much they had admired Don Hollinger—because even as scary as Ann Marie's father was, Donald dealt with it because he got to be with Ann. In other words, they saw themselves in him.

Teddy was a born jokester. A lot of our show took place in Ann's apartment, so I was constantly going to the door to let him in—and, of course, let

The Donald who all the girls loved.

The Teddy who made us all laugh.

him out, as we had to be absolutely clear that Donald was *not* spending the night. But often when I opened that door, even with the cameras rolling, Teddy would be standing there in some crazy get-up—a policeman's outfit, a Superman costume, a dress—anything to make me and the crew laugh.

After the series was over, Teddy briefly appeared on a short-lived sitcom about a dentist who lived with his wife and children—and a little monkey. I heard through the grapevine that Ted was unhappy with the show, so I called him to ask what was the matter.

"I can't believe they're giving me second billing to a monkey," he said. They've named the show *The Chimp and I.* I was your sidekick for five years. I'm not now going to be the sidekick to a friggin' chimp!"

God, it made me laugh. But he got the title changed to *Me and the Chimp.* I guess the chimp didn't have that good an agent.

Of the many signatures of *That Girl*—notably, the opening, in which a character would point at me and say the words "That Girl!"—one of the most popular was Ann's all-purpose exclamation, "Oh, Donald!" I would say that line to Teddy several times on every show—sometimes sweetly, other times angrily, often romantically.

When we were doing the series, I had no idea that this recurring bit of dialogue would become memorable. But it did. And to this day, I'm still regularly approached on the street by someone who says, "Please say 'Oh, Donald!' for me."

Whenever that happens, I remember all the great times with Teddy. And it always makes me smile.

Lew Parker

L ew Parker, who played my father on *That Girl,* was on Broadway in 1972, in the role of Senex in a revival of Larry Gelbart's *A Funny Thing Happened on the Way to the Forum,* starring Phil Silvers. He had started his career on the New York stage, so this was a wonderful homecoming for him.

Lew was a true Damon Runyon character. Dapper as hell. When we were doing *That Girl,* the rest of us would come to work in sweat suits and jeans. But Lew always showed up wearing a checked or tweed sport jacket with a pocket hanky, sometimes an ascot. And he loved the horses. Any day he wasn't on the call sheet, he was at the track at Santa Anita.

We'd had five terrific years together on the series. Lew played Lou Marie, the owner of a neighborhood restaurant, and I played his struggling actress daughter, Ann Marie. But before we found Lew, we saw a lot of actors for the role.

Early on in the casting, Billy Persky, the show's co-creator, came to me and said that Groucho Marx was interested in reading for the part of the father. Everyone involved with the show knew he wasn't right for it—but how could anyone refuse Groucho?

"I can't read with Groucho!" I said to Billy. "He's the Mount Rushmore of comedians. What agent had this brilliant idea?"

"It will be worse if we have him read with the casting director," Billy said. "You have to do it."

So out of respect, I read with Groucho for the audition—but I could barely look him in the eye. I'd grown up on the Marx Brothers—my whole family adored all of their movies—and it pained me to be put in the position of having to read with this legend, knowing that he wasn't right for the role. But I was touched, too, that he was game to do it. Someone once said that show business is not for sissies. And Groucho was no sissy.

Soon after, Lew came in to read—and from the first line, we all knew that he was perfect for the part. He was in almost every episode, and he and I not only developed a terrific on-screen rapport, but we grew close offscreen as well. Though married, Lew never had children, and I think he saw me as the daughter he'd like to have had.

I remember an episode of the show in which it was Ann's birthday, and her dad was taking her out for dinner, just the two of them. In the script, we had the following exchange:

Ann: Daddy, tell the truth. When I was about to be born, were you hoping for a son?

Lou: No. You were, and are, the only child I've ever wanted, and I loved you the minute I saw you.

When Lew got to his line, he couldn't say it without choking up. He tried it again, but still couldn't get through it. I held his hand under the table and gave it a squeeze. We started again. This time he delivered the line beautifully, and with a glimmer of tears in his eyes. It is a moment with him I will always remember.

Horrors! Dad (Lew Parker) finds Donald's pants in
Ann Marie's closet. It was the Sixties, and free love
was in the streets —but not on TV.

When I went to see Lew in *Forum,* it was clear he was just where he
wanted to be—on stage, with wonderful comic actors, in one of the
great guy comedies, having the time of his life.

But it was all cut short one month into the run when, during a performance, he became ill. The diagnosis was as bad as it gets: advanced
lung cancer. Lew had been a heavy smoker—I remember him always
with his pack of Kents nearby. I visited him in the hospital and asked
him what I could do for him. He said he just wanted some good ice
cream. So I brought him Baskin-Robbins every day.

Every day wasn't long enough. I got the call from his wife, Betty, on October 28, the day before his 65th birthday, telling me that he had passed in the night.

She told me that one of the last things he said was that he wanted me to do his eulogy. Of course, I said yes.

Then I panicked. I was very saddened by Lew's death, and I wasn't sure I was up to giving his eulogy. I had also never done one before.

I called my father for advice. He had done plenty. The old Catholic beatitude "Visit the sick and bury the dead" was something my father had taken as a personal command.

"I'm terrified to do this," I told Dad. "It's such a responsibility to speak on behalf of someone's life, especially this darling man."

"You're not giving a speech about his life," Dad said. "You're telling stories about him—the man you knew and worked with and loved. Tell funny stories. That's what the people who loved him want to remember."

So that's what I wrote.

The day of the funeral, I was still apprehensive about giving the eulogy. I was also very emotional and worried that I'd cry. When it was time for me to go to the pulpit, I walked unsteadily past the open casket, trying hard not to look inside. But I caught a glimpse of the hanky, and it hurt my heart to see it.

I collected myself, looked out at the congregation and began to read:

"Lew was my friend . . ."

But it wasn't my voice. Instead, the sound that came out of me was small and high-pitched. I cleared my throat and started again.

"Lew was my friend . . ."

Again that tiny, high voice. This time I kept going, trying to clear my throat along the way. I delivered my entire speech in that voice, until I got to the funny parts about him, and a few of the little stories my dad had given me. Then, miraculously, I clicked into the rhythm of a storyteller. Lew's friends laughed, and so did I.

My friend Elaine May was married to a psychiatrist at the time. I told him what had happened with my voice when I was giving the eulogy.

"That was the voice of the five-year-old inside of you, before you knew about death and funerals and eulogies," he said. "Of course, you would run to that safe place."

At one point in the eulogy, I had tried to tell the story about that birthday scene Lew and I did on the show, but, like Lew, I got too choked up to tell it. He wasn't there to squeeze my hand.

But I did tell a few of the stories my father gave me to weave into my comments. He said they would lift some weight off the hearts of the people who were there. And they did.

ONE OF THE STORIES DAD GAVE ME TO TELL LEW'S FRIENDS

There was a time when George Jessel was the Toastmaster General of the United States. At every important political and show business event, he was the master of ceremonies. And when an important person died, he was asked to deliver the eulogy, for which he was paid $5000.

One day an old man, in terrible grief, came to see Jessel.

"Oh, Mr. Jessel," he said. "I have had the most awful loss. I have lost my dearest companion of many years. I would be most honored if you would do the eulogy."

"I'm sorry for your loss," Jessel responded. "Who was it, your wife?"

"No," the man said. "It was my cat, Fluffy."

"No, absolutely not," Jessel snapped. "I would never do a eulogy for an animal."

The man begged him. "Please," he said, "I'll pay you double —$10,000."

Jessel said okay.

The service was held in the backyard of the old man's house with only his housekeeper and a few neighbors in attendance. He solemnly brought out a small box and placed it near a small hole he had dug in the ground. Jessel began his eulogy, and it was magnificent, as always. Everyone cried. It was beautiful.

When it was over, the old man handed Jessel the check.

"Mr. Jessel," he said, crying, "how can I ever thank you? How beautifully you spoke, it brought tears to my eyes. And not until today did I realize how much my Fluffy had done for Israel."

The Comedian's Comedian

W hat do Chris Rock, Jerry Seinfeld, Steven Wright and George Lopez all have in common? Every one of them reveres George Carlin as one of the greats.

On the set of *That Girl*, with a clean-cut, buttoned-up,
relatively unknown George Carlin.

Chris told me that Carlin once said to him, "I'm not in show business—I'm a comedian." Leave it to Carlin to make that distinction. He also said, "I think it's the duty of the comedian to find out where the line is drawn and cross it deliberately." It's hard to believe that a radical rabble-rouser like Carlin was once out there auditioning for jobs on episodic television. But he was, and, in fact, he landed such a job—as Ann Marie's agent in the first season of *That Girl*.

Because so many comics told me what an inspiration Carlin was to them, I went back and watched one of those early episodes. I'd forgotten what Carlin looked like in that part. How odd it was after all these years to see him with a close-cropped haircut and in a suit and tie, trying to play a buttoned-up guy. Every now and then you could see him break out of the straitjacket he was in. With a rasp in his voice and a hint of a mug, for a brief moment he would become what we would later admire as pure Carlin. Mostly, he was just trying to be a good boy and color inside the lines. But it wasn't his gig. And he knew it.

One day he just disappeared. We didn't hear of him again for a few years. Then all of a sudden, there was this startling new comedian rocking our world—and that's when we met the real George Carlin. You can only wonder how many great talents never had the guts to walk away and try to find their own voice. It wasn't that George couldn't play the part of Ann Marie's agent—it was that the form wasn't roomy enough for his genius. Like Seinfeld said, "If you can do stand-up, that doesn't mean you can do anything else. And if you can do anything else, that doesn't mean you can do stand-up."

WORDS TO LAUGH BY . . .

"Women like silent men. They think they're listening."
—*George Carlin*

"I celebrated Thanksgiving in an old-fashioned way. I invited everyone in my neighborhood to my house, we had an enormous feast, and then I killed them and took their land."
—*Jon Stewart*

"The guy who invented the first wheel was an idiot.
The guy who invented the other three, he was a genius."
—*Sid Caesar*

"I can't think of anything worse after a night of drinking than waking up next to someone and not being able to remember their name, or how you met, or why they're dead."
—*Laura Kightlinger*

"I always keep a supply of stimulant handy in case I see a snake, which I also keep handy."
—*W. C. Fields*

Q: What's the difference between a Rottweiler
and a Jewish mother?
A: Eventually, a Rottweiler lets go.
—*The Internet*

Growing Up Free

E ven though we traveled around the country, growing up in night-clubs, when Terre and I were little girls, one of our favorite things to do was sit on the floor with our portable pink phonograph and play story records.

Loretta Young reading *The Littlest Angel*. Bing Crosby's *The Happy Prince*. *Bozo the Clown, Cinderella, Snow White.* We'd lie on our backs and look up at the ceiling and see all the pictures in our heads. It was a great thing to do on a rainy L.A. day.

When Terre's first child, Dionne, was around five, I was reading to her from the books she had in her room, and I was shocked by how outdated they were. They all told the same old stories, starring the same old prince, promising the same old happy ending. None of the books had any new ideas encouraging Dionne to dream her own dreams.

"I can't believe you're giving her the same stuff we grew up with," I said to Terre. "Didn't it take us half our lives to get over these stories?"

"That's all I've been able to find," Terre said. "Why don't you try?"

Obviously, I thought, my sister hadn't looked hard enough. So off I went to the bookstore, confident that I would return with an armful of inspiration. But Auntie Marlo had a lot to learn. Not only had nothing changed, but in some cases things had gotten worse. One book I'll never forget was called *I'm Glad I'm a Boy! I'm Glad I'm a Girl!* The pictures were cute, but the captions were appalling.

"Boys are pilots, girls are stewardesses."

"Boys are doctors, girls are nurses."

"Boys can eat, girls can cook."

"Boys invent things, girls use what boys invent."

I almost had a heart attack in the children's book section.

Boys can eat.

Girls can cook.

Boys invent things.

Girls use what boys invent.

How could this be? After all the marches, the consciousness-raising, the literature? I thought back to Terre's and my old records and wondered, *How hard could it be to create an album for Dionne, with stories and songs that she could lie on the floor and listen to, and see pictures in her head that would awaken her imagination instead of putting her mind to sleep?*

Girls use what boys invent, indeed!

It couldn't be preachy. It would have to be entertaining and have some razzmatazz. This was not the *Littlest Angel* generation—these kids had rock concerts blaring from the TVs in their living rooms. And it would have to make kids laugh. That's the only way they'd get it—and *remember* it. Who was it who said, "What is learned with laughter is learned well"?

We'd make fun of all the old stories and outmoded ideas of what boys and girls can do. And we'd go to showbiz talent, not kids' writers, to create the material—people like Carl Reiner, Mel Brooks, Sheldon Harnick, Herb Gardner and Shel Silverstein.

My friend (and co-producer) Carole Hart and I began to develop the album by sitting around with the writers and talking about our own childhoods, and what we would have liked to change about them.

"I'd like to have heard that it wasn't a sissy thing for a boy to cry," Herb Gardner said. And Carol Hall wrote the terrific song "It's All Right to Cry."

"I'd like to have read one story about a princess who wasn't blond and didn't get married to the prince at the end," I said. And Betty Miles updated the ancient myth, "Atalanta," all about a king who holds a cross-country footrace, offering his daughter's hand in marriage to the young man who wins. But in Betty's version, the princess (now a *brunette)* joins in the race, so that if she wins, she can decide for herself whether she will marry at all.

I always loved the last line: "Perhaps someday they will be married, and perhaps they will not. But one thing's for certain. They will live happily ever after."

The ever irreverent Shel Silverstein wrote a piece called "Ladies First," about a spoiled little girl who insists on being given special treatment just because she's a girl—pushing ahead of everyone to be first in line and constantly announcing, "Ladies first, ladies first."

At the end of the story, tigers appear and surround a camp of children, and try to decide which one to eat first. Misunderstanding, our little heroine cries out, as always, "Ladies first, ladies first."

Shel's last line hammered home the point: "And so she was. And mighty tasty, too." (A tough punishment, but these were tough times.) The kids loved it. It was like a comic spin on a Grimms' tale.

We were all on a mission, obsessed with changing the world, one five-year-old at a time. For one track on the album, we came up with the great idea of interviewing kids and asking them questions to illustrate how children don't harbor sexist ideas.

We gathered a group of preschoolers and taped their conversations.

"What would you like to be when you grow up?" we asked one curly-haired four-year-old girl.

"I want to be a singer or an ice skater," she said. Good—nothing sexist there.

"Would you like to be a doctor?" we asked, leading the witness.

The little girl got an adorable look on her face and burst into giggles. "No!" she said. "Mans is doctors."

My God, she was four. We were already too late.

WHEN IT CAME TIME to cast the album, we recruited a terrific group of performers, including Harry Belafonte, football player Rosie Grier (who, playing against type, sang "It's All Right to Cry") and a sweet fourteen-year-old Michael Jackson. With his creamy dark skin and pillowy Afro, Michael winsomely sang "When We Grow Up" with Roberta Flack. A line of the song would one day be haunting.

"We like what we look like. We don't have to change at all." If only Michael had held on to that notion.

All of the pieces on the album came out of our own experiences, and we soon realized we were rewriting our childhoods. But it was lyricist

"When We Grow Up":
On the set with Michael Jackson and Roberta Flack.

Bruce Hart, Carole's husband, who came up with the timeless words, *Free to Be . . . You and Me*—and his title song, with music by Stephen Lawrence, spoke of rolling rivers and galloping horses, marvelously capturing a child's passionate desire for freedom.

I called Gloria Steinem and told her I wanted the money earned by *Free to Be* to benefit women and girls.

"Why don't you join me, Letty Pogrebin and Pat Carbine in forming the Ms Foundation for Women," Gloria said. "It will be the first women's foundation in the country." It was the perfect fit.

I broached with all of the artists the idea of donating their time and talent. They agreed enthusiastically to help out this new foundation called "Ms." But when Carole was working out the details with Mel Brooks, he said, "I'm happy to do this for Marlo, but I don't understand what it has to do with multiple sclerosis."

So much for my communication skills.

FREE TO BE . . . YOU AND ME became more than we had imagined, first a record, then a book, then an ABC-TV special—which turned out to be the most difficult version. The execs at the network were terrified of the program's messages. They begged us to take out "William Wants a Doll," a wonderful song written by Mary Rodgers and Sheldon Harnick. Telling little boys that "It's All Right to Cry" was bad enough. But telling little boys it's okay to cuddle a doll? That was dangerous.

Another Carol Hall song, "Parents Are People," featured Harry Belafonte and me singing the various verses in different locations around New

Anyone sounds good in a duet with Harry.

York City. The message of the song was unmistakable: Dressed identically and working at the same jobs, Harry and I happily declared that "Mommies and daddies can be anything they want to be."

In one of the scenes, Harry was pushing a baby buggy, singing about daddies, while I pushed a buggy alongside him, singing about mommies. That caused a furor. We were already "corrupting" little boys with songs about dolls and crying. But now we were insinuating that Harry and I were married. The racial implications were way too threatening to the network, especially for a primetime children's show.

Voices were raised and feathers flew—but in the end (and with the threat that we'd go to CBS), all of the songs stayed in.

And guess what? The world didn't come to an end.

The show won an Emmy and a Peabody, the book became number one on the *New York Times* best-seller list and the record went gold. We were floored by the impact it all had. My little message for Dionne had gone straight to the hearts of moms and dads and aunties and uncles and, most of all, teachers, who embraced it as a way to teach the kids in their lives a new way of thinking about themselves.

But for me the most astonishing reaction would come years later, when I interviewed Supreme Court Justice Ruth Bader Ginsburg for my book *The Right Words at the Right Time*. When I left a message at her office, I wasn't sure she'd even know who I was. But when she returned my call, she told me that she had always loved *Free to Be*.

"Really?" I asked. "Did you read it to your children?"

"Oh, yes," she said, "and I always take it with me when I speak on feminism." That was the best review of all.

But I'll never forget the words of the *Boston Globe* critic the day the show aired:

"Keep your children away from the set tonight."

In 1972, the world wasn't changing as fast as we hoped.

AROUND THIS TIME, my father was campaigning for a local Los Angeles politician whose platform, I thought, was particularly questionable. Dad was a conservative Republican, and I a liberal Democrat, so we usually left politics out of our conversations. But I had to comment on this.

"Dad," I said, "how can you campaign for this guy? He's a creep. And, frankly, I think it looks really bad for the whole family."

As usual, my father had the perfect comeback.

"Oh, I get it," he said. "I'm free to be you . . . not free to be me."

The man was hard to beat.

One-Girl Show

Over the years, we have all had the pleasure of meeting
the many outrageous characters that live inside the head
of Lily Tomlin—a snorting telephone operator, a
precocious little girl, a homeless bag lady. And though
each one is an offbeat creation, plucked from the
playground of Lily's boundless imagination,
we believe we know them all, and have as
much compassion for them as we have fun
watching them. That's because Lily never
judges them. She simply loves—and
lives—them. You can't help but wonder
where all these characters came from, and
when I asked Lily, I was swept up in a
colorful story, brimming with a cast of exquisite
eccentrics, and starring the little Lily herself.
—M.T.

LILY
TOMLIN

"I always wanted to be somebody, but I see, now,
I should've been more specific." *

Lily: When I was a little girl growing up in Detroit, my father used to take me with him to bars and bookie joints. And as any kid does with their dad, I entertained. He'd set me on the bar and I'd sing a little song.

My father was kind of a street guy, but always dependable in his work. He worked more than thirty years in a noisy factory. While my mom was light-hearted, sweet and witty—right up until the day she died—my dad was more morose. He was also a big drinker and gambler. That wasn't a great thing for him, obviously, but, as a teen, I never felt that I was affected by his drinking. I'd come home with friends, and he'd be passed out on the couch. So I'd just push his legs aside, and sit down.

"We're so good at it, the ability to delude ourselves
must be an important survival tool."

I'm not sure how other kids develop a sense of humor, but for me, it began when I started imitating the people in the old apartment house where I grew up. Later when we got a TV I'd see women doing comedy on *The Ed Sullivan Show*—comediennes like Beatrice Lillie and Jean Carroll. I was like a performance artist in that way. I'd wear my mother's slip, throw pearls around my neck and do their jokes. I especially loved Jean. She was very attractive, always dressed glamorously and had a real breezy style about her, like:

"I'll never forget the first time I saw my husband, standing on a hill, his hair blowing in the breeze, and he too proud to run after it . . ."

* Lily's italicized quotes, above and throughout, were written by her partner, Jane Wagner, author of *The Search for Signs of Intelligent Life in the Universe.*

I thought that was a scream. It still makes me laugh.

But most of my material came from that apartment house I grew up in on the west side of Detroit. It was a three-story building called the D'Elce—it was pronounced *Delsie*—and every single apartment was different, each with its own idiosyncrasies. All of the people in the building were different, too. I think my sense of curiosity and compassion was developed by seeing these people at their highest and lowest.

I instinctively recognized how funny everybody was, and so from the time I was six or seven years old, I'd put on shows and imitate the neighbors. I'd create a stage on the back porch of the building—I always wanted a stage—and use my mother's sheets as the curtain.

"If all the world's a stage, how come
so many people have to pay to get in?"

I used to love to hang out with Mrs. Rupert. She was my favorite, mostly because she was an eccentric. She wore a hat and fox furs to empty the garbage, and she'd often propagandize to me about the evils of progressive people. On her desk was a sign that said "Don't go away mad. Just go away." I thought that was great—it somehow appealed to me.

Another neighbor, Mrs. Clancy, taught French at a very exclusive girls' school. She was really out there, and pretentious, too. And then there was Jean Creek, who used to make me laugh just by the way she'd stand there with one baby up on her hip, while stirring a big old pot of oatmeal with her free hand. I'd go to Jean's apartment, play Rook, drink Pepsi and dance The Chicken.

I'd also go by Betty's apartment. She was the only woman in the complex who was divorced, and whose boyfriend, Frank, slept over. Back then that was really scandalous. Frank was a Jew and a communist who gave me all kinds of communist literature. He owned a chicken store, and every time I went down there, I'd beg him, "Please, don't kill the chickens! Please don't kill them!"

"The worst thing about dying must be that part where your whole life flashes before you."

And, of course, there was Mrs. Spear, who worked at one of the department stores and always wore a chignon. About three times a week Mrs. Spear would ring our doorbell and say to my mom, "Oh, Mrs. Tomlin, I'm sorry, I forgot my key." Mother would be fixing supper, and Mrs. Spear would say, "Oh, something smells good!" So my mother, who was an incredibly generous woman, would say, "Well, why don't you come and have supper with us?"

After she'd leave, my father would always say the same thing.

"Goddamn it, if old lady Spear rings that goddamn doorbell one more time to get a free dinner, I'm going to give her a piece of my mind."

I somehow took that as my marching orders. The next night when the doorbell rang, I beat my mother to the door, and told Mrs. Spear, "If you ring our doorbell one more time my father's going to give you a piece of his mind." Mother was mortified. Dad got a kick out of it.

"Maybe the reason we have a left brain and a right brain is so we can keep secrets from ourselves."

Another one of my early things was making sock puppets. When I'd go to visit family in Kentucky during the summer, I'd get socks and buttons from my aunt, and I could spend days and days making these puppets. And because people seemed to enjoy them so much, I learned to improvise little shows. I'd take my puppets and go across the field to where, say, some elderly woman was bedridden. I'd kneel down on the floor at the foot of the bed, then hold the puppets up, facing her, as if they were on a little stage. Then I'd entertain her. I'd sing "Shoo-Fly Pie" or something funny. I loved getting a laugh. I always did.

My brother was the same way. He's genuinely funny—naturally comedic—and we were always up to something. Because we lived in such a tough neighborhood, getting home from school without being beaten up was a good day. So when he was about seven and I was ten, we'd run home from school, take my mother's vacuum cleaner hose, drop it out our second-story window and taunt the tough kids who were out on the street.

"Hey you!" we'd yell through the hose. "Yeah, you in the blue jacket! I'm gonna kick your ass!" Then we'd duck down behind the window. The kids would be looking up and around, not knowing where the voice was coming from. My brother and I would be rolling on the floor, laughing.

But that was mild compared to some of my brother's other pranks. He once actually sawed our mother's couch into three pieces. With a hand saw. He thought it would look more glamorous as a sectional. My poor mother didn't. She wanted it up against the wall. In one piece.

"Things are going to get a lot worse before they get worse."

Then I became an entrepreneur. I learned very early on that there were lots of ways a kid could earn money.

It all started when I ordered a bunch of junk from the back of an old Red Ryder comic book, stuff like fake flies in plastic ice cubes and dog vomit; joy buzzers and soap that turned your hands black—all this crazy stuff that's designed to give a kid power. In the ad, they said, "Send no cash"—they'd send the package COD, which was great because I didn't have any cash and I didn't know what COD meant. I thought I was the only kid in the world who had figured this out. You get all this stuff for free!

So I sent in my order, and it came to about eleven dollars—which was a lot of money back then. I came home from school one day and my mother was standing there, looking at all of it.

"Did you order this junk from a comic book?" she asked.

"Yes!" I screamed, so excited I was practically levitating.

"Well, you can have it when you pay me back," Mom said flatly.

"Remember, we're all in this alone."

That stands in my mind as the greatest singular life lesson she ever gave me.

"How's a kid supposed to get any money?" I wailed. And that's when my mother gave me the idea of starting a little business, which is exactly what I did. I'd perform services around town. I'd walk your dog. I'd take out your garbage. I'd go to the corner store for you. Whatever you wanted me to do. It took a lot of dimes to get to eleven dollars, but I did it. I was very industrious.

One of my later jobs was to babysit, and I'd often ask my friend Susie to help me. After we put the kids to bed, we'd go through the parents' drawers together and see their private stuff. We'd find Trojans and sex manuals. But I'd been attracted to sex manuals for a long time before that.

*"I wonder if evolution is like a scientific experiment
that ran out of grant money."*

Of all the characters at the D'Elce, Mrs. Rupert was definitely the most mysterious. She was a botanist and the only person in the building who had venetian blinds, so you could never see inside her apartment. She'd only use her front entrance, the story being that someone had once walked in on her. So she kept her refrigerator pushed up against the back door. We never quite knew the details. To all the kids, she was just "the crazy lady."

One day, when I was about eight, Mrs. Rupert convinced my mother to let me come over to her apartment to walk her dog. I went over that first night and made a friendship that would last for the next four years.

After I gained entrance to her inner sanctum, we had a whole ritual. I'd go over after supper, walk her dogs for fifteen cents, then spend the evening with her. We'd listen to the radio and read the *New York Times*. She always made me look up the words I didn't understand. After we finished the *Times*, we would have tea and little petit fours.

Mrs. Rupert was like a girlfriend, but definitely an unusual one. She told me all sorts of wild stories. She said one of her plants was the same kind the pharaohs had used to silence their servants in Egypt.

"They'd put a piece of the leaf on the tongue, and it would paralyze the vocal chords," she said ominously. She once caught me trying to snap off one of the leaves. I guess I wanted to try it myself, or on my kid brother.

Mrs. Rupert's and my big weekly ritual was to go shopping together every Saturday. We'd go to Hudson's, and I'd have to wear a hat and gloves and carry a little girl's purse. She was teaching me to be a lady because she'd somehow decided I was the kid in the building who had the most potential to rise above my station.

We'd take the Hamilton bus downtown, and along the way she'd give me all these little pointers:

A lady never carries parcels if she can help it; and if she does have to carry a parcel, she uses only one arm so that the other arm is free.

A lady never crosses her legs, except at the ankles, and never sits with her back against the chair—which could encourage slumping.

And a real lady is able to open her handbag and reach inside and get anything she needs—without looking.

She even taught me how to blow my nose. We'd go to a little tearoom to have cocoa, and when it was cold outside, our noses would be running. So we'd slip up a side street, go into an empty doorway and blow our noses. Then, self-assured, we'd go into the tearoom and, sure enough, we'd see some poor, sniffling woman at the counter, struggling with the paper napkin holder. And, of course, Mrs. Rupert would give me a little elbow to make sure I noticed that the woman was not *composed*.

I just adored her. She was so wonderful and pixilated.

"Sometimes I feel like a figment of my own imagination."

By the time I was twelve, I was very big on magic. After I paid off the debt to my mother, I'd go down to Abbott's Magic Shop and buy tricks—like the rope that you cut into two, then magically restore. Or the trick where you raise an egg under a silk. I wasn't very good at sleight of hand, but it was fun.

Until now, I'd kept my showbiz life totally separate from my friendship with Mrs. Rupert. But one night I couldn't resist inviting her to see my magic act.

She flew off the handle.

"Magic act!" she gasped. "Don't tell me you've been spending your time and money on magic tricks! Don't you realize that it's all just an illusion?"

Then she said something that sounds apocryphal, and I've never forgotten it:

"If you're not careful, you're going to end up in show business!"

I was incensed. I felt like my dignity was eroded. "I'm not coming back!" I shouted. And I left.

Mrs. Rupert tried to win me back after that. One day, my brother and I were out in the backyard, and she peeped through one of her windows and said, "If you come tonight, I'll show you something very interesting." I was still pissed off, but I was curious.

So my brother and I went to her apartment later that evening. She took us into her dining room, which was tiny and had a table draped in a laced tablecloth, and a chandelier that was dark and gloomy, with a big silk hanging over it. She brought out a great big chest wrapped in chamois. After removing the fabric, she opened the box to reveal another box inside. Then she took out the smaller box.

"You must never tell anyone about this," she warned my brother and me. Then she opened the box.

By now, my brother and I were beginning to think we were about to see a dead baby's foot or something equally eerie. But in the box was a dagger and sheath, with something on it that could have been construed as blood. Or rust.

"This," she said, "is the dagger that killed Mussolini."

My brother and I were so disappointed. A dagger that killed Mussolini was nothing compared to a dead baby's foot.

That was my last encounter with her, and my family eventually moved to a new neighborhood. But one day after school I stopped by the old building and wandered over to Mrs. Rupert's apartment.

The plants were still in the window, and the venetian blinds were still drawn. I banged on her door, but no one answered. So I slid my school bus card under the door and went away.

I never saw Mrs. Rupert again. I wonder if she ever found out that her worst fear came true—that I wound up in show business. She'd probably be furious.

"Delusions of grandeur make me feel a lot better about myself."

Yes, they certainly do.

GUY WALKS INTO A BAR . . .

A drunk goes into a bar, stumbles over a few people, sits down and asks for a whiskey. The bartender tosses him out because he's too drunk. A few minutes later, the drunk comes back into the bar, knocks over a stool, sits down at the bar and again asks for a whiskey. Again, the bartender tosses him out. A few minutes go by and the drunk comes back, stumbles to the bar, sits down and asks for a whiskey. The bartender picks him up by the scruff of his neck and starts to throw him out. The drunk looks up at him and says, "How many of these bars do you own, anyway?"

•

A guy's sitting at a bar, and a farmer next to him says, "I've got a talking horse and I want to sell him for a thousand dollars."

"Yeah, sure," the guy says. "You have a talking horse."

"You don't believe me?" the farmer says. "Come around to my barn and I'll show you."

So the two men go to the barn and the farmer says to the horse, "Go on tell him."

The horse says, "I won the Belmont, I won the Preakness and I won the Derby."

"My God, that's amazing," the guy says. "That horse can really talk. Why would you want to sell him?"

"Because," the farmer says, "he's a bloody liar."

Rose Marie

When I went on the *Donahue* show in 1977, and the host walked into the green room with his shock of white hair and his deep blue eyes—well, let's say he made an impression. But what he casually said to me as he slid on his suit jacket impressed me even more.

"I'd like to talk about your mother. Is that all right?"

My mother?

No one ever wanted to talk about my mother. Not Johnny Carson or Merv Griffin. Not Mike Douglas or Dinah Shore or Tom Snyder. No one ever asked about Mom. They always had a million questions about my father.

Phil's show didn't air in Los Angeles or New York at the time, so I had never seen it. I didn't even want to go on because it would be a full hour with me as the only guest. *A whole hour?* I thought. *At 9:00 A.M.? Who's that interesting for an hour at that time of the morning?*

But I was in Chicago promoting the movie of *Thieves,* and my publicist, Kathie Berlin, insisted.

"You don't know him because he's not on the coasts," she said, "but this guy is the hottest thing in the country. You have to go on."

So I went on. And something happened. It was weird. It was alchemy. A couple drops of white hair and a dash of blue eyes. A tablespoon of Marymount girl, a splash of a smile. And it was done. He asked flirty personal questions. I giggled. It was like a first date. In high school. At the end of the show he held my hand.

"Well, you are just a fabulous guest," he said. I, of course, never one to demur from expressing myself fully, said, "You are wonderful and kind and you like women and whoever is the woman in your life is very lucky."

The women sitting in his audience watching us for that full hour knew that whoever that woman in his life might be, she'd better lock him up. That wouldn't be necessary. He was divorced, raising four boys and unattached.

And he wanted to talk about my mother.

MY MOTHER was an act unto herself. She was Italian—well, more than that. Sicilian. They're Italians, of course, just tougher and more suspicious. And don't ever cross them—they never forget.

My parents were friends with the Sinatras, especially Mom and Frank's wife Nancy, who had a lot in common. Rose Marie Cassanitti from Detroit and Nancy Barbato from Hoboken both married skinny, ethnic boys from the neighborhood who wanted careers in show business. Neither of these women had the slightest notion that their husbands would ever become as successful as they did. From where they began, they could never even have imagined it.

But Mom and Nancy adored these men and supported their dreams with all of their hearts. Through the tough times—and as each bore three children—they skimped and saved to make it all work. The Sinatras were Catholics, as we were, and my father was Frankie Jr.'s godfather.

Dad and Frank had a mutual respect for each other's work. They both played the top nightclub circuit, and frequently followed each other into an engagement, so they saw each other's shows often over the years. And they had great fun whenever they shared the stage for special celebrations—like the annual anniversary of the Sands Hotel in Las Vegas, which was always a wild, star-studded affair.

Our two families had houses next door to each other in Palm Springs. So when John Kennedy ran for president in 1960—and Frank was going to host him and his entourage at his house in the Springs—he asked my dad if the Bobby Kennedy family could use our house.

"I'll have to ask Rosie," Dad said.

Although my father was a typical Lebanese head-of-the-tribe kind of husband, my mother ran the house. It was her joy, her pride, her career. So no decision about the house was ever made without her approval. She said no.

"I don't want those shanties ruining my house," she said. (I told you she was tough.)

When I first brought home my very Irish boyfriend, Phil Donahue, that was all I could think about. But Phil understood. His grandmother referred to the Italians as the "Hytalians," and his mother said they "used the church but didn't support it." We both had maternal hills to climb.

My mother loved to sing, as did her mother and three sisters. Together they would perform at church, synagogues, Elks Clubs or any place that would have them. At 19, Mom had a fifteen-minute radio show called *The Sweet Singer of Sweet Songs*. That's where she met my father—he auditioned as her announcer. She once told me that she had urged the producer to choose him because he had "such sad eyes."

Soon the show was expanded to half an hour, and retitled *Sweethearts on Parade*. Mom and Dad became sweethearts away from the parade, as well. So when Dad wanted to go to the big city—Chicago—and take his shot at the big-time nightclubs, Mother packed up her things, left Detroit and the radio show behind and followed the love of her life.

But music would always be the other love of her life, and our house was filled with it. From the moment she woke up, music was playing, and it was a big part of the evening whenever she threw a party: Nat Cole or Sammy Cahn would be at the piano, accompanying Frank, Sammy Davis or Sophie Tucker. But no matter who took the stage in our living room, my mother—with the voice of an angel and the guts of a prizefighter—was never afraid to follow any of them. In truth, she relished it.

Mother's favorite singers were Sinatra and Cole, and their records played nonstop at our house. That is, until Frank left Nancy—then she never played him again. When Nat left Maria, he was gone, too. Sicilians are loyal. Those movies don't lie.

Mom and Dad outside WMBC, the Detroit radio station where they first met. They had no money, but they sure had style.

If there was an open mike, you can bet Mom would be singing
into it. What you see on her face is pure joy.

Mom's family wasn't poor like Dad's. Her father had a small produce
company—fruits and vegetables, a couple of trucks—so they never felt
the pinch that Dad and his nine siblings felt growing up. Still, her Detroit
neighborhood was a bit rough. Sometimes at around 5:00 P.M., if my
grandmother (the drummer) had forgotten something for the evening
meal, she would send her eldest, my mother, to the market to pick it up.
In order to get to the store, Mom would have to pass a bar and a pool hall
where there were always a lot of boys in leather jackets with slicked back
hair hanging around outside. My mother was a pretty little thing and

scared of those boys. So she devised a plan to keep herself safe. As she walked by the tough guys, she'd drag her foot behind her as if it was hanging by a thread. And they never bothered her.

When Terre and I were little girls, Mom would do an impersonation of this for us, dragging her foot around our living room floor. We would roll over laughing. It wasn't until we grew up that we realized it wasn't a funny story. It was a sad story of a sad time when girls had to limp just to live in peace.

My mother loved to laugh and to get a laugh. And she couldn't wait to tell you a joke or something she'd done—even if it didn't flatter her—as long as it would make you laugh. One of my most lasting memories of her was the morning she was to have an operation. We were sitting on her hospital bed, and I was combing her hair because she didn't want to "look a mess" when she went into the operating room. Then she told me a joke, wanting to know if I thought it was funny. I did.

"Good," she said "because I want to tell it when I get in there."

What a family.

DID YA HEAR THE ONE ABOUT . . .

A woman goes to the doctor and says, "Doctor, I have this problem.
I'm passing gas all day long. Just these silent little farts.
In fact, as I'm standing here talking to you, I've had three or
four silent, little farts. What do you think?"

The doctor says, "I think you need to have your hearing examined."

•

Mrs. Cohen's doctor called her and said, "Mrs. Cohen, your check
came back." Mrs. Cohen answered, "So did my arthritis!"

•

Two guys talking.
One guy says, "Doc, I need to have my eyes examined."
The other guy says, "I'll say. You're in a gas station."

The Book on
Kathy Griffin

Kathy Griffin is the girl we all knew in school—
the sassy, outrageous cut-up who made us laugh and had
the teachers tearing their hair out, even as they fought
the urge to crack up at her themselves. Awed by her
brashness and her impish grin, we wish we could be
just as fearless. But no matter how brazen
she gets—even when she makes us
squirm—we always forgive her, because
we've known her all our lives. And we
admire her insistence on being exactly who
she is and saying exactly what she thinks.
—M.T.

KATHY
GRIFFIN

Chapter One: Bad Girl

Marlo: You're known as a loose cannon. And, according to your own accounts, you've been banned from *The View* . . .

Kathy: A lifetime ban.

Marlo: . . . and barred from *The Tonight Show* . . .

Kathy: Because Jay and I had a fight.

Marlo: What's going on here?

Kathy: Well, it's usually a matter of me being inappropriate. Or exposing.

Marlo: What does that mean—"exposing"?

Kathy: I am their nightmare. I'm not afraid to say anything. It's not that I don't care anymore, it's just that I've already gotten into trouble as much as I can. I know what my boundaries are. I know that if I swear on a show, they're going to bleep it. When I swore on *Letterman,* they never had me back—and that was ten years ago. But they have Paris Hilton on the show, and she did a sex tape and shows her crotch when she gets out of a car. But because I swore, I was considered offensive.

Marlo: You mention Paris Hilton a lot. She's one of the celebrities you're absolutely brutal about. Then there's Celine Dion, Whitney Houston and Oprah. Why have you chosen these particular people?

Kathy: I would say that to be a candidate in my act, you have to be big enough so that people care. These people have unlimited amounts of fame and ego. And take Ryan Seacrest—he admits that he's famous for nothing!

Marlo: I see . . .

Kathy: It's so funny—some fellow D-List celebrity will come up to me and say, "You know, you better not put me in your act!" And I'll say, "Don't worry, you're not famous enough." But a household name—like Oprah or Whitney or Paula Abdul—they're candidates for my act because everybody knows who they are.

Marlo: But what I'm getting at is, what do these people have in common besides fame? Why would you go after Celine and Paula and Lindsay Lohan, but not someone like, say, Julia Roberts, who's very famous—not that I think you should go after her . . .

Kathy: Because they have it all and they're full of shit.

Look, the main reason I make fun of people is because of the choices they've made or the behavior they've displayed. Everyone gets that. People literally clapped with glee when they heard that Paris Hilton was going to jail. They look at Paris's behavior or Lindsay's behavior and think it's appalling, because you and I never could have gotten away with that stuff when we were 19 or 20.

Marlo: You seem especially fascinated with the sex life of big stars. Why is that any of your business—or anybody's business?

Kathy: I think it's because our real sex lives are so imperfect, that when you hear these celebrity couples say they have sex once a day, you're like, "Oh, bullshit! You can't have sex once a day!" And I love it when celebrities go on talk shows after they've been dating a month, and say, "This person is *the* one!" And you're just thinking, *Uh-huh. Tick-tock, tick-tock . . .*

Marlo: Yeah, that is funny.

Kathy: Right. And it's funny to everybody because the typical American viewer sees through this stuff so much more than the celebrities realize. Hollywood celebrity is so full of crap.

Marlo: But you're getting pretty big yourself. Are you going to have to change your shtick now?

Kathy: I have no worry about this at all. Two days ago I was at the airport and someone said, "Here's your ticket, Ms. *Gifford.*" So just when I start to think I'm getting a little big for my britches, the world bitch-slaps me back into my place very, very quickly.

Marlo: Does that make you feel bad?

Kathy: Absolutely not. It's the thing that amuses me most about Hollywood—that it's never enough, you're never famous enough. To me, that's a bottomless pit of funny.

Chapter Two: The *Seinfeld* Incident

Marlo: What was that whole *Seinfeld* thing about?

Kathy: I had a guest role on *Seinfeld* and I was a nervous wreck, because it was the number one show on TV, and those four people had become such giant stars. Their characters were national treasures, Jerry in particular. So when I went to the studio, I was really nervous. I mean, I'd never been to a set like that before—you know, where every piece of scenery is famous. Like the diner set. Or the apartment. You walk in and you want to steal a pillow, you know?

Marlo: That's so funny.

Kathy: So I'm taking pictures of myself holding a teapot from the diner set, right? Jerry was doing the warm-up for the audience—which by the way, I think is a very smart thing to do. I'm shocked at how many TV comedians don't do that.

Marlo: Yeah, my dad used to do it, too. It's great for the audience. So you're on the set . . .

Kathy: I'm on the set, and everyone is being very formal. Not that friendly. Even Jerry wasn't being friendly, so it was tough. I remember thinking, *Man, I've got to be on every second. I could get canned at any moment.* And, you know, Larry David is . . . I mean, I love him and all, but that first day, man, that was a tough room.

Marlo: So what happened?

Kathy: Well, I was so shaken by Jerry's behavior that after I taped the episode, I talked about it on my first HBO special. And, basically, the essence of my story was: Jerry Seinfeld is kind of a schmuck.

Marlo: Oops.

Kathy: Yup. And sure enough, he sees it.

Marlo: Oh, God.

Kathy: But here's the thing: He thought I was a riot! He even sent me this funny letter that I have framed in my office.

Marlo: Incredible. He's got such a great sense of humor.

Kathy: Right. So, next, they write a new episode where my character comes back and turns into a comedian who makes her living making fun of Jerry.

Marlo: Oh, that's great.

Kathy: Yeah, I know. So I have to say that was sort of an important moment for me. For once in my career—for one second, maybe—I had captured what my dad had: the ability to give someone the business—or as my parents would call it, "giving them guff"—and they actually took it in the spirit in which it was intended. Jerry didn't ban me from NBC or anything. He actually thought I was funny, and wrote a whole new episode about it. It was kind of amazing. *He's* amazing.

Chapter Three: The Pipeline

Marlo: You said you captured a bit of what your dad had. Tell me about that.

Kathy: My dad passed away two years ago, but he was hysterically funny. And he had the unique ability to be funny on cue. He was a natural wit. Very, very dry and sarcastic, and he never censored himself. That's where I get that particular . . . *affliction*. He had a little bit of what I call "the Don Rickles license to kill." But he was truly so likeable that he could get away with anything.

Marlo: Do you have a specific memory?

Kathy: Yeah. My dad was a pretty good fix-it guy, and he was always helping his buddies redo their bathrooms or rec rooms. One of these friends, Mr. Gillian, redid his rec room himself, and invited my father over one Sunday after church to take a look. My dad and I walk in—I was little and my father was holding my hand. And all the Gillians are there, watching, and Mr. Gillian says, "So, Johnny, what do you think?" And my dad looks around the room, takes this perfectly timed beat and says, "What a shit box!"

Marlo: Oh, no.

Kathy: The Gillians laughed, Dad laughed and I giggled and thought, "Oh, my dad is the funniest person in the whole world!" It didn't even occur to me as a little kid that he was using a curse word.

Marlo: Right.

Kathy: Nobody in the room cried. Nobody got offended. Nobody said, "How dare you!" Everybody just knew he was kidding. Of course, when my mother found out later, she said to my father, "You said *what*?!"

Marlo: So this is where your style of humor came from.

Kathy: Yes, it's a very direct pipeline from my mom and dad.

Marlo: Your mom is funny, too?

Kathy: She's funny, but she doesn't really know it. My dad was like a comedian, my mom was more of a *character*. Okay, here's an example: For my whole life, my mother has told me I'm not likeable.

Marlo: No—really?

Kathy: Really. And the way it comes out of her mouth is hysterical. She's not saying it to be a horrible person; she's just saying it like a director says when he's giving you a good note. Like "You're doing really well—we just need you to play the character a little bit more *likeable*." It's like my mom is actually directing me in life.

Chapter Four: The Town Crier

Marlo: Were there a lot of kids in your family?

Kathy: Yeah, I'm the youngest of five kids.

Marlo: And you were the one who entertained everybody, right?

Kathy: Not really. Growing up, I was more like . . . Do you know that book *The Alcoholic Family*? It lists all the roles family members take on—like, one person is "The Peacemaker." Another is "The Mouse." Another is "The Clown."

Marlo: And you were the clown?

Kathy: No—I think I was the mouse, because I was more interested in getting people to hear whatever outrageous thing was happening, or whatever I thought was the truth. That's what I do in my act today. So in our family, I'd say everybody was probably wittier that me. I was more like the town crier.

Marlo: When did you first get the idea that you could make people laugh? Were you the class cut-up?

Kathy: I was definitely the class cut-up—but it was the classic survivor story. I was this little, spindly, freckly, pale kid with kinky bozo hair. Completely picked on. Never in a popular group or anything.

Marlo: So getting laughs made you popular.

Kathy: It never made me popular—but it made me not get picked on anymore. I remember the specific tipping point. I was nine or ten, and the mean girls' clique was really coming down hard on me, one girl in particular. So I made this clever joke about her, and sort of packed the joke with facts—like she'd gotten a bad score on a test, or something. And I did it in front of her girlfriends.

Marlo: And?

Kathy: And she backed off. That was kind of a big moment for me, you know? I wasn't making them laugh to be popular. I just thought, *Well, if I can keep them distracted by laughing at my jokes, then maybe they won't be so focused on kicking my ass after school.*

Chapter Five: Griffin vs. Kidman

Marlo: Your whole act is built around being on the celebrity D-List, and you really are the queen of self-deprecation. When did that start?

Kathy: That's something from my parents, too, and I think it's kind of an Irish-Catholic thing. There's this kind of philosophy they all have—a strong edict about keeping everyone in their place. My mom still uses the expression "Don't get so high and mighty."

Marlo: Right.

Kathy: Or, "Look at herself—she thinks she's the queen of England!" That's the attitude I grew up around, and I just felt it was funny. I could never understand these households where the parents would say things that were, like, supportive. I thought it was hilarious when kids would say, "My parents tell me I can grow up to be whatever I want to be!" I'd just roll off my chair laughing. I'd think, *Well, they're kidding with you! You can't be whatever you want to be! You have to be what they tell you your limitations are!*

Marlo: That's very funny.

Kathy: You know, when I was in high school, I used to tease my mom. I'd say to her, "Why didn't you guys ever tell me that I could grow up to be a ballerina?" She'd say, "Because you have piano legs." I just sort of laughed and said, "Oh, I guess you're right."

Marlo: Why do you think people find self-deprecation so funny?

Kathy: Because they can relate to it. I think more people can relate to me than they can to Nicole Kidman. I mean, if you're going down the line and ask women, "Well, who do you really relate to?" they're not going to say Nicole or Charlize Theron or Jessica Biel . . .

Marlo: Right, right . . .

Kathy: I mean, I wish I was Nicole Kidman! And I think women admire those people who are all perfect and put together. I just don't think they look at those people and say, "Hey, she's just like me!"

Marlo: So in a way, they need you.

Kathy: Yes. And I need them.

Capra, Orson (the Other One), and Me

I got a call from Fred Silverman, the programming chief of ABC.

"I'd like you to make a Christmas special for us," he told me. "Something we could play for a few years."

"Me?" I said. "I'm not Sammy Davis. I don't sing and dance. What kind of Christmas special could I possibly make?"

"Just think about it," Fred said.

"All right," I responded, "but it's already February. You mean for a year from this Christmas, right?"

"No," he said. "I mean *this* Christmas."

Really?

IT SEEMED IMPOSSIBLE to create a brand-new anything in such an incredibly short time frame, but I talked it over anyway with Carole and Bruce Hart. We had done the *Free to Be* album, book and TV special together a few years before. Both of them were writers who were sharp on story and structure, and Bruce was a lyricist, as well. I loved working with them, and we were also good pals.

We agreed that a musical show was out of the question, unless I wanted to play host, like the Ed Sullivan role. So we started thinking about classic movies we might remake. We didn't have much time, and coming up with the perfect Christmas movie for me wasn't so easy. I was too old to play the little girl in *Miracle on 34th Street*, too tall to play Tiny Tim, and no matter what the film, Santa always had to be a guy.

We finally hit on it—we'd remake the Frank Capra classic *It's a Wonderful Life*. It wasn't really a Christmas story, but the plot builds to a moving and memorable scene on Christmas night. And the message was pure Capra— that each and every life mattered, and if one person was removed from the tapestry, all the other lives around him would never have been the same.

In the original, Jimmy Stewart played George Bailey, the man whose life mattered. For our movie, we'd turn George into a part for me, and call her Mary Bailey.

But remake Frank Capra—wasn't that a mortal sin?

I'd grown up on Capra's films—*Mr. Smith Goes to Washington, You Can't Take It with You, It Happened One Night*. They were Dad's favorites, along with Preston Sturges's films. Terre and I could recite almost every line from Sturges's *Miracle of Morgan's Creek*, starring Eddie Bracken. We'd even practice Bracken's famous triple takes in our bathroom mirror. (Anybody can do a double take, but only Bracken could do three.)

Universal owned the rights to *Wonderful Life*, but Freddie loved our idea, so he arranged for us to produce it with Universal as our partners. "Partners"—they keep the money.

Out of respect to Mr. Capra, I knew that I had to let him know that I was going to remake his film. So I called him and asked if he'd have lunch with me. He lived in Palm Springs, but was coming to L.A. the following week, and he agreed to meet me. What a thrill it was to talk with him about his movies, and to have this icon all to myself. I asked him why he wasn't making movies anymore. There was no one like him, and we needed more of him.

His answer was fascinating. "A good director doesn't just shoot the script," he told me. "He has his eyes and ears open to any new idea that might come along. For example, you remember the school dance scene in *Wonderful Life?*"

"Of course," I said. "What Capra buff doesn't remember when the gymnasium floor opens up, and Stewart and Donna Reed fall into the swimming pool underneath it?"

Capra smiled. "That wasn't in the script," he said. "I didn't even know they had that sliding floor at Beverly Hills High. But when we got there that day to shoot the scene, someone on the crew told me about the pool, and I knew I had to use it. We had already shot the scene that came after it, when they walk home from the dance. So we'd have to reshoot it, because now they'd have to have wet hair and be dressed in robes."

I was confused. "What does that have to do with not making movies anymore?" I asked.

"I wouldn't do that today," he said. "I'm too old. I'd just shoot the script. And that's not the way you make a good movie."

Sigh.

I then told Capra that I was planning on remaking that very movie, and I asked if he'd consider being a consultant on it. It would be such an honor to work with him, I said. His response was a most definite no.

His answer saddened me. I not only wanted to spend time with him, but even more, I wanted his approval.

"Well, do you have any advice for me?" I asked.

"Yes," he said. "Don't do it."

I tried one more time to convince him, by comparing his classic film with all the classics in literature that had been retold many times through the years, some of them for centuries. But his stand was clear. He wasn't angry. He was, well . . . Sicilian. And if there's one thing I'd learned from my life experience, it was that you don't talk a Sicilian into or out of anything. I really couldn't blame him. He just didn't want to be a part of the remaking of his own classic. I loved him, I honored him, I had wanted him to be a part of it. I hoped now he wouldn't blame me for wanting to remake it.

So we forged ahead.

One of the most memorable characters in the picture is Mr. Potter, who was played in the original by the great Lionel Barrymore. Potter was a true villain. He owned everything in the small town of Bedford Falls, and delighted in buying up even more, no matter how much it destroyed other people's lives. He was the original "greed is good" character.

In my mind, no one could replace Barrymore in that part but Orson Welles. The head of ABC movies, Brandon Stoddard, bet me a hundred dollars I would never get Welles—and for a while, he was winning the bet. At first, I couldn't even *find* him, but Cybill Shepherd (who lived with Peter Bogdanovich, a great pal of Orson's) sneaked me his home number. I tried him at all different times of the day, but he was never there, and I didn't want to leave a message. The surprise attack is always your best chance.

Frustrated, I tried him at eight in the morning. *Oh God,* I thought as I listened to his phone ring in my receiver, *what if he gets mad at such an early call? What if he just hangs up on me?*

A groggy voice answered the phone. It was unmistakably Welles. I immediately dove into my pitch, chirping on about how I was producing a television remake of the movie, and no one but him could possibly replace Barrymore, and that we'd schedule the shoot so he only had to work five days—I was talking as fast as I could. And the poor man was just trying to wake up.

Finally I took a breath, and he spoke.

"How much will you pay me?" he asked.

"How much do you want?" I said.

"Ten thousand a day."

"Sold!" I said.

I already had a hundred dollars from Brandon. Now I just had to find the other $49,900.

WE CAST WAYNE ROGERS as my husband, and he was terrific in the part. But as we started to work on the script, what was really interesting was to see how our gender-switch underscored the difference between men's and women's roles. For me to play the George Bailey part, our screenwriter, Lionel Chetwynd, barely had to change a line from the original screen-

Orson Welles and me. There's something I never thought I'd say.

play. The character was in financial ruin, brought on by the greedy Mr. Potter, but was so loved in the town that his neighbors all stepped forward to rescue him. That scenario could happen to a man or woman, so it wasn't hard to change the gender for that character.

Bailey's wife was another matter. In the original, all Donna Reed's character needed to do was support George's dreams and dearly love him. But for Wayne to play my husband, he couldn't just be supportive on the home front. We had to give him a job, his own goals and new lines. Many of them.

The day Orson Welles came to the set, everyone was very excited. I had personally overseen all the goodies to put in his trailer. Then I saw Barney, who worked the cue cards on a lot of variety shows. I asked him what he was doing there.

"I do Mr. Welles's cards," he told me.

Mr. Welles uses cue cards? I thought. *On a movie?* I was flabbergasted. I was about to act in scenes with the great Orson Welles, and he was going to be reading from cards! Sure, Bob Hope and Dean Martin used them all the time on their TV specials, but this was a dramatic film. I felt sick to my stomach.

I needn't have worried—they didn't call him Orson Welles for nothing. When we began to rehearse our first scene, it was clear that the way he held his head to read the cards—with his chin slightly down and his eyes peering at me from beneath his intense brow—he looked perfectly right from the camera's view. And it didn't hamper his great acting style in any way.

I, on the other hand, didn't know where the hell to look. His eyes weren't available to me, and I could hear the cards constantly flipping behind me. I've always known that an actor's performance is in the eyes of the other actor. I remember when I was first studying acting, I asked my father what he did when the actor he was working with didn't give him anything back. His reply: "I fire him." Funny, but not practical.

Luckily, in all my scenes with Orson I had to be in a very anxious state. Mr. Potter was the bad guy and I was the little guy being beaten down by him. I barely had to prepare. The real situation had everything I needed to be fearful and anxious.

THE SHOOT WENT SMOOTHLY. Well, we went over budget and over schedule, but the network was thrilled with the rough cut. We were in post-production, and all we had left to do was put in the music. We had hired Johnny Mandel, one of the great movie composers, to create the score. And after that, we'd be done.

I was looking forward to finishing. Carole and I had been working on the movie full-force for nearly nine months, and we were exhausted. Our plan was to deliver it to the network by Thanksgiving, which was late for promotion, but there was no way we could have done it any faster. It was a miracle that we made it in time for Christmas.

One other reason I was eager to be done was because I was thinking a lot about Phil. We had met in January—just a month before all of this had started—and had been quietly dating throughout. Things were getting serious—so much so that he wanted us to finally come out of the closet with our romance. So he decided to throw a party at his house—rent a tent, hire a band, make it a big bash—to introduce me to his friends and some of the interesting Chicago people he thought I'd like to meet, like Roger Ebert, Gene Siskel, Mike Royko and others.

Phil's party was scheduled for the weekend right after we would finish the final mix of the movie—which included the music.

What's that old saying? "If you want to make God laugh, tell him your plans." The Friday before the scoring session, Johnny Mandel had a heart attack.

We were in shock. Johnny was such a lovely man, and Carole and I had spent many hours spotting the music with him, and had been eager to hear what he was writing. I called the hospital to see how he was. He sounded relieved to be there, but very weak. He was such a pro—he felt terrible to have let us down.

"Don't worry about us, and just take good care of yourself," I said. "There will be other pictures for us to work on."

Okaaay. Panic. We not only had to get a new composer, but we had to have the work done in just a few days or we would miss our mix date. And if you miss your mix date, it can take weeks to get another one. So we needed to move fast: find a composer, sit with him, watch the movie several times, select the right moments for music, then go over every theme. It was a gargantuan task.

Carole and I begged Stephen Lawrence to take it on. Stephen had composed such great music for *Free to Be,* and he was our friend. You could never tackle this with a stranger. So he was our best shot. But the idea of going to Chicago for Phil's party was now out of the question. There was simply no time. I wouldn't even be able to sleep for five days.

I had to call Phil. *Well,* I thought, *this could be the end of it.* Being with an actress is a lot of trouble for a guy. My brother, who produced many TV series and spent most of his time with actors, told me once that he went out of his way never to date an actress. And when Phil and I started dating, he always got a laugh with his line "I never knew a woman who had so much energy for so many things other than me."

Phil picked up the phone. I told him about Johnny's heart attack and that it would be impossible for me to come to Chicago for his party.

"You're kidding, right?" he said. "Can't someone else oversee it just for a day?"

"No," I said. "There are no extra days. I have to do it. I'm the producer. The buck stops here."

Phil was silent. I felt awful.

"I don't know if you've ever been in a spot like this," I offered, "when your work life suffocates your personal life. But I'm hoping you'll understand."

I waited, hoping. Finally, Phil said, "Yes, I have—more times than I'd like to admit. But when they pass out the disasters, I'll take this one."

How do you not love this guy?

It was too late to call off the party, so we decided that I would phone the party and tell my story to the assembled guests. There were a lot of obsessives there that night—so they got it. Phil said it was a great evening. I wish I had been there.

As disappointed as I was to miss the party, the sacrifice paid off. The work sessions with Stephen were thoroughly successful, and he quickly turned out a vibrant score. One melody was so beautiful, and Phil was so charmed by it, that he shipped the sheet music to a company in Switzerland and had it made into a music box as a gift for me—in time for Christmas. Obsessives were *everywhere*.

OUR MOVIE, which we renamed *It Happened One Christmas,* aired on ABC two weeks before Christmas. It got an incredible 46 share of the audience, and played for four successive seasons after that—just as Freddie had wanted. Some critics were abashed that I had monkeyed with the gender in a Capra film, some thought it ingenious. But most important, the audience took the film's message to heart as passionately as they had with the original. And the mail we received was all about Capra. So I guess he was part of our movie, after all.

A few months later, Orson Welles was a guest on *The Tonight Show.*

"So you appeared in a movie with Marlo Thomas as the producer," Johnny Carson said to him. "What was that like?"

"She's an interesting woman," "Orson answered. "She's a cross between St. Theresa of the Flowers and Attila the Hun."

The Wright Stuff

All comedy buffs think they're the one who discovered Steven Wright. And once we've made that discovery, it's hard to let go of him. He's addictive—hear one Wright joke and you need to hear another. There have been other comedians who built their acts on a string of one-liners, but Wright's are different. More than just zingers, each line tells a miniature story—at first bizarre, then eye-opening, then finally brilliant, as we get a deeper, funnier look at the things we thought we knew.
—M.T.

"I like to reminisce with people I don't know."
—Steven Wright

Marlo: You know, preparing for this interview wasn't so easy. Your bio on your website was about as short as your jokes. The whole thing is twenty-eight words—twenty-six if you don't count "The End." Why? Don't you want anyone to know about you?

Steven: Well, my publicist wrote this really long biography of all the stuff I had done, and I felt self-conscious about it, like I was making a speech about myself. So I made a smaller version. I didn't do it to be mysterious. The other one just seemed too self-centered.

Marlo: Well, that's sort of what a biography is, you know? There are a lot of them on Winston Churchill, like twenty-seven volumes. He must have been a very self-centered man.

Steven: Yeah. That's hilarious.

"I remember when the candle shop burned down.
Everyone stood around singing 'Happy Birthday.'"
—Steven Wright

Marlo: You can say in one sentence what it takes most comics to say in a paragraph. Your one-liners are like gold. How many rough drafts do you go through to get it so perfect?

Steven: Something in my mind starts to edit down the joke so I can get the point across with the fewest amount of words. I don't like standing there if they're not laughing. I don't like doing big, long set-ups.

Marlo: It's so economical, what you do. You take us from the beginning to the end in such a short amount of time. And you embrace the absurdity of life. If the world were more normal, would you be out of work?

Steven: Probably. There are so many weird things in life—from the time you wake up till the moment you go to sleep. So many pieces of information go by, and some of it just jumps out at me as a joke.

Marlo: How many of these lines do you do in a typical show—like eighty?

Steven: A typical ninety-minute show has a couple hundred lines, probably.

Marlo: Wow.

Steven: To do a five-minute thing on *The Tonight Show,* that would be about twenty, twenty-two jokes.

"I had a friend who was a clown.
When he died, all his friends went to the funeral in one car."

—Steven Wright

Marlo: What's the longest Steven Wright joke on record?

Steven: It was a pretty traditional story.

Marlo: Tell it to me.

Steven: I was on a bus and I started talking to this blond Chinese girl and she said, "Hello," and I said, "Hello, isn't it an amazing day?" And she said, "Yes, I guess." And I said, "What do you mean, 'I guess'?" And she said, "Well, things haven't been going too well for me lately." I said, "Why?" She said, "I can't tell you. I don't even know you." And I said, "Yeah, but sometimes it's good to tell your problems to a total stranger on a bus." And she said, "Well, I've just come back from my analyst and he's still unable to help me." And I said, "What's the problem?" And she said, "I'm a nymphomaniac, and I only get turned on by Jewish cowboys." Then she said, "By the way, my name is Diane." And I said, "Hello, Diane, I'm Bucky Goldstein."

That's, by far, the longest joke I've ever done. It was worth it because the laugh was huge. I did it so many times, I kind of retired it.

"It was the first time I was in love and I learned a lot.
Before that I never even thought about killing myself."
—Steven Wright

Marlo: People always call you deadpan. How did that start?

Steven: It was an accident. I was so afraid of being on stage that I'd talk very seriously, even though I was saying these insane things. I was concentrating so hard on trying to say them in the correct way, and in the correct order, that it came out deadpan. And that became my trademark.

Marlo: You don't ever appear nervous. I mean, when I'm nervous, I talk as fast as possible. How did you keep that kind of unflappable calm?

Steven: A friend of mine gave me some good advice when I would do *The Tonight Show.* I would be so nervous that I'd almost get, like, numb. So my friend told me to play the studio audience like I was playing in a little club. There were 500 people in the studio, so I just ignored the idea that it was going out on TV. And once they started laughing, it became just like in the clubs. If you stop to think that 10 million people are watching you, you'd get so nervous you couldn't even function.

"I was reading the dictionary.
I thought it was a poem about everything."
—Steven Wright

Marlo: How did it all start for you?

Steven: From TV. I have two brothers and one sister. My brother controlled the television because he was older, so I had to watch what he watched. And I liked it—Johnny Carson's monologue, and all the comedians he had on, like Robert Klein, David Brenner and George Carlin.

Also, there was a radio show in Boston every Sunday night. The host played two entire comedy albums, and I kept a little radio in bed with me.

I guess I was studying it all without knowing I was studying. I loved Woody Allen the best. I also loved Bob Newhart's albums and Carl Reiner and Mel Brooks's *2000-Year-Old Man*. By the time I was sixteen, it was my fantasy to be doing this.

Marlo: But your work is so different from theirs. How did you find your style?

Steven: I started listening to the way Woody Allen structured jokes. Then I got into surrealistic painting. I loved the way the artists combined different realities that couldn't be combined in the real world. Years later, when I started writing jokes, I did the same kind of thing.

Marlo: That's really interesting. Sid Caesar and other comics have talked about comedy in terms of music, but no one has talked about it in terms of painting.

Steven: Well, I've always been very visually stimulated. Drawing helps my comedy, because when you draw something, you examine it in a much closer way.

Like, if you're drawing a table that has a wine bottle on it, and a wineglass beside the bottle, not only do you see the glass and the bottle, you also see the shape in between them. Exercising that part of my mind helped me with my comedy, because it taught me to notice things more closely than I normally would.

"I went to the museum where they had all the heads and arms from the statues that are in all the other museums."
—Steven Wright

Marlo: Were you the funny guy in school?

Steven: I was always joking around with my buddies and making them laugh. I wouldn't make the whole class laugh, because I was a shy kid and didn't want the attention.

Marlo: What's a Steven Wright joke, circa junior high?

Steven: I made up a joke that made my friends laugh, about a flock of false teeth. I remember thinking that, even though there was no such thing, the words were assembled in a funny way.

Marlo: So what did your flock of false teeth do?

Steven: I have no idea. Just fly by, I guess . . .

"I was at my uncle's funeral and I was looking at the coffin and thinking about my flashlight and the batteries in my flashlight. And I told my aunt, 'Maybe he's not dead, he's just in the wrong way.'"
—Steven Wright

Marlo: Okay, so here's this kid in school who knows he's funny, and has his own craft. What was your first professional gig like?

Steven: When I did my first open mike, I tried about three minutes of jokes, and the audience laughed at, like, half of it. I thought it was a failure because they didn't laugh at all of it. One of the other comedians pulled me aside and told me that I was pretty good for never having done it before.

Marlo: After that, did you think you'd make it?

Steven: You never know what's going to happen. I wanted to try stand-up. I wanted to give it a shot. And I didn't want to wonder my whole life about what would've happened if I had tried it. I've had this whole career and this whole life because I took that initial risk.

> "I went to a restaurant that serves 'breakfast at any time.'
> So I ordered French Toast during the Renaissance."
> —Steven Wright

Marlo: Last question: Have you ever owned a comb?

Steven: Used to as a boy.

Marlo: What happened to it?

Steven: I think I lost it.

> "I'm writing a book. I've got the page numbers done."
> —Steven Wright

ANOTHER STORY FROM BOB NEWHART

There was a comic who called himself Professor Backwards. His name was actually Jimmy Edmondson. In his act, people in the audience would call out their state or city, then Jimmy would instantly pronounce it backwards. He was probably dyslexic, but he made a small living from the act.

Jimmy was always hard up for funds, so during the era of person-to-person telephone calls, he figured out a way to avoid paying for calls to his agent. Whenever he needed to know when his next club date would be—and what he'd be paid—he'd speak in code to his agent, through the operator.

"Person-to-person call from Jimmy Edmondson," the operator said on one occasion.

"He's not in right now," the agent answered.

"Do you know where I can reach him?" interrupted Jimmy.

"Yes, he'll be at the Fontainebleau Hotel on January 1st through the 13th," the agent said.

"Do you know what room he'll be staying in?" asked Jimmy. (This was the code for how much money he'd be paid.)

"Yes, he's in room 750," the agent said.

"Wait!" said Jimmy. "I thought he was supposed to be in room *1500*." To which the agent replied:

"Tell him he's lucky he's not in room 500 . . ."

Growing a Feminist

W here's she gonna go?"

That's what my uncles (all eight of them) would say whenever they had an argument with their wives. And no matter how angry those women might get with their husbands, the bottom line was: Where's she gonna go?

Was it then? Sometimes I think it *was* then that I became a different kind of female from all the women in my family. As a girl growing up, I witnessed sixteen marriages—nine on Dad's side, four on Mom's, two sets of long-married grandparents, Italian and Lebanese. And, of course, my parents' marriage. And in every one of them, the husband was *numero uno*. There wasn't any abuse or that kind of thing. Just the everyday drip, drip of dissolving self-esteem.

I made up my mind somewhere in the middle of all this that the whole domestic scene was not for me. I had things I wanted to do and didn't want to do.

I knew I didn't want to give up my dreams for love and miss them for the rest of my life, like my mother.

I knew I didn't want to be dominated by another person.

And, most important, I knew I always wanted to have a place to go. That above all. No one would ever say about me, "Where's she gonna go?"

So when I told my mother I had fallen in love with a divorced man who lived with his four young sons, she said, "Oh, what a joke on you!" A below-the-belt punch line if there ever was one, but it still made me laugh. My mom knew a good set-up when she heard one, and my life had been the perfect set-up for that line.

Not only had I always had a fight-*and*-flee response to commitment and marriage, I was also the girl who had a stockpile of sassy remarks, like "Marriage is like living with a jailer you have to please." And "Marriage is like a vacuum cleaner—you stick it to your ear and it sucks out all your energy and ambition."

I was "pinned" in college, but that was the fun, romantic thing to do. And romance I liked. I also liked men—their soft, fuzzy necks, their strong legs, their firm behinds. And in the morning there was something about a man in a terry-cloth robe—I always had a strong genetic urge to start squeezing orange juice. But still . . .

My eyes were on the horizon, not on the hearth. And I actually felt betrayed by my best girlfriends as they dreamily walked down the aisle.

Hey, what about that swell loft we were gonna get together?

How 'bout that great trip to the Far East we had planned?

One by one they deserted me. Sometimes I wondered if I was the only girl in the world who felt like I did. Then I read *The Feminine Mystique* by Betty Friedan. And I knew I wasn't.

Around this time, I was screen-tested for a TV pilot for ABC called *Two's Company*. I was thrilled when I got the part, and the pilot was terrific. It didn't sell. No big news—most pilots don't sell. But the show brought me to the attention of Edgar Scherick, the head of programming for ABC. Scherick told me that he and the people from Clairol, one of the network's prime sponsors, thought I could be a television star, and he described a few ideas they had for a show for me. In all of the shows, I'd be playing the wife of someone, or the secretary of someone, or the daughter of someone.

I hesitated for a moment, then charged ahead.

"Mr. Scherick, did you ever think about doing a show where the girl is 'the someone'?" I asked. "You know, a girl like me—graduated from college, doesn't want to get married and has a dream of her own."

Scherick looked at me like I was speaking in Swahili.

"Would anyone watch a show like that?" he said. I asked him to read *The Feminine Mystique*—which he did. He was a one-of-a-kind executive. He called me after he finished the book and said, "Is this going to happen to my wife?" He was so intense he made me laugh. Then he said, "Everybody thinks I'm crazy, but I'm going to go with you on this."

Edgar (by this time he was Edgar) was the true father of *That Girl*. And a true mentor of this one.

Despite Edgar's support, there wasn't a lot of enthusiasm for the premise of the show. And the research proved it. Television audiences didn't like show business stories, they didn't like girls without families and they didn't much care for shows starring actors no one ever heard of.

But the night we premiered, we won our time slot. What happened? What happened was that this girl, who seemed like a revolutionary figure to the men in suits who did the research, was not a revolutionary figure at all. She was a fait accompli. There were millions of *That Girls* in homes across America. We were not our mother's daughters. We were a whole different breed. As Billy Persky would later proudly note, "We threw a grenade into the bunker and cleared the way for Mary Richards and Kate and Allie and everyone else to walk right in."

Once we began taping the series, the mail started pouring in—and it was startling. We got the usual "I love your haircut" type of letter. But I was also receiving mail from desperate young females unloading their secrets.

"I'm 16 years old and I'm pregnant, and I can't tell my father. What should I do?"

"I'm 23 years old, and have two kids, no job and a husband who hits me. What should I do?"

I didn't expect it. I was doing a *comedy* show. But the more I read these letters, the more I realized that these young women had no one to go to but this fictional young woman they identified with on TV. They laughed with me, so they felt they knew me. I was close to their age. And I felt responsible.

So my assistants and I tried to find places of refuge for these young women. We hunted in city after city, but there weren't any such places. This was before the term "battered wives." Back then, it was just called "unlucky." That mail politicized me. And as much as anything else I had witnessed in my life, it was the seed for much of what I'd put my energy toward in the years ahead.

Even though the show was doing well, the battles went on. Some at the network wanted my character to have an aunt move into her apartment with her.

"Why?" I asked.

"Because people would prefer to see a girl living in a family unit."

"A family unit?" I countered. "*The Fugitive* doesn't even have a city. Why do I have to have a family?"

The debates weren't just in the executive offices. We were finding our way in the writers' room, as well. One week, we were reading the script for the next episode, when I stopped cold at a joke. The story was about computer dating. Ann Marie sends in her picture, as does a handsome young man (played by comedian Rich Little). On the night of the big date, Ann is getting dressed when the doorbell rings. So her neighbor, Ruthie (played by Ruth Buzzi), runs to answer the door. Ruth had become famous for her funny characters on the variety show *Rowan & Martin's Laugh-In*. An audience favorite was a funny-looking biddy who was suspicious of all men and rapped them on the head with her purse.

In our script, when Ruth opens the door, Rich was to look at my picture in his hand, then at her, and mutter, "She must have gone right through the windshield." The guys in the room thought this was very funny. I hated that joke. It undermined everything I believed we should be saying to girls. And I didn't want Ruth to feel insulted.

"I want to take this out," I said.

"Why?" Ruth asked. "It's funny."

"It's not funny, Ruth, it's demeaning."

"Hey, c'mon," she said. "It's my bread and butter."

I should have known. I grew up with comedians. Phyllis Diller had made a livelihood with this kind of self-deprecating routine. The joke stayed in, but I was always uncomfortable that it was in my show.

AFTER THE FIRST successful year of *That Girl,* an agent had the idea of my playing the part of Gloria Steinem, a young reporter who had gone undercover as a bunny at the Playboy Club and revealed what young women were being put through on the job. The agent set up a meeting to discuss the deal with Gloria and me. This would be the first time Gloria and I met.

We sat across from the agent at his desk. He beamed appreciatively at us.

"Boy," he said, "I don't know which one of you I'd like to fuck first."

Gloria and I go glam—wind machine and all.

Boy, did he pick the wrong two women to say that to. I don't think we heard anything else he said that day. The meeting—and the idea—came to an immediate end. But Gloria and I were at the beginning of a long and deep friendship.

SOON AFTER, Gloria called me and asked if I would pitch in for her at a welfare mothers event in New Hampshire.

"Welfare mothers? Are you crazy? They'll hate me," I said. "I'm a kid from Beverly Hills and I don't have any children. What will I talk to them about?"

"Trust me," Gloria said. "They'll love you—and you'll love them. You're all women."

I was terrified. But I wanted to rise to the occasion, and I think I was curious to see if these women and I would be able to connect. So I started by talking about family.

I told them about my grandmothers, and made them laugh with stories of Grandma the drummer, and how independent and eccentric she was.

Marching for the ERA in Chicago, with Bella Abzug (IN HAT, SECOND FROM THE LEFT), Phil, Betty Friedan (FAR RIGHT) and thousands of women warriors.

I told them about the time my mother had received a beautiful silver picture frame, and how she'd asked Grandma for a photograph of her to put in it. I knew what my mother wanted. She wanted a mother-like portrait of Grandma in a lovely dress and a string of pearls, her hair in a neat bun. But what Grandma sent was a picture of herself dressed as a fortune-teller—with wild scarves, gypsy earrings, a crystal ball and a mischievous grin.

"This is the show woman who is your mother," Grandma was saying. "Frame that!"

And my mother did. She put it right on the piano in our living room. When my little friends came to our house and asked me who the lady in the picture was, I didn't even hesitate.

"That's my mother's fortune-teller," I'd say.

I also talked to the welfare mothers about the other women in my family. About my mom giving up the work she loved to be with my dad. About my aunts and their marriages, and how they had been dismissed because they were women. By the end of the night, we were laughing and crying, and Gloria had opened my eyes and my heart to the connections that we women have with each other.

AND THEN I met Bella.

Bella Abzug was a big, strong, brilliant woman. She was a lawyer and a fearless congresswoman from New York who fought for women's rights and all the causes she believed in with a fierce sense of justice and outrage. For those of us who worked alongside her, she was both an inspiration and a mentor. Some people would describe Bella as "the one with the big hat." They didn't know Bella. She wore dozens of hats, and shielded all of us with her broad brim.

She also had a great sense of humor that she often used to make a political point. It was in the midst of the heated fight for the Equal Rights Amendment that she made that memorable quip: "True equality will

At a backyard fund-raiser with "Tanta Bella" and Carol Burnett.

come not when a female Einstein is recognized as quickly as a male Einstein, but when a female schlemiel is promoted as quickly as a male schlemiel."

I called her "Tanta Bella." She was the loving, demanding aunt, always advising Gloria and me about everything, including marriage. She was happily married to Martin Abzug, the most supportive man in the world, and they had two great daughters. She saw no reason why Gloria and I couldn't do the same.

She was crazy about Phil, and taunted me about marrying him. "What's wrong with you?" she said. "You think you're going to do better than this?" Bella was something else.

Shortly after I was married, I was on a flight to Chicago. I'd just been seated, when Bella bounded onto a plane (everything she did was big), and when she saw me, she bellowed in her loudest voice, "When are you going to have a baby?!" Everybody looked at us. I was mortified. So I bellowed back, "I got married. Make Gloria have the baby." One of the few times I got in the last word with Bella.

Phil and I were married quietly at my parents' house in May of 1980, with just our families present. The night before, I wrote Gloria a letter. I was worried that when she heard the news, she would feel abandoned, as I had felt when all my friends got married many years before. We had both been single for such a long time, and we'd reveled in it. A lot of young girls had written me, saying that when their mothers nagged them about settling down, they'd use me as an example.

ABOVE: A happy coalition (from left), Letty Cottin Pogrebin,
Gloria and Pat Carbine, all of us cofounders of the Ms. Foundation.
BELOW: With matching cigars: the men in my life.

"Marlo Thomas isn't married, and *she's* not crazy."

I think Gloria and I felt we always had each other to point to, as well. It was a bond between us. And now I was breaking it. But she was happy for me, and when Phil and I returned from our honeymoon, she and Bella threw me a bridal shower. They made little posters with every disparaging comment I'd ever made about marriage and hung them around the room. What a shock it was to see them all together like that. No wonder I never wanted to marry.

But I don't think anyone was more surprised that I was getting married than my mother. She kept asking Phil at our wedding, "How did you get her to do this?" Dad was simply happy that I had found this lovely man and that I was finally settling down. He celebrated in the Lebanese tradition by taking his handy old shotgun outside and firing it three times into the sky. Of course, the neighbors called the police, but it was good to know that the years had not lessened "Orson's" sense of the dramatic.

WHEN PHIL AND I were on the plane to Greece for our honeymoon, he left his seat to go to the bathroom. The woman sitting across from us noticed my wedding band.

"You're Marlo Thomas, aren't you?" she said. "Did you get married?"

This was the first person outside of our families to know about our wedding. I blushed, in my new bride role.

"Yes," I said shyly. "We were married yesterday."

"Why?" she said. "I am *so* disappointed. Why would you get married?"

I was stunned. *Oh my God,* I thought, *what have I done? Women like this have been looking to me to set an example of independence. And now I've let them all down.*

But then Phil returned to his seat. And I got over it.

The Joke on Me

My mother was right. The joke was on me. Me, who had carefully built a life around being on my own. *Miss Independence.*

When I was doing my TV series, I had used my first money to buy myself a beautiful, big house on Angelo Drive in the hills above the Beverly Hills Hotel and, without the use of a wedding registry, had picked matching china, crystal and a silver pattern. Take that, traitorous girlfriends!

And now here I was in Winnetka, a suburb of Chicago, moving in with a man who was raising four boys, ages 12 to 16—Michael, Kevin, Danny and Jimmy. His daughter, Mary Rose, lived with her mom in New Mexico. It would have been nice to have had one more female under our roof. I'd never seen so many jockstraps in my life. Or wet towels. It was like living in a frat house.

But they were sweet, and they had done *some* organizing. They had all put their names on their underwear. It was the first time, however, that I had been with a man who had "Dad" written on his jockeys.

But I adjusted fast. I took to hiding bottles of Coca-Cola under the bed. With four boys and assorted pals, it was them or me.

I went into Jimmy's room, where his socks stood up by themselves, and there were discarded pizza boxes under his bed. I told Phil about it.

"Try not to think about it," he said.

It was all I thought about. I'd fall asleep with images of maggots dancing in my head. I had been raised by a drill sergeant kind of mother. "A place for everything and everything in its place" was her mantra. Maybe some place underneath all this mess I'd find *my* mantra.

Terrified of being any part of the fantasies of teenage boys, I found the mornings especially challenging. I never left the bedroom in a robe or any kind of casual wear. I was always completely dressed, hair in place, as if their father and I had been having an all-night meeting in that room down the hall.

And I was working hard to keep my feminist values up front, teaching Phil the smallest of things. Like what a hamper was for. What really got to me, though, was that all of them kept asking me where their things were.

"Where are my shoes?" Phil would constantly ask.

What is it about men? They think we women have a radar attached to our uterus. And the thing that killed me was that I knew where they were. I knew where Phil's shoes were. I knew where *all* four boys' shoes were.

How did this happen? Had my mother secretly planted a chip in me at birth that would activate when I said "I do"? I was beginning to understand why there hadn't been a female Shakespeare or Mozart. There wasn't room in their heads for symphonies and sonnets—their brains were cluttered with where everyone's shoes were.

And through it all, I kept thinking, *Now my mother is completely happy.* Terre and Tony had been settled for some time, but that hadn't stopped her one bit from continuously nagging me to join the betrothed battalion. And when her rhapsodizing about the glory of it all hadn't made a dent in my resolve, she brought out the big guns: "You'll die alone!" Nice.

So when Mother called me in Chicago, where Phil and I were living the first summer after our May wedding, I regaled her with my marital adventure. I was *Marloizing* Phil's house with new closets. I'd gotten the boys to come out of their rooms *at the same time* for the family dinner hour. I'd color-coded the towels.

And brimming with newfound maternal pride, I told my mother that Phil was bragging to everyone about how I could talk to his sons individually.

"She got the book on each of them very quickly," he'd say. "Most people speak to them as a flock."

As I went on and on to my mother, knowing how thrilled she'd be by all of this, she interrupted.

"What about your career?" she crisply asked.

Yep, it stopped me, too. This woman had hounded me to get married for most of my life, but here it was: Underneath it all, she had been as conflicted about it as I was.

I had always made the joke that I was "my mother's revenge." But like all good jokes, it was rooted in truth.

ROUGHHOUSING with RITA . . .

"I love being married. It's so great to find that one special person you want to annoy for the rest of your life."
—*Rita Rudner*

"I think men who have a pierced ear are better prepared for marriage. They've experienced pain and bought jewelry."
—*Rita Rudner*

"I want to have children, but my friends scare me.
One of my friends told me she was in labor for 36 hours.
I don't even want to do anything that feels good for 36 hours."
—*Rita Rudner*

"It wasn't that no one asked me to the prom,
it was that no one would tell me where it was."
—*Rita Rudner*

"Marriages don't last. When I meet a guy, the first question I ask myself is: Is this the man I want my children to spend their weekends with?"
—*Rita Rudner*

"When I eventually met Mr. Right,
I had no idea that his first name was Always."
—*Rita Rudner*

... and ROSEANNE

"As a housewife, I feel that if the kids
are still alive when my husband gets home
from work, then hey, I've done my job."
—*Roseanne Barr*

"Experts say you should never hit your
children in anger. When is a good time?
When you're feeling festive?"
—*Roseanne Barr*

"The quickest way to a man's heart
is through his chest."
—*Roseanne Barr*

"Women complain about PMS,
but I think of it as the only time of the
month when I can be myself."
—*Roseanne Barr*

"My husband said he needed more space.
So I locked him outside."
—*Roseanne Barr*

The Making of a Wisenheimer

Like the rest of America in the fall of 2008, I couldn't wait for the weekend to watch Tina Fey's dead-on send-up of Alaska governor Sarah Palin, on Saturday Night Live. *Tina's channeling of Palin was by far the best female impression I'd ever seen, and almost overnight, her winks and "You betcha's" turned her from a star into a superstar. But nothing about Tina's remarkable rise qualifies as "overnight." She worked her way to the top from the scrappy improv circuit in Chicago (including Second City), where she honed her performing and writing skills. For all the comedy writers that roamed through our house—and our lives—when I was growing up, there never was a woman at the table. Tina not only made it to the table of* SNL *writers—in just a few years she moved to the head of it. But to her it's not about gender, it's just about getting the laugh. That's something she's been doing her whole life.*
—M.T.

TINA FEY

Step One: Come from a Funny Family

Tina: I grew up in Upper Derby, Pennsylvania, outside Philadelphia, and I think there's something about the Northeast—New York, Philly, Boston—where everyone's a little bit of a smart aleck. I went to college in the South, and my roommates would always say, "How come when your family's here, if you ask them a question, they'll always give you a sarcastic answer?" I'd say, "I guess that's just how we do it up there. Everybody's kind of a wisenheimer."

Step Two: Have Greek Uncles

I had an Uncle Pierre and an Uncle Napoleon—I don't know why they were named that; we're a Greek family—and they were very funny, in a cutting kind of way. They were great at take-down humor. Like, when Uncle Pete would come over, he'd play my mom in Scrabble, and when he'd start winning, he'd turn to me and say, "Go comfort your mother. She's crying."

Step Three: Find Your Comic Groove

When I was 12 or 13, I decided that I wanted to try to be funny. That's the age that you realize, *Oh, I get it—some girls are going to be very pretty, and then the rest of us have to figure out what our coping mechanism is going to be.* Looking back, having greasy skin and getting your boobs at ten is actually a good way to grow up. It builds character.

Step Four: Do Your Research

My brother always made me laugh. He'd imitate everything he saw on *Saturday Night Live*—he did a great Steve Martin. But we were all big fans of comedy shows. We watched everything on TV. Old Burns and Allen, classic sitcoms, Marx Brothers movies, Laurel and Hardy, and all of the Monty Pythons. We practically lived on Channel 48.

Step Five: Try Out Your Material

I wasn't exactly the class clown, but I was definitely funny—I just wasn't up front about it. I'd mutter things under my breath so my friends could hear it, and they'd always laugh. Basically I think I became funny to get people to like me. I especially remember being a cut-up in algebra class. That's because I wasn't great at math, and getting a laugh was a lot easier. My favorite joke was: "Two peanuts were walking down the street, and one was a-salted." Okay, it's a really, really dumb joke, but it always made me laugh.

CHRIS
MORRIS

Step Six: Make One Last-ditch Effort Not to Be a Comedian

In college, I thought about becoming a serious actress, but it quickly became clear to me that that wasn't the right path. My problem with learning how to act was that I was never sure what you were supposed to be thinking about when you were doing a role on stage—unlike with improvisation, where your focus is always on your scene partner. So eventually I began to write, and wound up studying playwriting. And most of my plays came out funny, as opposed to serious.

Step Seven: Take It to the Next Level

In the early Nineties, I moved to Chicago and started studying at Second City. I had a day job, working the front desk at the [Evanston] YMCA, which left my nights free for classes. I'd take the train to work every morning at 4:00 A.M., always with the same group of Polish cleaning ladies. I somehow convinced myself they were looking out for me.

For a brief period, I tried stand-up—at a very, very amateur level. I enjoyed it and really respect it as an art form. But to go out there alone is really tough. The highs are high, but the lows are *really* low.

Step Eight: Be Discovered

I began working on *Saturday Night Live* in 1997. I was a writer there for a few years before I moved to on-camera. It took some adjusting moving from performing full-time to writing full-time. It's tough giving away your best material to someone else—though when they're a better performer than you, that makes it a lot easier. When the job opening came up to co-anchor the "Weekend Update" news segment, [producer] Lorne Michaels asked me to do a screen test. I wasn't that nervous because I'd been working there for three years. I knew the room and the people I was auditioning for, and I knew I had a job to fall back on. I was lucky in that way because, if I'd come in out of the cold, I would have been really, really intimidated. To audition in that room is scary. There's, like, two people watching you and nobody laughs. It's the worst.

Step Nine: Become a (Gasp!) Sex Symbol

I was extremely amused when people in the media started calling me "a thinking man's sex symbol." Obviously, it was because of my glasses, but glasses make anyone look smarter. Put a pair on a *Playboy* model and she becomes a paleontologist.

But the most hilarious thing for me was when *People* magazine named me one of the 50 Most Beautiful People of the year. Every year, there's always a person on the list who makes you roll your eyes and say, "Yeah, right." I guess I was that year's person. Still, I'm not going to complain about it. I've decided to stash all those magazines in a trunk, and then show them to my daughter one day.

Step Ten: Learn to Do a Dead-on Impersonation of a News-Making Vice Presidential Candidate

People were fascinated with Sarah Palin, regardless of whether they loved her or not. The weirdest thing for me was when everyone kept commenting on how similar we looked. Hello? This woman has perfect teeth and a great tan—and she's got really long legs. I will admit, however, that we have similar noses.

THE BOOK OF PAUL

One of the quickest minds ever to light up a television game show was comedian Paul Lynde on Hollywood Squares, *hosted by Peter Marshall. Let's go to the tape . . .* —M.T.

Peter: Paul, what is a good reason for pounding meat?
Paul: Loneliness.

Peter: Do female frogs croak?
Paul: If you hold their little heads underwater long enough.

Peter: If you were pregnant for two years, what would you give birth to?
Paul: Whatever it is, it would never be afraid of the dark.

Peter: According to Ann Landers, what are two things you should never do in bed?
Paul: Point and laugh.

Peter: Paul, how many men are on a hockey team?
Paul: Oh, about half.

Peter: What did the Lone Ranger always leave behind when he left town?
Paul: A masked baby.

Peter: Why do Hell's Angels wear leather?
Paul: Because chiffon wrinkles.

Peter: Paul, in ancient Rome, bakers were required by law to bake something into each loaf of bread. What was it?
Paul: A Christian.

The Reluctant Interview: An Improv

W hen Elaine May and I first met, we didn't like each other. She was directing a revival of Herb Gardner's play *The Goodbye People* at the Stockbridge Theatre in the Berkshires. I had just started going out with Herbie, and each day we would watch the rehearsals together. Later that night, he'd ask my opinion of what I had seen, and I would give him my comments, never dreaming he would tell them to Elaine. Unfortunately, he did.

Elaine wanted to kill me—here was this girl from Hollywood, swooping in and critiquing her work. But by then the feeling was mutual. I didn't like her either because, from the moment we'd met, she called me "Margo." I had just finished my TV series and was pretty well known, so I took her getting my name wrong as a personal—and intentional—knock.

The following year, we were thrown together quite a bit because of her close friendship with Herbie. One night she heard someone call out my name.

"Wait—your name is Marlo, not Margo?" she said. "Why didn't you tell me that?"

"I just assumed you were mad at me for giving my notes on the play," I said. "I thought you were being hostile."

Elaine answered back, "Well, I think it was hostile of you not to correct me for a solid year."

And so it began . . . a forty-year friendship.

At one point, Elaine moved into my house on Angelo Drive for six months. It was very early in our friendship, so we were still being pretty careful with each other. Actually, I was careful. *She* complained constantly that there wasn't enough surface space for her papers. And she smoked. We were like Felix and Oscar. She was Oscar and I was the one with the broom and the dust pan.

It was during the third week of her stay that I met David Geffen. What a force he was. He was just hitting his stride as a movie and music mogul, and I had never met anyone who was so sure of who he was and where he wanted to go. And going out with me was one of the things he definitely wanted.

So we made a date.

"But I'd rather not go into your house if Elaine May is there," he said.

It seems they had met—and fought—at a restaurant a few nights before. Great. What a houseguest—a complainer, a smoker and now my dates don't want to come into my home.

So, for a couple weeks, I would meet David in front of the house. Then one night, when I thought Elaine was out, he came inside. I ran up to get my coat, and when I came back downstairs, there they were in the living room, the two of them, chatting away. And they were both complaining about me.

David eventually became a part of my life, and he won Elaine and me over with the sheer power of his energy and optimism and love. And he was an obsessive. Perfect.

But even when Elaine is inciting a domestic comedy, she's like a sister to me. We have worked together, lived together, strategized together, played together and cried together. When my dad died, everyone tried to comfort me by reminding me of what a great life he'd had. But Elaine was the one who said the very right thing.

"This is awful," she said. "There is no consolation. It's just horrible."

Exactly. That's *exactly* how I felt. And by her understanding that feeling, she actually comforted me.

But of all the things Elaine and I do together, the thing we do best is laugh . . . like hell.

In 1990, we co-starred in a movie, *In the Spirit,* written by Elaine's daughter, a gifted actress herself, Jeannie Berlin. As with any project, we needed to promote the film, but Elaine is famous for never doing interviews. So our producer and dear pal, Julian Schlossberg, landed on a great idea: Elaine and I should do a faux interview, with me as the eager journalist and Elaine as my reluctant subject. We loved the idea, turned on a tape recorder and began to improvise.

What follows is that conversation, as it appeared in *Interview* magazine.

Marlo: Elaine, I know you're nervous about being interviewed, but it's just me, and you're a highly articulate person who makes her living putting words together, so I'm just going to throw the ball to you and let you run with it O.K.?

Elaine: Great.

Marlo: What was it like working together?

Elaine: Great.

Marlo: Was it fun working together?

Elaine: Yes.

Marlo: Were there any surprises in our working together?

Elaine: No.

Marlo: Well, there must have been some surprises.

Elaine: Oh. Well, maybe there were.

Marlo: What were they?

Elaine: What do you mean?

Marlo: I mean, you know me so well. Did anything I do surprise you?

Elaine: Oh. Yes. I was surprised by the power of your acting.

Marlo: Thank you. In what way?

Elaine: It was so very good.

Marlo: What about our friendship?

Elaine: It was fine.

Marlo: Do you recommend friends working together? I mean, there are some people who think you shouldn't mix business with friendship. Or that if you give a friend a dollar, if you loan money to a friend, it will ruin that friendship. Would you recommend taking that risk?

Elaine: Well, I think a dollar is such a small amount to lose.

Marlo: No, no I mean . . . I shouldn't have said a dollar. I mean, you know, people lend money to friends, right?

Elaine: Yes.

Marlo: Then, somehow, that changes the friendship. So they say you shouldn't mix business with friendship. Do you think we should mix moviemaking with friendship?

Elaine: Is this the same as the dollar?

Marlo: Forget about the dollar. This has nothing to do with the dollar. I'm just saying that, do you think our being friends made the scenes better or worse?

Elaine: You mean our scenes?

Marlo: Elaine, you're so nervous. You're listening so hard that it's making you seem stupid.

Elaine: I see.

Marlo: Now, just relax and listen to me. Did we have more fun doing our scenes together because we were friends? For example, in the scene

In the Spirit: With Elaine—up against the wall.

where you had to grab me by the neck and bang me up against the wall, would you have had as much fun doing that to a stranger?

Elaine: No. That's true.

Marlo: Yes. What?

Elaine: It was more fun grabbing you by the neck and slamming you up against the wall than a stranger.

Marlo: Really? Why?

Elaine: Well . . . because you aren't a stranger.

Marlo: Aside from that.

Elaine: There is no aside from that.

Marlo: You know, if you don't expand on these questions it's going to be a very boring interview. I mean, if I ask you why it was fun to grab me by the neck and bang me against the wall, you have to give me a better answer than "because you aren't a stranger." What else made it fun?

Elaine: Well, it was fun . . . because . . . you're smaller than I am.

Marlo: We've always fought about this, Elaine. I am not that much smaller than you are. I think I'm only an inch shorter, that's about it.

Elaine: That's smaller.

Marlo: Well, it's not that much smaller. It's not small enough for you to have that smug expression on your face.

Elaine: And you're weaker than I am. That's always fun.

Marlo: I like the idea of myself being weak and vulnerable.

Elaine: And it's always fun to take a weak, vulnerable person and slam them up against the wall.

Marlo: I don't think you are going to like the way this looks in print. "It's always fun to take a weak, vulnerable person and slam them up against the wall"? Spoken like a true guy.

Elaine: I really think it's unfair for you to ask me if something is fun and then tell me I have to expand on it, and then when I do, you attack me for it. I mean, I barely know what I'm saying. I'm very nervous.

Marlo: Why? I don't understand why you're so nervous. I'm still you're friend Marlo. This is just like we're talking on the phone.

Elaine: No, it isn't. You don't call me on the phone and ask me if it was fun the last time we talked.

Marlo: No, no, but I . . .

Elaine: You are very direct on the phone. You say, "I've been sent two scripts. One of them is a true story of a woman who's dying and one of them is a true story of a woman who's paralyzed—"

Marlo: "—which one sounds like more fun?"

Elaine: What?

Marlo: I'm kidding. I'm just making a little joke. Elaine, look at how tense you are. You're actually clutching your clothes. And you're not breathing. That's why you've stopped thinking. There's not enough oxygen getting to your brain.

Elaine: These are very hard questions.

Marlo: Are they?

Elaine: Yes.

Marlo: All right, here's an easier one. How do you feel about being a writer and a director in what is predominantly a white-male-dominated world?

Elaine: You mean . . . is it fun?

Marlo: No, forget fun. We're off of fun. I mean, most of the executives, directors and screenwriters in Hollywood are men. So how do you feel about being in what is mostly a men's club?

With Elaine, doing what we do best.

Elaine: Can we turn off the tape for a minute?

Marlo: No. Bella Abzug once said, "Real equality is going to come not when a female Einstein is recognized as quickly as a male Einstein, but when a female schlemiel is promoted as quickly as a male schlemiel." What's your feeling about that?

Elaine: Well, I think there are probably more female schlemiels in high positions now than when I started, although it's true that there are no female schlemiels in the highest position. But I think that, in time, there will be.

Marlo: That's not the point I'm making.

Elaine: It isn't?

Marlo: No. I don't want incompetent women to rise to the top. Look, everybody knows how I feel about this issue. How do you feel about it?

Elaine: Fine.

Marlo: You know, I really worked hard on these questions . . .

Elaine: And they're excellent.

Marlo: Thank you. And I'd like you to work a little harder on your answers. "Yes" and "No" and "Fine" aren't really good enough.

Elaine: Well, I just gave you some long answers and you didn't like them.

Marlo: Well, they were terrible. Did you like them? You'll kill yourself when you read the quote about female incompetents being promoted to high positions in time. And the one where you said it was fun to pick up a smaller person and bang them against the wall? You'll get letters on that one.

Elaine: Can't you cut that one out of the interview?

Marlo: No, I can't. I mean, I could but I won't. I'm part of the media now, Elaine. See? You're sitting that way again. You're all hunched over and you're not breathing.

Elaine: Can we turn the tape off for one minute?

Marlo: No. What would you like to do next?

Elaine: Eat.

Marlo: No. I mean as an artist. Don't cross your eyes. Just answer me. See, this is why I won't turn off the tape or edit it. The only meaty part of this interview is your reaction to the questions you don't want to answer. Now, I'm going to ask you again—would you like to direct? Write? Act?

Elaine: It doesn't matter to me.

Marlo: What does matter to you, Elaine?

Elaine: Money. Living forever. And there's a third thing.

Marlo: Money matters to you?

Elaine: Look, I don't want to go on with this unless you promise me you'll cut those answers out of the interview.

Marlo: All right.

Elaine: You promise? You will?

Marlo: You have my word as a reporter. Now let's go on to another question. Are you working on something now?

Elaine: I . . . uh . . .

Marlo: You'd rather not say? Have I hit a nerve? I know when you shimmy your shoulders like that I've made you uncomfortable.

Elaine: Yes, it would be better for me not to say what I am working on now.

Marlo: Well, what's left? How about your personal life? What's the most important thing to you, personally?

Elaine: Grooming. Lifestyle. A well-decorated and gracious home.

Marlo: Well, that's not true. I've seen the way you dress and I've been to your apartment.

Elaine: Look, you want me to expound on your questions and then you argue with everything I say.

Marlo: But it's not the truth.

Elaine: Well, nobody tells the truth in an interview. Except people who have never been interviewed. And they only do it once.

Marlo: Elaine, *Interview* magazine has given me the responsibility of doing this with you. I can't knowingly hand in answers that I know are lies.

Elaine: Why not? Don't you tell lies in interviews?

Marlo: Of course I do. But I'm not being interviewed now. I'm interviewing. I've been given a sacred trust. For this moment in time, I am the media. And as my friend, I'd like you to help me.

Elaine: I have helped you. Now I'm going to eat.

Marlo: All right. Well, then, I'll just wind up here. You say you were surprised at "the power of my acting . . ."

Elaine: Yes.

Marlo: Well, at least I got the truth out of you twice.

The Storyteller

It is nearly impossible not to love Whoopi Goldberg, and a good reason for that is because she's both unusually hilarious and hilariously unusual. That voice that buzzes like an alto sax, those killer sidelong glances. Comic talent is rewarded and awarded in many ways but rarely with an Academy Award. Whoopi vaulted over that barrier when she captured the Oscar for Ghost more than twenty years ago, with her portrayal of a brazenly phony psychic. It was just one of the countless compelling characters she's been inhabiting for the span of her career. And each one has spoken to our common humanity—our dreams, our fears, our deepest secrets. I've never forgotten the little girl Whoopi summoned up in her first big stage show—the one who dreamed out loud about wanting to be beautiful. I knew from the first line that Whoopi was telling me a little bit about myself.

—M.T.

**WHOOPI
GOLDBERG**

"Normal is nothing more than a cycle on a washing machine."
—Whoopi Goldberg

Whoopi: When I was born, upon emerging from my mom, I found the light and put my face up into it and smiled—half in and half out. I've been that way ever since. I live in a very strange and wonderful world in my head.

It all began with my mother and her funny accents. When I was little, my mom and her cousin Arlene did dialects all the time, just to make themselves laugh. They would talk as little, old Jewish ladies, or Spanish guys, or Hungarians. What's funny is that they'd do these dopey foreign accents, but neither of them had ever left the country. I just loved that. I always wanted to go to the places their accents were from.

I'd hear them pretending to speak French, and I'd think, *Oh, I can speak French, too!* But when I'd try, they'd look at me like I had four heads.

"How did you learn all these languages?" I'd ask.

"What languages?" my mother would say.

What's funny is that my mom is very straightforward and deep. But somehow, when she got together with Arlene, they'd become two of the silliest people I knew.

"I used my imagination to make the grass
whatever color I wanted it to be."
—Whoopi Goldberg

As a child, I wasn't very fast, and I was kind of quiet—but I could act. I remember when I was about eight or nine, I told my mother, "I'm going to Hollywood to become a star!" And I believed that could really happen—I had seen it on *The Little Rascals*! But what I really wanted to be was Jean Harlow, coming down that enormous staircase in *Dinner at Eight*. That is my first cognizant movie memory. I wanted to have that effect, floating down the stairs—where everything in the room just stops. But I didn't become that actress. All I did was tell great stories.

When I was a little girl, I loved to hear my mom read, and then I would make up the most wonderful tales—about fairies and dragons and princes, all sorts of magical people. I'd also have full conversations with inanimate objects, or animals, which is something I still do. I like to give voice to animals because I truly believe I can see what they're thinking. My cat is a Russian Blue—he's gorgeously grey—and I have these great conversations with him. I do most of the talking. He just looks at me and sort of sucks his teeth. But I know what he's thinking.

"I don't have pet peeves, I have whole kennels of irritation."
—Whoopi Goldberg

I didn't go to high school. Like many comedians, I was sort of a disciplinary problem. My mother would try to drag me to school, but somewhere along the line, she recognized that school just wasn't for me, and that it was better to know where I was than to have me hiding out.

So we made a deal: She wouldn't make me go to school as long as I kept myself occupied with something that interested me.

So I would go to museums, or hang out at home and listen to Richard Pryor or Moms Mabley. Moms made me laugh, just insanely. And Richard would tell these great stories.

I also liked watching old movies. Back then, movies were on TV all the time. You had the *Million Dollar Movie*, *The Early Show*, *The Late Show*, *The Late, Late Show*. And then there was that great program in the middle of the day, hosted by Gloria DeHaven. She'd come on-screen to introduce the movie, wearing a caftan with her hair coiffed. She looked amazing.

But it was always hard for me to figure out what I was as a performer. I didn't want to do stand-up comedy because, in stand-up, you have to be really brave. When you're a storyteller, you can be semi-brave.

So when I was 25, I wrote a show to demonstrate what I thought I could do. One of my characters was the little girl who wanted long hair. I'd always wanted to be a Breck girl, because I dreamed about being on the back of a magazine. But it was pointed out to me, fairly early, that I was perfect—except for one thing. I thought, *Oh, so if I had blond hair maybe . . .*

So my little girl character wore a half-slip on her head, tossing it around, as if she had long, beautiful hair.

When I started doing that little girl in my act, I discovered something interesting—that lots of girls felt like that, whether they were white girls with straight black hair, or straight blond hair, or curly hair. It didn't matter. Everyone wants something they don't have.

"I am an artist. Art has no color and no sex."
—Whoopi Goldberg

I had a life-changing experience on a trip to Amsterdam that I wanted to share on stage, but I couldn't figure out the best character to tell the story. It was about the Anne Frank House, and traveling on an airplane, and the crazy stewardesses that I'd had. So I decided to be a junkie and have that person tell the story—because who's the last person you'd ever expect to have that kind of an experience?

It's all about trying to convey bits and pieces of information that I've discovered in the world in an interesting way. Whether it's the little girl, or the junkie, or the surfer chick who ends up giving herself an abortion because no one will talk to her about what's happened to her, I've kept doing it.

For me, this is an evolutionary process that I've been building from the age of five or six. I'd hear adults say things that I thought were interesting or fun, and they laughed a lot—mostly at themselves.

And that's how it started. I wanted to be in that conversation.

"We're here for a reason. I believe a bit of the reason
is to throw little torches out to lead people through the dark."
—Whoopi Goldberg

Against the Odds

From my dad's first foray into TV in the early Fifties, with the *Four Star Revue* variety show, he and Mother got red-carpet dressed and attended the Emmy Awards every year. Dad had won a few of the coveted statues himself, and his production company produced many winning shows—*Make Room for Daddy, Dick Van Dyke, Gomer Pyle, Andy Griffith, The Real McCoys* and *Mod Squad*. So he was an active and upstanding member of the Academy.

But in 1986, when my brother Tony's show *The Golden Girls* was nominated for Best Comedy Series and I was nominated for Best Dramatic Actress in a TV movie, *Nobody's Child,* my parents decided to sit it out. The odds were against both Tony and me taking home Emmys, and they just couldn't bear the thought of one of us winning and one of us losing.

So Mom and Dad made the decision to put on their pajamas, open a bottle of wine and, for the first time, watch the show at home.

The program had just begun when they got a call from their neighbor and pal Ted Mann. Ted owned the Mann Theatres, so he was one of the first in the neighborhood to have a satellite dish with an East Coast feed. He was already in the middle of the show, while my parents and everyone else on the West Coast were only seeing the start.

"Tony just won the Emmy!" Ted shouted into the phone.

Mom and Dad were so excited that they put their coats on over their PJs and ran over to Ted's house to watch the rest of the show. They got there just in time to hear the nominees being read for my category—Katharine Hepburn, Vanessa Redgrave, Gena Rowlands, Mare Winningham . . . and their little girl. They could hardly breathe as Tom Selleck opened the envelope. And guess what—it was me.

My parents were bowled over and did what any ecstatic mother and father of two Emmy winners would do. They ran home, took off their pajamas, put on their tux and gown and drove to the party.

Brother and sister winners. I said in my acceptance speech:
"Someone's going to have to go to our parents' house
and pick them up off the floor."

Legends of Comedy

Well into their seventies, Dad and two of his best pals, Milton Berle and Sid Caesar, teamed up to form a new act called *The Legends of Comedy*. Exactly what the title implied, the show was a celebration of the careers of three men doing what they did best—entertaining people. And now for the first time they were doing it on the same bill. I went to see the show in Atlantic City and sat in the audience more spellbound than I would have thought. I had seen them all perform countless times, but never side by side. It was an amazing experience—like attending a one-night, crash-course comedy school—as these veterans of the craft tore up the stage, each in his own unique style.

Milton came on first, exploding with energy—banging out one-liners, walking on the sides of his feet, making faces, crossing his eyes, prancing and dancing, licking his hand to slick back his hair, and all with a look of sheer delight on that rubbery mug of his. He was a marvelous rat-a-tat clown—a master of Berlesque burlesque—who the audience adored and he adored back. As I watched him, I could almost see the six-year-old boy standing up in his parents' living room, making his whole family double over in awe at this precocious and genuinely funny kid.

Then came Dad, Mr. Sleek, in his pressed black tuxedo with his red satin pocket hanky. He strode to the mike and good-naturedly welcomed his audience. *"Good evening, ladies and gentlemen."* They immediately quieted down to hear what he would say next. Dad adored making an audience laugh, but he also loved bringing them to a hush. He used to tell me that a good storyteller knows how important the silences are, and is never afraid of them. Dad controlled his audience like an orchestra conductor. He was Mr. Cool.

I remember once being with him in the dining room of the Sands Hotel when a young comic approached our table.

"Mr. Thomas," he said nervously, "I'm just starting out as a comedian, and I'm having the hardest time beginning my act. I never know what to say when I first come out. Can you give me some advice?"

My father looked up at the young comic.

"I'll tell you what," he said. "I'll give you, free of charge, what I open with."

"Oh, my God," the kid said. "Would you really? What is it?"

Dad said, "Good evening, ladies and gentlemen."

Third on the bill was Sid Caesar, who couldn't have been more different from his two friends. No rat-a-tat, no gentlemanly welcome to the audience. Instead, Sid came out in character—a German professor—then gave us another of his characters, and another, and yet another, all from different countries, all with different accents. The audience was transfixed.

And it was interesting knowing where all those voices came from. Sid had told us the stories of growing up like my dad, as the son of immigrants, in the same kind of melting-pot neighborhood. His father owned a small restaurant in Yonkers called the St. Claire Buffet and Luncheonette. When Sid was a boy of nine he worked there—for a quarter a day—clearing tables after school. As he went from table to table, he'd hear the customers chattering in a smorgasbord of accents—French, Italian, German, Polish, Spanish, Hungarian, Russian and Yiddish—and he liked to mimic them. He picked up the rhythms, the intonations, the musical nuances of each dialect, then he'd talk to each group in his own double-talk version of their language.

At first the customers thought Sid was actually speaking to them in their language, but soon they realized that this little pisher was faking it. They loved it—and Sid loved making them laugh. He couldn't wait to get there after school every day. He had found his way into a comic device that would become a signature of his career.

Milton, Dad and Sid, always together, this time on stage.

On stage that night in Atlantic City, we never saw the man, Sid Caesar, until the final moments of his act, when he bid us "Good night." But he was brilliant. He gave us not only a cast of colorful and funny characters, but also a touch of the rich cultures that came along with them.

In their brief but memorable engagement as a team, Milton Berle, Danny Thomas and Sid Caesar painted a remarkable picture of the distinct ways in which a comedian can approach comedy. They also made it clear that each one of them was destined to do it his own way. And it was certain, as you watched them up there on that stage, that they were also destined to spend their lives making us laugh.

SID'S MOST MEMORABLE JOKE

I asked Sid Caesar if he remembered the first time he got up in front of an audience. He told me that he made a speech at his Bar Mitzvah, and though much of it had to be serious, he did manage to slip in a few jokes from the pulpit.

But the real headliner that day, Sid remembers, was the rabbi, who told a joke that still makes Sid laugh. —M.T.

There were mice running all over the synagogue, and everyone was in a panic. Women were terrified, kids were hiding and the men didn't know what to do.

"Don't worry," the rabbi announced. "I'll take care of it."

Sure enough, the next day all the mice were gone. The people in the shul were astonished! An older gentleman stood and asked, "Rabbi, how did you do it? How did you get rid of all the mice?"

"Easy," the rabbi answered. "I Bar Mitzvahed them. And as everyone knows, once they're Bar Mitzvahed, they never come back."

The Elm House

I t's very odd when someone dies suddenly. Your brain can't compute it. It's like they've been kidnapped, plucked out of your life. They were here yesterday. Now they're not.

Dad had been on the road promoting his new book, *Make Room for Danny*. And he was having a ball—big crowds, the book was selling well. He seemed healthy and very happy. You could hear it in his voice.

Then the call from the doctor at 1:30 in the morning. I dropped the phone and screamed. My father had died of heart failure. I fell to the floor and began rocking back and forth—like I was davening, I think, which I'd never done in my life. It must be primal. Phil climbed over me to get to the phone and I heard him saying, "Who died? . . . Oh no!"

It was February 6, 1991. Daddy was 79.

I got on the plane to L.A. and cried all the way. Phil stayed behind to dedicate a *Donahue* show in remembrance of Dad. So I was alone. My pal Kathie Berlin wanted to fly with me, but I couldn't wait—I had to get there. She took the next plane. The flight attendants were dear—hovering with Kleenex and water. I was inconsolable. An open faucet of tears. Then cocktail napkins started being passed over my shoulder, with notes written on them.

"I loved your father."

"He was like a father to me."

"I grew up on your Dad."

"I'm so sorry for your loss."

They were my first condolence notes. It was so sweet, it made me cry more. Something I didn't realize till much later was that, when we landed, though I was sitting in the front row and the door was at the center of the plane, there wasn't a line. I walked right off. The attendants must have asked the passengers to let me off first. And they did. What a kind thing for all of those people to do.

I walked dazed off the plane, to where Terre and Tony were waiting for me. We drove to the house, which was filled with people, and all I could think of was *What do I drink to make this pain go away?* No one ever tells you that grief is physical. I felt like I'd been hit with a plank. I'm not much of a drinker, so Father Pat, our family priest since we were small— and a pretty good drinker—introduced me to mixed drinks. Scotch—too bitter. Vodka—too hot going down. Same with gin. We settled on Seagram's 7 and ginger ale. I remembered that from college—a kid's drink, but I could get it down. I got a *few* down. It wasn't yet noon.

My best pal since childhood, Camille, was already there, passing food, making drinks. Of course Camille would be there. We'd shared so much growing up. And now her presence brought some kind of normalcy to this otherworldly tableau.

Dad's comic pals started coming in, red-eyed, telling stories, forcing a laugh. But it was too soon.

Thank God for Terre. She was taking care of Mom, walking her around the courtyard. Mom had the stunned look of a boxer who had hit the mat, and Terre was trying to keep her on her feet. Tony and I went to Good Shepherd Church and began to arrange the flowers. So many flowers had arrived, it looked and smelled like a florist shop. Or a funeral parlor. We put all the white ones, for resurrection, on the altar. We sent out for white ribbon to arrange bows on the ends of all the pews. We had a piano brought in so Roger Williams could play Dad's favorite song, "Autumn Leaves."

Then we made a list of the speakers. Tony looked at me.

"You know what we're doing, Mugs, don't you?" he said.

"No," I said. "What?"

"We're producing Dad's last show."

Yes, I guess we were. We hugged each other tight and continued producing. Then we got a call from the archbishop's office and were pleased to learn that he would attend the service. That was nice—Dad would have liked that. But they informed us that, for this honor, only one person would be allowed to speak other than the archbishop. Guess he had a busy day.

"Thanks, anyway," we said, "but we have a couple of presidents and several comedy legends who will be speaking on behalf of their friend, so we understand if this makes it impossible for the archbishop to attend."

Presidents Reagan and Ford spoke. So did the archbishop (yes, he came anyway). So did Bob Hope and Milton Berle.

Phil emceed—beautifully. If ever a man was put in a spot to fail, this was it—taking on the role of speaking on behalf of a family's adored patriarch. But it was as if he had reached into our hearts. He expressed it for all of us. I'll always remember him saying, "He made us believe that he would live forever. But two days ago he proved us wrong and broke our hearts."

The first speaker Phil called on was Milton, who walked up to the pulpit and said, "Thanks, Geraldo." Good ol' Uncle Miltie. He knew what to do. Everyone laughed. They needed to.

There were a lot of laughs that day from the comics. Bob Hope said that Dad was so religious he had stained glass windows in his car. There was also a memorable laugh that did not come from the pulpit. It started when Mother's lipstick fell out of her purse, hitting the ground with a noisy clack, then began rolling across the floor. Terre, Tony and I watched it roll and started to giggle. As it made its way past the grandkids—first Dionne, Jason and Tracy, then Kristina and Kate—they started to giggle, too. And trying as hard as we could, none of us could stop, until we were all laughing hysterically. It was terrible. Our bodies were shaking, tears of laughter streaming down our faces. We must have looked crazy. We were.

For hours and hours, day after day, friends came to offer their condolences, eat heartily and make us laugh. And what good friends—Elaine, Herbie, Chuck, Julian, Barry, Kathie all came from New York to be with me. After a while, Terre, Tony and I decided to duck out and take a drive to the old Elm house. We just had a need to see it again. It had been, what, thirty years, since we had all left and Mom and Dad had built their big beautiful dream house on the hill, atop Beverly Hills, overlooking the city.

We drove to the corner of Elm and Elevado and parked across the street. I could see my old bedroom windows that faced the street. How many times I had watched from that window as a boyfriend rode away on his bike. It looked smaller. Does everybody's childhood home look smaller when they're all grown up?

We got out of the car. *Let's knock on the door. Maybe the owner will let us go inside. No, that's crazy. We don't even know these people.*

We walked to the door and knocked. A nice-looking blond woman opened it.

"We're the Thomas kids," we said. "We grew up in this house. We just lost our dad and we felt a very strong urge to visit this house."

The nice lady smiled. "I was wondering when you'd come," she said.

"What do you mean? You were expecting us?"

"Oh, yes," she said. "Your father used to drop by all the time, and he'd sit in the den and have a vodka with us, and talk about the old days. He loved this house."

We were floored. We should have known. Dear, sweet, sentimental Daddy.

We entered the house.

"We'll go outside," the woman said. "Feel free to walk around."

So we sort of meandered. I walked into the den first, where on Friday nights we had watched all the Capra, Sturges, Chaplin and Three Stooges movies. I remembered how I used to run the projector. Because I was the oldest, Dad had taught me how to work it, so when he was on the road, we could still watch movies.

Then the living room, with the big black piano that held Grandma's picture as a fortune-teller on top of it, and where all the pianists and singers would sit on the bench and perform after dinner, and where the comics would tell stories and make everyone laugh. At the far end of the room, in front of the glass doors, was where we put our Christmas tree each year—with the mountain of gifts from family, friends and Dad's colleagues.

Then the dining room, which faced the street, with the windows that let in such a pretty light through the panes. I could almost see the U-shaped table, built that way so that no one sat with their back to the huge, wall-to-wall carving of the Last Supper that hung there. Me always on Dad's right. On Sunday after Mass, we'd have to close the drapery so the movie guide buses wouldn't look in at us having our brunch. "Monkeys in a cage," Dad would say.

I walked up the stairs and remembered Mom sitting on the top step, holding baby Tony in her arms that Christmas, just two weeks after he was born, so he could be a part of our Christmas morning.

I went into my parents' bedroom. It didn't look like it did on all those school mornings when I'd go in for my allowance, or something extra to go to the movies with Camille and Moya, or to negotiate staying out later than they wanted me to. But the bed was in the same place as it was when we used to climb into it to keep Mom company when Dad was away.

What I hadn't expected was the burst of emotion I felt when I walked into Dad's bathroom–dressing room, where I used to sit on the edge of the tub, watching him shave and listening to his stories about being on the road, or telling him how I felt about something that no one else seemed to understand. It was the room most untouched by the new owners—the "oatmeal"-colored tile (Mom called it that), the big glass shower with the tile bench inside, the pane-glass window overlooking the street, where I would glance at our circle driveway and the brick house across from ours. Oh, how many times I had sat there transfixed and laughing and happy to be with him. Dad's bathroom. How funny that it was this room that held the sweetest memories of my childhood home.

I couldn't stop weeping, but I was glad I had come. Because for those few moments, the flowers, the eulogies, the box that held him were washed away, and I was transported, and as close to him again as I could get.

I went downstairs, and Terre and Tony looked as I must have. Drained. But it was good. We had made a visit to relive, not just to bury, our father. We were ready to go back and finish the ritual at home.

CHAPTER 50

Mother and Marge

After my father died, I brought my mother to New York to stay with me and Phil for a while. She didn't want to sleep alone in a room, so we thought it would be good for her to invite her old friend, Marge Durante, to come along with her.

Jimmy Durante, the legendary comedian, had left Marge widowed many years before. She and my mother had always been close friends, and now Marge was a great comfort to Mom.

We took walks in Central Park, Mother and Marge in their boxy mink coats, looking every bit like that other era they came from. We even took a carriage ride. They loved it, but Mom felt sorry for the horses.

One day, they disappeared from our apartment for a few hours, and I became worried. When they finally got back, I asked them where they had been.

"We walked over to the Copa, just to take a look at it from the outside," Mom told me. I was very touched by that.

"Did it look like it used to?" I asked.

"I don't know," Mother said. "Back then, we only saw it at night."

A few days later, Phil invited Mother and Marge to a taping of his show. He said he'd also like to introduce them in the audience. Mother was against the idea. She didn't want a fuss—she just didn't feel up to it. Phil tried to persuade her by telling her that people would love to see her and Marge—they had been married to men who many people remembered with great affection.

Mother remained reluctant, so I told Phil not to push her. She'd been doing pretty well, and I didn't want her to get upset. Phil agreed, and off they all went to 30 Rock. I was working, so I wasn't able to go with them, but I heard all about it when I got home later. Phil told me that once they got to the studio, and Mom and Marge felt all the excitement of the audience, they decided that it was all right for Phil to introduce them. I was delighted.

"How was it?" I asked my mother.

"They stood!" she said, proudly.

You can take the girl out of the club . . .

Not long after that, I decided it would be a good idea to take Mom to the movies, as another distraction. I scoured the paper for a film that wouldn't bring up any sad memories for her. No love stories, no showbiz stories, no family stories. I finally found a lightweight comedy that I thought she might get a laugh or two out of; and even if it wasn't any good, at least it would be harmless, and not anything that would make her emotional.

We bought our tickets, settled into our seats and the movie began. Just as I had hoped, the film was pretty bland, and I was feeling good about my choice.

Then suddenly, Mother burst into tears. I was dumbfounded.

"Mother, Mother, what is it?" I frantically whispered.

"These people are so untalented," Mother wailed, "and *Daddy's* dead!"

GEORGE BURNS

January 30, 1995

Dear Phil & Marlo-

Thanks for the lovely flowers. When
you're 99 you get a little confused, you
don't know whether to smell the flowers or
eat them. But I figured it out, and they
were delicious.

Thanks again.

Love,

George

The Only Jew in the Neighborhood

He's got wit, charm, savvy and bottomless smarts. But there's one thing Jon Stewart doesn't have: a fourth wall. He's removed it. He looks right at us, rolls his eyes, shakes his fists and plays the joke directly to us, as if we were sitting across the desk from him. And because of this rapport, we feel we can trust him. We know he'll call the game the way he sees it. His Daily Show *fan base has come to depend on him for their nightcap of laughter, whether he's cracking wise or expressing outrage. But he's also a comedy guy who is taken very seriously, often hailed as a dominant voice in 21st century America. But he sure doesn't take himself seriously. From our first "Hello," I felt I was talking to an old friend. One who can always make me laugh.*
—M.T.

JON
STEWART

Marlo: Do you have any idea how many comedy addicts adore *The Daily Show*?

Jon: Actually, we try to keep ourselves in as much of a bubble as possible. If I start feeling like, *Oh my God—people like me!*, I'll start screwing up for sure.

Marlo: Most comedians found their comic voice in their childhood, some of the older ones in their immigrant neighborhoods. What about you?

Jon: My childhood was different from the days of the old comics. I grew up in the suburban Seventies, and the stories about it are so banal. In the old days, there was much more romance. More character. People spoke with old world accents; there was more of a connection to our roots.

Marlo: I know, my grandma used to spit on my head when people said I had beautiful eyes.

Jon: See, I never got that! Why wouldn't anyone spit on my head?

Marlo: Clearly you were deprived.

Jon: Exactly.

Marlo: Was there anyone in your childhood who could make you laugh?

Jon: My grandfather possessed this really dry sense of humor. Everybody has two weird sides of their family. One is the loud, screaming, Lower East Side family; the other is your stereotypical, newspaper-reading, quiet side. It's sort of like the two Jews—the Sephardic and Ashkenazic, you know?

Marlo: Right. So you made your grandfather laugh?

Jon: I tried desperately. But I think it was him who made *me* laugh. Billy Crystal always talks about how he used to perform in front of his family, but I think the suburbs were a more isolating existence. For me, there wasn't this sense of the family hearth, with everybody sitting around, and Aunt Sylvia flapping her arms and telling stories. That was much more of a traditional Billy Crystal–Sid Caesar way to grow up.

I grew up more as an outsider. I was the only Jew in the neighborhood, as opposed to, you know, living in a family of people who got chased out of their homeland by the pogrom and were now living in Massapequa. I guess it's a generational thing.

Marlo: Still, being the only Jew in the neighborhood had to help make you funny.

Jon: Well, being small and Jewish is a good recipe for developing a wit. Most of my laughs came from my classmates.

Marlo: So you were the class clown.

Jon: Actually, my friend was voted class clown. I was voted best sense of humor. And I take great pride in that distinction.

Marlo: You should.

Jon: I did. My fart humor back then was very sophisticated. I did top-notch stuff. But what passes as wit when you're younger is really just obnoxiousness. Then you slowly learn the difference between something that will make people laugh and something that will get your ass kicked. There's a very fine line there.

But, yeah, the stories of my childhood lack any real magic. I was very much like a bad *ABC Afterschool Special*. Latchkey kid, basically unsupervised, most of the time thinking up ways to entertain my friends. It all feels so clichéd. Even the way my family got divorced. My dad got laid off and then had an affair with a secretary. It was Philip Roth, you know?

Marlo: Conan O'Brien told me that he spent his entire childhood making fun of himself so nobody else would.

Jon: That's exactly right. If you had the best Jew joke in town, or the best short joke in town, at a certain point nobody wanted to compete with you. I mean, my last name is Leibowitz. Just about every fun curse word for a little kid rhymes with that. "Tits." "Shits." So unless you could top the other kids material-wise, they'd be relentless.

Marlo: Did you have a couple of standard lines that you defended yourself with?

Jon: No, it was all situational. We didn't write stuff back then. It wasn't the Orpheum Circuit. But you did have to be quick on your feet. In some respects, that was good training for stand-up comedy, because it's all in the moment. You're just trying to deflect things.

Marlo: You do that a lot on your show.

Jon: Yeah. In some ways I think you're always the kid you were when puberty first destroyed your life. That sense of esteem you were searching for is always a part of you, no matter what happens. I remember my life before I got on television, and how much harder it was to get laid then. So believe me, I have a decent sense of my own self-worth.

Marlo: Maybe you weren't getting laid, but you were always getting laughs.

Jon: Yeah, well I gotta tell you, getting laughs was cold comfort to getting laid. The one thing I can remember from high school was that being the funny guy got you access to the party, but typically in some sort of advisory or service role.

Marlo: Meaning?

Jon: Meaning, the first time I got to second base with a girl, I was actually driving and watching my friend do it.

Marlo: Really?

Jon: Yes—that was the first time I saw a breast: as my better-looking friend felt someone up in the back of my Gremlin while I drove.

Marlo: That's hysterical.

Jon: But I was a great lure. Have you ever seen the old angler fish lure? It's got that weird little thing coming out of its head. That was me. I would do the dance and draw in the people. Then they would come in and say, "Wow. Now, can we go fuck your friends?"

Marlo: Ah, so you were the pimp, really.

Jon: That's right. Or the carnival barker. You sort of bring people in for the ride, and then they say, "Oh, you're so funny. Now . . . is there anyone we can actually go out with?"

Marlo: You mention being the only Jew on the block. When I was growing up, all the best comedians were Jews. But look around now: There's Letterman, Colbert, Leno, O'Brien. You're the only Jew.

Jon: But that's always been the case on a national platform. You know, the Jews were the tummlers, they were the guys in the clubs battling it out. But when it came to national TV, they wanted the guy from Nebraska. They wanted Johnny Carson, not Joey Bishop.

Marlo: So how did you sneak through?

Jon: Basic cable, baby! The world changed when basic cable came around, and suddenly you didn't have to appeal to the widest swath of people anymore.

Marlo: You know, my dad was Lebanese, which made him an unusual looking choice to play a father on prime-time TV, especially in the era of *Father Knows Best* and *My Three Sons*.

Jon: Yeah, that was shocking. Back then, the image of family was *Ozzie and Harriet*, then your dad comes along and shows the real face of America. The immigrant face.

Marlo: Well, he had a good agent. But let's get back to you. You're not only funny, but you're incredibly ballsy. You went on CNN's *Crossfire* and told off the hosts.

Jon: I think that was more hypoglycemia than anything else. I've got to eat more before I go on these things.

Marlo: But what's interesting is, you weren't trying to be funny. You actually reprimanded the hosts for being partisan hacks masquerading as genuine news analysts. If you weren't a fan of the show, why did you go on in the first place?

Jon: We had a book [*America: The Book*] to promote, so it was one of those odd dares, where we thought, "Wouldn't it be kind of interesting to promote the book on the sort of show that reflected what we were writing about?" Like if Charlie Chaplin had opened his movie on Hitler at the Reichstag, you know? Like, "Hey, man why don't we slip it right into the belly, and see what happens?"

Marlo: But things got heated very quickly.

Jon: Well, they began coming after me for not having enough ethics as a journalist. And my feeling was *You know what? I have a job. Why do I have to do yours?*

Marlo: Then one of the hosts criticized you for asking politicians softball questions. You said, "You're on CNN! The show that leads into me is puppets making crank phone calls. *What is wrong with you?*"

Jon: Well, I couldn't believe they were suggesting that, by not holding politicians' feet to the fire, I was somehow as guilty as they were. You can judge my show on many things. You can say it's not funny, you can say it's not interesting. But to say it lacks journalistic standards? Yeah, well, guess what . . .

Marlo: Speaking of political analysts, tell me the one difference between you and MSNBC commentator Chris Matthews. You rag on him a lot.

Jon: Well, obviously there's the reach difference. His jab could probably keep me at bay. But, you know, I really don't know him well enough, so I'd be hard-pressed . . .

Marlo: Come on.

Jon: Okay, put it this way: When I talk, typically the oxygen masks don't drop from the ceiling, and people aren't warned to put them over their child's face first.

Marlo: [*Laughing*] That's what I was looking for.

Jon: That's what I figured.

Marlo: I'm cheap, you know. I'm a comic's kid.

Jon: I hear you.

Marlo: Your former *Daily Show* colleague Stephen Colbert became a star himself. What do you think you could teach Stephen about the art of comedy—and before you answer, you should know that I asked him the same thing about you.

Jon: I'm going to go with . . . nothing.

Marlo: Really?

Jon: That man is doing something that has never been seen on television before. He's literally rendering this character in real time as he goes along. It truly is one of the most remarkable things I've ever seen. And, you know, as good a performer as Stephen is, he's an even better producer. I have nothing but admiration for him.

Marlo: I'll let him know you said that. Tell me about your kids. Are either of them starting to show signs of being funny?

Jon: My little girl is almost three, and she's a real performer—singing songs from *Sleeping Beauty,* dancing and spinning, putting on shows. She's already memorized her patter. She came to the studio the other day, sat in my chair and said, "Ladies and gentlemen, boys and girls, please turn off your cell phones and welcome to the show!" She sat for a minute longer, then looked up at me and said, "Uh . . . I don't have any jokes."

Marlo: How great! Well, at least she knows the game.

Jon: Right. I thought that comment was very prescient from someone who's not even three, because I've certainly had that feeling behind that desk.

Marlo: What I find interesting is that you're doing satire on television. When I was growing up, people in the business were condescending about satire. The old adage was: Satire is what closes on Saturday night.

Jon: [*Laughs*]

Marlo: Hadn't you ever heard that?

Jon: No.

Marlo: I think if those old comics were alive today, they'd be astounded that satire is actually making it on TV.

Jon: People are so sophisticated now that you have to win them over with volume, and I think that's the secret to it. If you can make satire part of the language, part of the culture, then it becomes a regular part of their diet. That's how *Saturday Night Live* has been able to do it. That's how we've been able to do it. It's a volume game. You become a part of people's digestive process.

Marlo: But you're also steering them. You're educating them to understand—and appreciate—satire. I was once in a play that I thought was really funny, but then it got bad reviews. I said to a screenwriter friend of mine, "Why did the critics pan it?" And she said, "Because they weren't clear that it was *supposed* to be funny." It's almost like you have to announce it to people.

Jon: I think that's absolutely true. We spend so much time on our show trying not to be explicit—but to be *clear*. We try hard to process the material and put it back out there as comedy. But intent is really an important part of it.

Marlo: And you're obviously succeeding. *Time* magazine named you one of the most influential people in the country. That had to surprise you.

Jon: Listen, we do a show that's about media culture. So I'm never surprised when the media responds that way. It's like they're saying, "This man is making fun of us. He's chosen a very good subject to make fun of. He must be very important." By considering it as flattery, they elevate *themselves*. I think that's what the media does. And in the process, we sort of become outsized in whatever they think our influence is.

Marlo: Still, did you ever imagine that you would have this kind of impact?

Jon: No, none of this ever seemed possible to me. Even when I told my family what I was doing, there was this sense of "For *what*?"

Marlo: So what was the lure?

Jon: It was a language and a rhythm that I thought I understood. It's like music, you know? You hear it and you feel like, "Yeah, man, that makes sense to me." You know how some musicians can play by ear? I felt like I had that—like there was a certain "comedy by ear" that I knew how to do. And producing our show is somewhat of a musical process. The most important time for us is between rehearsal and the show, when the song is rewritten to sound a little bit better.

Marlo: It's such a kick to watch you on your show, especially when the camera catches you trying not to crack up at something that's going on. Which makes me want to know: What do *you* find uncontrollably funny? What gets to your funny bone?

Jon: Sadly, what I love most is when something bombs. Watching the bomb. Loving the bomb.

Marlo: I love bombs, too. Why is that?

Jon: Having worked in the clubs for so long is sort of like being a magician for a lot of years—you know all the tricks. So I always found it funny when I was bombing, or one of my friends was bombing. It's something that's different—like being caught in a sudden snowstorm.

Marlo: And if it happens on your show?

Jon: I enjoy it the most when things go wrong on the show. I relish it. It's reminds me that "Oh, right, this isn't neurosurgery." Like, we're making jokes about, you know, the Elmo puppet that we re-jiggered to be a Guantánamo detainee, and the beard accidentally comes off. Now, that's funny.

Because, inherently, we're like the Little Rascals: We're just a bunch of idiots in the backyard putting on a show.

St. Jude Children's Research Hospital

I
t is not possible to think about my childhood without thinking about
St. Jude Children's Research Hospital. Although, like any hospital, it
shoulders its share of sadness, St. Jude is also about laughter. Laughter
built the place.

Getting ready to go on, backstage at "The Shower of Stars"
—with Dad, Frank Sinatra and Jerry Lewis.

Dad raised the early funds to build St. Jude from benefit concerts he gave, both on his own and with his pals from the world he knew best— nightclubs. Milton Berle, Bob Hope, George Burns, Sid Caesar, Jack Benny, Frank Sinatra, Dean Martin, Jerry Lewis, Sammy Davis, Jr. Even young Elvis.

Frank did so many of these events that there is a floor at St. Jude named for him. My father called these fund-raising galas "The Shower of Stars," and they carried a message of hope for the most helpless of all— little children with hopeless diseases.

My father began to build his dream of St. Jude by making a simple sketch of the hospital on a piece of cardboard that came from the cleaners

In 1983, the U.S. Congress voted unanimously to award my father with the Congressional Gold Medal for his work as founder of St. Jude Children's Research Hospital. Ronald Reagan presented it at the White House. A proud day for our family.

with his shirts. Talk about low-tech. He showed the drawing to every potential donor he could find, but mainly to the Lebanese community, encouraging them to build a place of hope for America's children, in gratitude to this country for embracing their immigrant parents.

But it was his passion that sold it. He lived and breathed the hospital. Dad talked so much about St. Jude when we were growing up that Terre, Tony and I thought he was one of our uncles.

His belief that he could accomplish this is astounding—that a poor kid from Toledo, with one year of high school, a nightclub comedian, would be able to build a world-renowned cancer research hospital. Where does that kind of chutzpah come from?

Same place his humor came from—his immigrant childhood, where no one in his poor neighborhood ever went to a doctor. Dad's mother gave birth to all ten of her children without a doctor. Children he knew and played with died of influenza and rodent bites. He saw firsthand the inequity of poor health care and was galvanized by the experience. He was going to fix it. And he used his gift of laughter to pay for it.

He named the hospital after St. Jude, patron saint of hopeless causes, to whom he'd prayed when his budding performing career had stalled. *Give me a sign to help me find my way in life, and someday I'll build a shrine in your name.* He soon found fame, and kept his promise. And he built the hospital in Memphis, Tennessee, because he'd once read a news item about an eight-year-old black child in the South who was riding his bicycle and was struck by a car. But no emergency room in the area would take him, and he died. My father carried that clipping in his wallet for years.

When I became *That Girl* in 1966, Dad called me his "bonus kid," because, whenever he was unable to attend a St. Jude event, he'd send me to take his place, to pick up a check or make a speech on behalf of the hospital.

At Phil's and my wedding, Dad clinked his glass and said, "Today, I haven't lost a daughter. I've gained a fund-raiser." Everyone laughed. He

The two "bonus kids" on their wedding day.

did, too. But he wasn't kidding. He knew he had just acquired another *bonus kid*.

Gloria Steinem, who has raised millions of dollars for every form of civil rights, for candidates across the country and for a myriad of causes she believes in, calls fund-raising "the second oldest profession in the world." It's a funny line, but somehow it rings true.

After my father died, I came to realize something that I'm sure everyone who has ever lost someone they loved has learned. And that is—love endures. Even years later, the love remains as before. It doesn't diminish. It doesn't divert. It endures, intact.

Then I found out something else. Friendship endures, too. A few months after Dad died, there was a benefit for St. Jude, and I got the news that Bob Hope was flying from L.A. to New York to emcee the event. All through the years, Dad had always called Bob and all of his friends—personally—to ask them to perform at these fund-raisers. But Bob, the emeritus of all things funny, was now doing this without a call from Dad. I was very touched, and phoned Bob to thank him.

"I can't tell you how moved I am," I said.

"Are you kidding?" Bob said. "I love Danny."

Maybe his pal was gone, but their friendship was very much alive.

My siblings and I had never intended to carry the torch of St. Jude. In fact, Dad had been quite clear to us that the work of the hospital would not be our burden to carry after he was gone. We accepted that, and I

Friendship endures. "The Boys"—Milton, Sid, George and Jan—
continued to attend St. Jude dinners even after Dad was gone.

Terre, Tony and I followed Dad's heart to St. Jude.

think each of us was relieved. St. Jude had taken the second half of Dad's life to build and maintain, and with him gone, the responsibility would be even greater.

But soon after he died, Terre, Tony and I thought we should go to Memphis to talk to everyone at the hospital, and let them know that we would be there if they needed us. They had all worked so closely with Dad, been inspired by him, and his death was as much of a shock to them as it was to us. He hadn't been ill, and had just been with them two days before, celebrating the hospital's 29th anniversary.

When I got to the driveway at the hospital, with the fifteen-foot statue of St. Jude standing tall at the entrance, I sat in the car, paralyzed. I didn't want to go inside. It was all too fresh. I also didn't want to cry in front of the children or their parents. They had enough of their own heartache.

So I pulled myself together and went inside. In the lobby, a party was going on. There was ice cream and cake. Confetti. Balloons. And the happy clamor of children running around in party hats.

"Whose birthday is it?" I asked the nurse.

"Oh, it's not a birthday party," she said. "It's an off-chemo party."

I had never seen anything like this before. Here were all these little children celebrating and deriving strength from one child's turn for the better, with their parents and grandparents standing by with tears in their eyes. If this child could make it, maybe their beloved child would, too.

In that moment, I breathed in what my father had been holding in his heart for so many years. I had walked into a place, a community, where hope lived. A place that families had traveled to from all over the country, terrified, carrying death sentences for their babies. I looked around at the fairy-tale murals painted on the walls, at the red wagons, instead of wheel-chairs, carrying children down the hallways.

I saw a part of my father that hadn't been as clear to me before. I had always thought of him as a good man, a philanthropist, but I hadn't truly understood how deeply personal this was to him. How thoroughly he had given his heart to this place, to these people.

And I knew now that his spirit would always live here.

A few minutes later, a mom brought her little girl over to me.

"Do you know who this lady's Daddy is?" the mother said to her daughter.

"Yes," the little girl said.

"Who?" the mom asked.

The little girl proudly answered, "St. Jude."

In the background I heard the children singing.

"Pack up your bag, get out the door, you don't need chemo anymore."

Then I cried.

EPILOGUE

A few months after my father died, two of the grandkids were graduating from high school—Jason, Terre's son, and Tracy, Tony's daughter—and they had asked me to be the commencement speaker. Like all things with us, it was a family affair.

But we weren't yet ready for a big celebration. Mother certainly wasn't up to it. So after the ceremony, we all went to Hillcrest Country Club for lunch. Hillcrest had always been a favorite haven for our family, so it seemed fitting that we should gather there for Jason and Tracy's big day.

We took a private room away from the lunch crowd. Given Mom's emotional state, we were all still treating her as if she were made of glass that might shatter if we moved it the wrong way.

Suddenly, the door swung open and in walked George Burns. We were all so happy to see him, but he barely acknowledged us. He walked straight to Mother.

"Hey Rosie," he said with a mischievous smile. "I hear you're single again!"

We all froze in terror, almost afraid to look at Mom.

She threw her head back and roared.

And then we all did. What a gutsy, smart thing for George to do.

Like they always did. They knew how to find the funny.

God bless a sense of humor.

Marlo Thomas graduated from the University of Southern California with a teaching degree. She is the author of five best-selling books, *Free to Be . . . You and Me, Free to Be . . . A Family, The Right Words at the Right Time, The Right Words at the Right Time Volume 2: Your Turn!* and *Thanks and Giving: All Year Long*. Ms. Thomas has won four Emmy Awards, a Peabody Award, a Golden Globe and a Grammy, and has been inducted into the Broadcasting Hall of Fame for her work in television, including her starring role in the landmark series *That Girl*, which she also conceived and produced. She is the National Outreach Director for St. Jude Children's Research Hospital. Ms. Thomas lives in New York with her husband, Phil Donahue.

Credits and Permissions

Passages from the book *700 Sundays* by Billy Crystal, reprinted with
the permission of Grand Central Publishing. Copyright © 2005 by
Billy Crystal.

Passages from Larry Gelbart's essay about Danny Thomas, reprinted with
the permission of Larry Gelbart.

Al Hirschfeld's illustration of the cast of *Thieves*, © Al Hirschfeld,
reproduced by arrangement with Hirschfeld's exclusive representative,
the Margo Feiden Galleries Ltd., New York, www.AlHirschfeld.com

Photograph of George Carlin in concert courtesy of HBO.

Reproductions from *I'm Glad I'm a Boy! I'm Glad I'm a Girl!*, text copyright
© 1970 by Windmill Books, Inc., illustrations copyright © 1970 by Whitney
Darrow, Jr. Published by Windmill Books/Simon & Schuster.

Marlo Thomas's interview with Elaine May, originally published in
Interview magazine, April 1990.

Comedian caricatures by: Tim Foley *(Steven Wright)*, Chris Galvin
(Whoopi Goldberg), Bob Kurtz/Kurtz & Friends *(Lily Tomlin)*, Chris Morris
(Tina Fey, Kathy Griffin), Stephen Silver *(Joy Behar, Billy Crystal, Jay Leno,
Jon Stewart, Ben and Jerry Stiller, Robin Williams)*, Brian Smith/Bullz-Eye.com
(Don Rickles, Chris Rock, Jerry Seinfeld), Taylor Smith *(Conan O'Brien)*,
Zach Trenholm *(Alan Alda, George Lopez, Elaine May, Joan Rivers)*, Greg
Williams *(Stephen Colbert)*.

All other photos and reproductions are from the collection
of Marlo Thomas, reprinted with permission.